THE NUCLEAR CHALLENGE

For Alison

The Nuclear Challenge

US-Russian strategic relations after the Cold War

CHRISTOPH BLUTH
University of Leeds

Routledge
Taylor & Francis Group
LONDON AND NEW YORK

First published 2000 by Ashgate Publishing

Reissued 2019 by Routledge
2 Park Square, Milton Park, Abingdon, Oxon, OXl 4 4RN
52 Vanderbilt Avenue, New York, NY 10017

Routledge is an imprint of the Taylor & Francis Group, an informa business

A Library of Congress record exists under LC control number:

ISBN 13: 978-1-138-72165-4 (hbk)
ISBN 13: 978-1-138-72161-6 (pbk)
ISBN 13: 978-1-315-19432-5 (ebk)

Contents

Acknowledgements

This book marks another stage of a long journey to unravel the complexities of nuclear weapons policies, their far-reaching real and potential consequences for the whole of mankind and the steps that can be taken to avert the risks and dangers that we all face, whether we are aware of it or not.

I have been encouraged and helped in my endeavours by many friends and colleagues. I especially want to single out William C. Potter, whose enormous commitment to the cause of nuclear safety and non-proliferation and whose support of my work in various small but significant ways has made this book possible, and Nikolai Sokov who shares my fascination with Russian nuclear weapons programmes. The late Oumerisik Kasenov, formerly Director of the Kazak Institute of Strategic Studies, was a good friend who introduced me to the complexities of Central Asian politics from the inside.

Others include Roy Allison, Pavel Baev, Debbie Ball, Bruce Blair, Emily Ewell Daughtry, Andrea Ellner, Rose Gottemoeller, Irina Isakova, Yelena Kalyuzhnova, Roman Laba, Murat Laumulin, Ronald Lehman, John Lepingwell, Dov Lynch, Steve Miller, Robert O'Neill, Vyacheslau Paznyak, Alexander Pikaev, Robert Rinne, Scott Sagan, Hans-Henning Schröder, Jane Sharpe, Jessica Stern, Anton Surikov, Dmitri Trenin, Heinrich Vogel, David Yost. Obviously I have sole responsibility for any opinions expressed in this volume, and any errors it may contain. Natalie Hey and Lorraine Sherriff helped with preparing the typescript for publication. Thank you to Alison Williams for putting up with my obsession with the topic of nuclear weapons and your enduring love and support.

1 The Strategic Paradox

The strategic nuclear 'arms race' was arguably the most dramatic feature of the Cold War. It was the existence of two large and growing arsenals of strategic nuclear weapons and the capability to inflict total devastation at any part of the world that gave the East-West confrontation its global character and imbued it with an apocalyptic quality. One of the peculiar paradoxes of the political processes whereby the Cold War ended is that while the military confrontation in Europe was effectively ended by the Soviet withdrawal from Eastern Europe and the Conventional Forces in Europe (CFE) treaty regime, the strategic nuclear force postures remained virtually intact. Communism has virtually disappeared as a political force, the Warsaw Pact has been dissolved. Eastern Europe is now free, and the Soviet military machine that kept the Communist regimes in power and threatened to roll over Western Europe at short notice has removed itself from the scene. Indeed, the might Soviet Union itself has fallen. And yet, vast arsenals of strategic nuclear weapons are still in place, capable of destroying the economic foundation and annihilating the population of the other side. The end of the Cold War should in principle also mean the end of the strategic nuclear confrontation. As the Russian government is seeking a close co-operative relationship with the United States, the political function of large strategic nuclear arsenals needs clarification. It seems strange for two countries who are partners or even allies to target nuclear weapons at each other. Although there has been a symbolic agreement between Russia and the United States not to target weapons at each other, the technical means for mutual destruction at short notice are still in place. So far, the United States and Russia have found themselves unable to emerge from the eerie twilight zone of mutual assured annihilation.

An additional problem arises from the fact that Russia is passing through a profound economic and social crisis. In this context, the huge arsenal of advanced nuclear and conventional weapons produced and deployed or stockpiled by the former Soviet Union represents a potential security risk of enormous magnitude in an environment where governmental control over all institutions in society has become weak and uncertain. To provide for the security and safety of nuclear weapons and materials, to prevent the illicit smuggling of plutonium and highly enriched uranium and to prevent nuclear scientist from selling their expertise to other states has become the focus of a concerted joint effort by the United States and Russia.

This purpose of this study is to look at the role of strategic nuclear arms control in US-Russian relations. The principal assumption here is that after the Cold War this relationship is in a process of transition from a fundamental mutual antagonism to one of partnership. The fate of nuclear weapons and the formulation of nuclear weapons policies must of course be seen in the context of the international security environment as a whole. It is the purpose of this chapter to look at some of the principal features of this environment and explain the fundamental directions of nuclear weapons policy that suggest themselves with a high degree of urgency.

The end of the Cold War has raised very fundamental questions for the security and defence establishments, particularly in Europe and North America. First of all the new international security environment has to be understood. This must involve an analysis of the end of the Cold War and its implications, the range of threats or potential future threats to national security and the proper instruments required to meet them. Then a reassessment of the requirements for military capabilities may be possible.

Interpreting the end of the Cold War

Neo-realist analysis, such as it has been recently expounded by, for example, John Mearsheimer and Kenneth Waltz,[1] explains the Cold War on the basis of the basic principles of how states interact in the international system and the role of the balance of power. According to realism, anarchy prevails in the international system and therefore relations between states are inherently prone to conflict. This manifests itself in a behaviour of the maximisation of power and security. Since no international organisation is ultimately capable of enforcing order, every state has to provide for its own security. In order to achieve this, a state constantly seeks to improve its relative power position. This requires building up military capabilities and at times the use of military force.[2]

In the neo-realist understanding of international relations, the East-West conflict, which emerged in the aftermath of World War II was a natural consequence of the post-war balance of power and is best understood as the rivalry between two Great Power systems.

The explanation given for the fact that the East-West confrontation did not result in military conflict between the main protagonists (hence the term 'Cold War') and the absence of war in Europe during the last 45 years (described as the 'Long Peace' by John Lewis Gaddis) is the bipolar distribution of power which is seen as contributing to stability and the development of large strategic nuclear arsenals which raised the cost of war to an unacceptable level.[3]

This interpretation of the Cold War leads to a very specific analysis of the post-Cold War security environment. The collapse of the bipolar system may result in instability and large-scale conflict if no balance of power emerges that can hold the emerging inter-state rivalries in check. The policy prescription advanced by Mearsheimer is that to re-establish the stability of the international system in Europe, the United States and the Western European states (in particular Britain and Germany) should balance the multipolar system emerging in Europe with military forces (including nuclear forces) against states that threaten to start a war. This implies a new balance of power arrangement to compensate for an apparent Russian inability to continue to function as a Great Power. John Mearsheimer suggested for example the acquisition of nuclear weapons by Germany. Together with a continued American commitment to Europe and a continuation of NATO these are the conditions deemed necessary for coping with ethnic conflicts, potential inter-state rivalries in Europe and for maintaining stability in the region as a whole.[4] There are important reasons why the neo-realist analysis and policy prescriptions should not be accepted. First, the stability of the bipolar world is generally overstated. The global nature of the bipolar conflict meant that while direct military confrontations between the principal protagonists were avoided, there were major proxy wars at the periphery and many regional conflicts became polarised along Cold War lines and were fuelled with the influx of large quantities of high-technology weaponry from both sides. While the 'long peace' prevailed in Europe because of the risk of nuclear war, there is no reason to assume that there would have been unending conflicts in Europe without the Cold War. On the other hand, the conflicts that exist now are at least in part a product of Soviet imperialism and the Cold War.

Realist analysis is misled in its interpretation of the bipolar conflict. The East-West conflict cannot be understood simply as the natural rivalry between two great power systems. It was a more fundamental antagonism involving the legitimacy of different types of socio-economic organisation and the legitimacy of certain political élites for which the pursuit Great Power interests was an essential instrument to perpetuate their own existence and ambitions. Neo-realist analysis fails to explain these specific features of the East-West conflict.[5]

Furthermore, neo-realist analysis completely fails to account for the end of the Cold War.[6] While the power of the Soviet Union and its empire were clearly in decline in the 1980s, and while this decline would no doubt at some time in the future have rendered the Soviet empire unsustainable, these systemic factors do not account for the timing and direction of the changes.[7] As long as substantial strategic and theatre nuclear forces were deployed by the Soviet Union, together with conventional forces sufficient to quell any rebellion in Eastern Europe, the military position of the Soviet Union was not under imminent threat. The economic crisis *followed perestroika* and the restructuring of Soviet foreign relations. If the Soviet Union had decided to use the political and military instruments of power in the same manner as before Gorbachev assumed the leadership, it could have easily defended its position. The collapse of Soviet power and the dissolution of the Soviet state itself therefore fundamentally contradicts neo-realist analysis, according to which the perpetuation of their own existence and the maximisation of their power is the most fundamental objective that states pursue.

The long-term decline in Soviet power could have led to a variety of different responses, but the kind of political reform which occurred was perhaps the least expected one. Indeed, in continuity with the long established parameters of Soviet foreign policy a greater assertiveness abroad and a more sustained endeavour to improve the economy by a more determined use of the authoritarian instruments of government and the ideological structures for political socialisation would have been expected. It is both the timing and *peaceful* nature of the end of the Soviet empire that defy explanation by the neo-realist or the structural realist paradigm. The changes in the international system were not inevitable consequences of changes in the balance of power.[8]

The interaction of the Soviet state with the international system cannot be satisfactorily explained on the properties of the international system alone, but needs to be based on an analysis of internal developments. One theoretical framework that seeks to provide the connection between domestic and international politics is David Easton's systems theory of international relations which defines political interactions, as distinct from other kinds of interaction, as being principally oriented toward the 'authoritative allocation of values for a society'.[9] The values of Soviet society were defined by Marxism-Leninism as interpreted by the Communist Party, which meant Stalin until March 1953. The policies of Stalin's successors Malenkov and Khrushchev could be understood as an attempt to redefine the basic values of Soviet society in order to pursue policies that they believed would resolve the dilemmas that the Soviet Union faced. The development of the doctrine of 'peaceful co-existence' and the emphasis on economic and political rather than military competition with the

West can be seen as part of the system of values Khrushchev was advocating which affected both domestic and foreign policy. The role of the Soviet Union in the international system can be accommodated within this approach. Despite the official adherence to the goal of 'world socialism' in which the Soviet Union would play a leading role, there were evidently deep differences about the how the Soviet Union should adapt to the international environment. The Khrushchev period is instructive because there were two clear alternatives advocated by different parts of the Soviet élite. One was the pursuit of a more overtly hostile policy towards the West, accompanied by greater investments in military production; the other was the line of 'peaceful co-existence', accompanied by a shift in resources towards agriculture and consumer goods production. It was not self-evident that the Soviet Union was forced by the external environment to follow one or the other; their distinction lay primarily in the consequences for Soviet society.[10] A similar analysis applies to Gorbachev's New Political Thinking. New Political Thinking challenged both the realist and the Marxist-Leninist theories of international relations (as hitherto understood) by proposing a new set of values based on global interdependence and human values. The logical corollary of New Political Thinking was the demilitarization of East-West relations. It implied the abandonment of the unilateral maximisation of national security on the basis of military forces and the search for mutual security based on political relations. This was accompanied by domestic political reform beginning with a campaign for *glasnost'* and leading to the introduction of major elements of genuine democracy.[11]

The consequences of these changes were clearly not foreseen by Gorbachev and his supporters in the Soviet political élite. While the policies were successful in so far as they did radically alter East-West relations, the application of new thinking to relations with Eastern Europe exposed the political fragility of Soviet control and resulted in the disintegration of the Warsaw Pact and Soviet military withdrawal. The introduction of genuine elections and the promotion of *glasnost'* allowed the development of a political culture which destroyed the homogeneity of the existing political system. The failure of the economic reforms intensified the process of social and political disintegration, resulting in the end of the Soviet Union.

It is important to emphasize that the transformation of the role of the military factor in East-West relations and particularly on the continent of Europe can be interpreted as a change in the value system on which Soviet foreign relations were based. The most potent manifestation of this was no doubt the abandonment of the 'Brezhnev doctrine' in relations with Eastern Europe. Another was the endeavour by the Soviet Union to integrate with rest of the world community, particularly in the context of a variety of multilateral institutions which it once opposed. It also manifested itself in a fundamental change in Soviet behaviour in the United Nations, the most prominent example of which was the support of UN Security Council resolutions and the measures taken for their implementation against Iraq after the invasion of Kuwait in 1990.[12] The crisis of the Soviet system was not merely one of economic decline, but also one of political legitimacy. The collapse of Soviet communism was not only the collapse of a hegemonic power bloc, but also the rejection of one system of values and norms in favour of another.

Towards a new international system in Europe?

The misinterpretation by the neo-realists of the nature of the Cold War and the reasons for its end leads to a false characterisation of the system of states in Europe after the Cold War. The potential for inter-state conflict predicted by John Mearsheimer is nowhere apparent in Europe except on the territory of states which have now fallen apart, such as certain parts of the former Soviet Union and the former Republic of Yugoslavia.[13] These conflicts can be interpreted either as civil conflicts or post-colonial conflicts. It is therefore correct to say the collapse of the Soviet Union and the Yugoslav state, which created stability on their territories by the constant threat of force has resulted in instability and conflict. On the other hand it is important to emphasize that European states after the Cold War do not seem to be naturally prone to military conflict. Quite the opposite appears to be the case; the principal objective of virtually all Central and Eastern European state is to join various Western multilateral organisations such as NATO and the European Union and thereby accept the consequent constraints on their foreign policies.

The critique of neo-realist analysis could be expressed by stating that a realist approach to international relations based on the Hobbesian analogy is not readily applicable to relations between liberal democracies. Not only have there been no wars between liberal democracies, but they are not perceived to threaten one another and the balance of power between liberal democracies has been relevant only in the context of responses to other external threats.[14] Although the common external threat and the conscious endeavour to overcome the national enmities in Europe which have resulted in two world wars were undoubtedly important factors, a deeper structural principle seems to be necessary to account for this difference in the role of military force. Among the factors that may be part of the explanation are:

- a shared value system which includes the acceptance of international norms
- the existence of institutional mechanisms for the resolution of conflicts
- the more diffuse nature of political power in liberal democracies that makes it difficult to sustain military conflicts, unless they are relatively limited in time and their objectives are widely accepted by the population. This generally rules out the acquisition of territory by force owing to the difficulties of absorbing hostile populations in the political system and the violation of political norms involved.[15] It also means that domestic consent to a war depends highly on the nature of the regime against which war is to be conducted
- i.e. it has to be credibly described as an aggressive and authoritarian (non-democratic) regime
- the vulnerability of high-technology societies and their high standard of living has resulted an unwillingness to support the costs of war, both in terms of casualties and damage to the society itself.

The Gulf War, although on the surface a contradiction of the notion that the world may be moving towards an inherently less conflictual state, is a good illustration of these principles. Iraq was in the grip of a tightly controlled dictatorship which imposed its own agenda on the Iraqi population by means of terror. It did so without any regard to the possibility of casualties or damage to the civilian economy. The United States and its allies were only able to muster such a determined response because the Iraqi annexation of Kuweit constituted such a clear violation of international norms that there was sufficient acceptance of military action by the populations of the allied states. The war plans were designed to ensure the absolute minimum of casualties on the Allied side and maintain military operations on the territory of Iraq, to the extent of introducing sophisticated tactical anti-ballistic missile systems in the (not wholly successful) endeavour to defeat Iraq's sole means of striking at surrounding states.[16] Opinion remains divided on whether the Gulf War demonstrated a 'New World Order' and whether it was justified. The point here is that the case of the Gulf War confirms, rather than refutes, the existence of the kinds of constraints on the use of force imposed on liberal democratic political systems outlined above.

All this suggests that the neo-realist approach underestimates the potential for international co-operation to resolve the new security dilemmas and that co-operative collective security regimes can be established to incorporate newly emerging international norms, a commonality of values among new and old democracies as well as an increasing functional interdependence.

Russian in the international system: a period of transition

Russia's relations with Europe cannot be separated from its relations with the West as a whole and the broad features of its foreign policy in general. Russian foreign policy is still in a state of flux. Like the other former republics of the Soviet Union, the Russian Federation has had to come to terms with being an independent state needing to define its national interests and foreign and security policy objectives.

The principal element in the new frame of reference for Moscow is the disintegration of the Warsaw Pact and the Soviet Union itself. The Russian Federation is now virtually surrounded by former Soviet republics, all of them with deep political, social and economic problems, some of them highly unstable and subject to violent civil conflicts. The territory of the Russian Federation itself, about 75 per cent of the territory of the former USSR with about 60 per cent of its population, is still not properly defined, given that significant sections of the borders are purely notional, and the degree of control that Moscow can exercise over the entire Federation is uncertain.[17]

Both the external and the domestic environment faced by Moscow's policy-makers have been transformed. Russia has emerged from a tremendous global conflict with the highly industrialized countries of the West, which endured for over forty years, and from an even longer period of totalitarianism and mismanagement of all aspects of government. In this context, Russia, as the largest and by any measure most powerful of the Soviet successor states, has to deal with the many issues arising from the loss of empire: relations with the former Soviet states and eastern Europe, policy towards the former adversaries of the Soviet Union, and the extent of any remaining global role that Russia might play. More fundamental and important is how the Russian people, having been defeated in the struggle with the West and betrayed by the totalitarian misrule of their own leaders, and having rejected the most basic values on which their society had supposedly been based, redefine their own national identity, and how this determines their relations with the rest of the world.

Russia and the world

It did not take long for a general consensus to emerge in Russia that it does not have the resources to play a global role. Accordingly, Russian involvement in third world countries not contiguous to its own borders, including allies of the former Soviet Union, has virtually ceased. Nor is there any interest in resuming a hegemonic role in eastern Europe. More importantly, from the point of view of relations with the West, the confrontation with the West, and with the United States in particular, is considered to be over.[18]

The first two years of the Yeltsin government were characterized by a foreign policy in which the development of closer relations with the West dominated everything else. The continuing decline of Russia's economy and the bitter conflict between Yeltsin and the parliament which was resolved by the use of force have resulted in a political climate marked by disillusionment with economic and political reform. Since the events of October 1993, when President Yeltsin broke up the sit-in at the parliament, forcibly dissolved it and restructured the Russian political system by means of a new constitution, Russian democratic forces have been continuously losing influence. This trend has been accompanied by an increasingly assertive foreign policy which stresses Russia's role as a great power on the world stage and its special interests in 'the former Soviet space'. At the same time, relations with the West have cooled somewhat, and the concept of a partnership between Russia and the West has openly come into question.

There are a number of factors that account for these developments. The first is the emergence of new conceptions of Russia's national interest. We can discern several elements crucial to Russian national security policy. The first of these is that Russia is and remains a great power. This means that while Russia seeks a co-operative relationship with the West, it does so on equal terms and it will not toe the Western line in international organizations. The second is that Russia claims the right to a dominant position in the former Soviet space, which remains its special sphere of influence. This claim has a range of implications. For Russia, the external border of the Commonwealth of Independent States is perceived as the geopolitical boundary of the Russian Federation. Russia sees itself as the sole guarantor of security within that area, bearing the main responsibility for conflict resolution and peacekeeping in the CIS. This assumption has an economic dimension as Russia increasingly asserts a right to be involved in the disposition of major reservoirs of natural resources in the CIS, such as oil and gas. Another facet of this stance is the intention to exclude any external powers from major influence in the periphery of the former Soviet space. The perception that these are vital elements of a strategy designed to safeguard Russian national security, which is perceived to be under threat especially at its southern periphery, explains to some extent the shifts and changes in Russian policy towards the West.[19]

The second factor is the reassertion of the conservative institutions of the *ancien régime*. These include the armed forces, the military-industrial complex, the gas and oil industries, the agricultural sector and the security services (the successors to the KGB). These institutions do not have a common agenda, but they exercise a great deal of influence on policy outside the democratic process. This is exacerbated by the fact that the middle layer of the bureaucratic apparatus in all the ministries is dominated by people from the Soviet era who largely dislike the West and who share the objective of restoring both Russia's great power status and a new union of the former Soviet states. Given that the influence of the parliament is more restricted under the new constitution, it is now believed by many expert observers that democratic control over the policy process, in so far as it ever existed, has largely been lost. The extent to which power struggles in the Kremlin impact on policy was vividly demonstrated by the short period during which Alexander Lebed headed the Security Council after the presidential elections in 1996. Although Lebed's efforts to concentrate power in his own hands were ultimately defeated, this episode, which coincided with Yeltsin's prolonged and severe illness, demonstrated the deficiencies of the political process.

The third factor is the sharp and prolonged downturn in the Russian economy. There was an expectation that market reform; Western economic aid and Western capital investment would transform Russia's economy. This has not happened, partly because of gross mismanagement, partly due to systemic factors. The entire industrial base of Russia, which is dominated by military production, needs to be fundamentally restructured in order to be able to produce goods capable of competing in the world market. The investment capital required to retool Russia's industry is enormous and the entire process will require decades. Although Russia has undertaken systematic reform of the economy and industry has been privatized on a huge scale, this is only the beginning. So far the principal outcome of the reform process has been a rapid fall in the level of production, government insolvency (which translates into insolvency for the major companies which relied on government orders), unemployment, a precipitous rise in the cost of living and a concomitant fall in the standard of living. Attempts by the Russian government to control inflationary pressures have been rather uneven, although this element of economic policy has been comparatively successful since mid-1995.[20] The fragility of Russia's efforts to halt economic decline were exposed in the financial crisis in August 1998 when the ruble collapsed in the wake of the Asian financial crisis and prospects of returning to economic growth vanished. Another fundamental problem has been the absence of an effective legal system to regulate economic activity. These difficulties are exacerbated by the growth of organized crime and corruption, which pervade every aspect of economic activity in Russia today.

The consequence has been that Western investors have remained reluctant to become involved. Cumulative foreign investment in the Soviet Union and

Russia from 1988 to 1994 amounted to a mere $2.7 billion. Of particular symbolic significance has been the Russian perception of the rather small scale of Western aid and credits. Germany has been the most substantial and reliable donor, providing DM81.2 billion to the former Soviet states between 1990 and 1993.[21] The United States has been hesitant to commit major sums, partly as a consequence of its own large deficit, partly from a lack of confidence that a larger financial commitment would benefit the Russian economy. The conclusion drawn by many in the Russian political élite is that the hope for Western aid is illusory and that Russia will have to rely on its own resources, while among the general population the failure of the Russian economy has resulted in a general disenchantment with reform.[22] Although economic constraints still provide a powerful motivation for good relations with the West, this is less strong now than it was in 1991 and 1992. In particular, what is remarkable about the more recent trends in Russian policy is that Russia is willing to pursue the reintegration of the CIS as a priority objective, despite the potentially high costs and despite the detrimental consequences on Russia's extended integration into the world economy.[23] The Russian government appears to be willing to take greater risks in pursuit of a more independent foreign policy.

One consequence of this shift is that Russian policy towards the West has become less predictable and co-operative. This does not mean that Russia will threaten the West directly, although it may act against Western interests in international organizations; certainly, the return to a more adversarial relationship with the West cannot be ruled out, but remains very unlikely so long as the economic interests of the state, the interests of the main power groups and the personal interests of much of the political élite remains highly dependent on the influx of Western money and close relations with the West. Another danger lies in the outbreak of internal conflict in the Russian Federation that may get out of control altogether, or complete societal breakdown. Although fundamentally co-operation with the West and integration into the international remains fundamental to Russia's foreign and security policy, basic disagreements about the future of European security continue to affect relations with the West. However if there is a threat from Russia, it does not arise from political ambitions supported by aggressive military power, but rather in the potential for political, social and economic breakdown, resulting in civil conflict (including, potentially, the loss of control over nuclear weapons).

Towards a new system of international security

The security policies of Western countries have, on the level of threat perception at least, adapted rather quickly to the new security environment. Whereas during the Cold War period they were defined on the basis of a specific substantial military threat, with forces deployed and configured to meet this threat, this is no longer the case now. Very soon after German unification a consensus emerged that Western Europe was no longer facing a serious military threat. The optimism of the immediate period following the collapse of the Berlin Wall was rudely shattered by the Gulf Conflict in 1990-91, which proved stubbornly and dangerously unsusceptible to political instruments alone. Even worse were the conflicts in the former Yugoslavia and the former Soviet Union which brutally exposed the inadequacies of European collective security arrangements and raised deep questions about the very concepts underlying them. As a consequence, the confidence in pan-European collective security and a New World Order declined.

One important argument in favour of more formalised arrangements for collective security in Europe is that a higher degree of institutionalisation of a relationship of strategic co-operation, and the more Russia and other states from Eastern Europe can get locked into a system of collective security involving international institutions, norms and instruments of enforcement of human rights and international law could prevent the resurgence of fundamentally antagonistic relations based on a military confrontation. A successful political and economic partnership with the West is the best hope of preventing the resurgence of authoritarian and nationalist regimes or the descent in chaos.

It would be fair to say that Western policymakers share the view that after the Cold War the non-military aspects of security are likely to assume much greater importance. There are two key aspects to this. First of all, the instruments of foreign policy and power projection have changed. Economic power has become the key to political influence in the restructuring of international relations. The second aspect is that the threats to *societal security* are primarily non-military, resulting from economic dislocation, ethnic rivalries and, as a consequence, large migratory movements. This has important implications for Western Europe. It has to face a new role arising from the fact that Eastern Europe sees it as the source of its future economic security. At the same time, it is facing new sources of insecurity, which question the existing political philosophy based on the ideas of tolerance, human rights, social justice and the welfare state and require new and politically unpalatable means to deal with them.

The international system in the early post-Cold War era therefore faces the enormous paradox that while on the one hand virtually all the states in the region have abandoned older forms of international conduct in which military force played a dominant role, at the same time the transition of the European system of states requires a system of collective security with effective military instruments to enforce and keep the peace. This is what we might term *the central dilemma of European security*. The problem results from the fact that while a value-free commitment to balance of power politics is deemed unacceptable, there is neither the intellectual analysis nor the political commitment to build effective structures of collective security in Europe, neither in Germany nor in its partner countries. As long as this is the case, the countries of Europe are helpless as new conflicts erupt and remain unable to take the necessary steps that it takes to ensure effective conflict prevention and management. This was a real challenge for European security policy after the Cold War.

This suggests precisely the opposite approaches to policy from those advocated by John Mearsheimer and some other neo-realists. Any sustained endeavour to recreate military balances of power in Central Europe would be detrimental to this process. Let us briefly consider the military instruments involved in Mearsheimer's policy prescriptions.

Nuclear forces

Neo-realist analysis provides the clearest statement in support of the retention of nuclear weapons capabilities.[24] Nuclear weapons are seen to have an indispensable role in a new balance of power arrangement to compensate for the collapse of the bipolar order. Many analysts would agree that nuclear weapons are necessary to continue to exercise a fundamental restraining influence on inter-state conflict in the uncertain decades to come. They would point to the absence of war in Europe during the last 45 years. The argument is that nuclear weapons will continue to be an indispensable source of security in Europe and on a global basis.

There is an even more basic argument in favour of retaining nuclear weapons. It is difficult, if not impossible, to get rid of them. As Sir Michael Quinlan argued in a recent article:

> There would always be a latent menace, even if nuclear weapons were no longer in existence at all, implicit simply in the fact that they could be rebuilt...[25]

In other words, it is not possible to 'put the nuclear genie back in the bottle' because it is always conceivable that some state will secretly reacquire nuclear weapons even after complete nuclear disarmament. Thus it could be argued to be prudent for Western states to retain at least some nuclear capability for the indefinite future. This argument also fits in with a neo-realist analysis, which would predict that states would ultimately resort again to the deployment of a nuclear arsenal in pursuit of their national interests.

In response to the arguments advanced above, a number of points need to be made.

First, the stability of the bipolar world is generally overstated. While the 'long peace' prevailed in Europe because of the risk of nuclear war, there is no reason to assume that there would have been unending conflicts in Europe without the Cold War. On the other hand, the conflicts that exist now are at least in part a product of Soviet imperialism and the Cold War.

Even if one were to accept that the risks inherent in the production, deployment and targeting of nuclear weapons systems were justified by the nature and scale of the threat from a totalitarian state seeking to destroy the international order, it is less clear that this can be maintained in the absence of such a threat.

The ultimate impact of nuclear weapons on the international system may not necessarily prove benign. It is evident that nuclear weapons did fundamentally influence the way in which Western and Soviet policymakers thought about the role of military force as an instrument of foreign policy. In this sense they were a source of stability and in the international system and security for the protagonists. But the avoidance of global catastrophe during the Cold War was by no means inevitable. During the early years of the strategic nuclear confrontation, nuclear weapons were deliberately used as an instrument of diplomacy. Consequently there were a number of nuclear crises, which could have ended differently.[26] Furthermore, there was a doctrinal commitment to early nuclear use in the European theatre both on the Soviet and US side at least until the late 1960s. While acting as a deterrent, such nuclear planning also raises the risks of unintended escalation.

The strategic nuclear relationship between the United States and the Soviet Union/Russia was and to a lesser extent remains an extremely dangerous phenomenon. In particular, the shift to launch-under-attack postures at the strategic nuclear level which was complete on both sides by 1983 increased the possibility of nuclear use in a crisis or accidental nuclear launch.[27] American strategic nuclear planning, as embodied in the so-called SIOP (Single Integrated Operational Plan), was premised on the rapid launch of the bulk of available forces at very short notice, with decision times of at most ten minutes.

A detailed analysis of the technical features of the early warning and command and control systems shows that errors can occur in each and every element of the system. Sensors can and have given false warnings. There are known instances both from the United States and the Soviet Union where missile launches were reported that never took place. The false warnings did not result in the decision to launch a 'counterstrike' because of the lack of strategic warning (i.e. there was no crisis or other indication that an attack was imminent or likely) and negative corroboration by other sources (e.g. radars). However, procedures developed to a point where in the presence of strategic warning (e.g. during a crisis when forces had been put on alert) a false warning could conceivably have produced a launch decision. Strategic warning, on the other hand, is notoriously unreliable and the history of the US-Soviet confrontation is littered with false interpretations of force dispositions and alerts by the other side. The fact that strategic nuclear forces remained under control and were never used does not mean that this outcome was inevitable. It was not inevitable that relations between the Soviet Union and the United States would not get out of hand. Moreover, a close analysis of planning for nuclear operations shows that a nuclear war started unintentionally was a real possibility.[28]

No amount of geopolitical analysis therefore should be allowed to obscure the fact that fundamentally the strategic nuclear confrontation between the United States and the Soviet Union was incredibly dangerous, fraught with the potential for the destruction of human life and the terrestrial environment on an apocalyptic scale.

A strong argument can be made that the presence of nuclear weapons is not a factor of stability in the kinds of conflicts erupting in the wake of the Cold War. Contrary to neo-realist analysis, as has been pointed out above, the evidence so far seems to point to a low potential for inter-state conflict in Central Europe in which deterrence could play a major role. The crisis regions are characterised by intra-state conflicts or post-colonial conflicts caused by the break-up of the former Soviet and Yugoslav states. Nuclear weapons are not a source of security or stability in the context of such conflicts. The fact that Russia is a nuclear state does not help it to secure its southern borders. The Afghan rebels were not deterred by Soviet nuclear forces, nor are the Tajiks currently operating from Afghan territory. Nuclear weapons have no relevance in the conflict between Georgia and Abkhazia or Armenia and Azerbaijan. The same applies in the Balkan conflicts. Four nuclear powers are involved in the conflicts in the former Yugoslavia, but this has no relevance. The opposite conclusion must be drawn - the presence of nuclear weapons in such crisis regions constitutes a major source of danger and insecurity. In particular the safety of the former Soviet nuclear arsenal represents a security problem of the highest magnitude.[29] Although there are many immediate measures that could be taken urgently to render the existing stockpile of weapons more secure, this problem can ultimately only be resolved in the context of a 'co-operative denuclearization' which provides both the political context and the level of international technical co-operation necessary for nuclear safety.[30]

Conventional forces

The build-up of substantial conventional forces to create a military balance of power in Europe is also not in the interests of future European security. First of all, it would not be required in terms of the military security of NATO Allies. One of the reasons why NATO members were initially reluctant to extend membership to Central European countries is precisely that this is not perceived as enhancing the security of the Alliance. Indeed, enlargement had the potential for reducing Alliance security in so far as Western Europe might be drawn into conflicts from which it would otherwise remain isolated. There is currently an extensive conventional arms control regime in place (the CFE Treaty) which is in principle capable of preventing local arms races in Central and Eastern Europe and particularly constrains Russian military deployments west of the Urals. It is in the security interest of all European countries that this regime remains in place and that Russia remains an adherent to it.[31]

There remains the issue of the use of military force in crisis regions in Europe, i.e. in the former Soviet Union and the former Yugoslavia. As far as the latter is concerned, the reluctance by leading members of NATO to assume a peace-making role did much to discredit the idea of collective security. The reluctance of Western European states to get involved in anything other than peace-keeping and humanitarian actions was a consequence of the perceived difficulty of legitimising such potentially costly and controversial actions at home and of the fact that at present West European and US security interests are not directly affected. The Dayton peace agreement and the intervention in Kosovo have gone some way to restoring NATO's credibility, but consensus on collective security in Europe remains elusive.

It is true that the conflicts in the former Soviet Union and the former Yugoslavia cast a substantial shadow on the optimistic picture of a Europe without major military threat characterised by political and economic integration and the transition from national defence to collective security. They do not necessarily contradict the conclusion, however, that both an idealist and/or institutionalist perspective proved to be a better guide to the future of Europe than Kenneth Waltz's and John Mearsheimer's dire neo-realist predictions. The first point to be made is that these conflicts were associated with the dissolution of states and were not inter-state, but rather intra-state conflicts. They are therefore special cases that do not necessarily permit conclusions for the European system of states as a whole. The former Soviet Union and the former Yugoslavia otherwise are quite distinct. The conflicts in the FSU were concentrated in regions of the Caucasus and Central Asia in which central government had become incapable of enforcing order. This is the antithesis of the neo-realist case, where a government fails to use all of its resources to maximize its power and authority. From a neo-realist perspective the relatively peaceful dissolution of the Soviet is a remarkable and in many respects paradoxical event. There was no war of dissolution the Soviet Union; to the contrary, the core state, Russia, was one of the principal agents bringing about its dissolution. It is true that since then Russia has sought to exercise a hegemonic influence over the former Soviet territory, and that its involvement in various conflicts (Georgia and Abkhazia, the Transdniestr dispute and the Tajik civil war) had the intent to consolidate its influence and support its perceived security interests as an important determining factor. But this was never pushed to the point of removing governments or destroying the national sovereignty of the newly independent states, and when push came to shove there was no appetite in Moscow for the reestablishment of the Soviet Union.[32] While democratization in the former Soviet states remains incomplete, and pockets of regional anarchy and potential conflict zones persist, the reality is that the newly independent states have integrated into the international system in a peaceful fashion and with an increasing acceptance of accepted norms of international conduct.

This in stark contrast to the dissolution of Yugoslavia which was resisted by the core state, Serbia, with ferocious violence. While the events in the former Yugoslavia have important consequences for the whole of Europe, they are not evidence that international anarchy in Europe is going to be the norm, and that new balances of power and new nuclear weapons states to provide an ordering power will be required. In this sense the Yugoslav 'war of dissolution' is very much the exception rather than the rule.

Neo-realist analysis can draw more comfort from the failure to develop adequate institutional mechanisms for collective security and the reluctance of Western powers to commit to peace enforcement in the former Yugoslavia. This accords with Mearsheimer and Waltz's belief that state will always prefer the maximization of autonomy and therefore pursue autonomy-seeking policies. Moreover, European states and even more so the United States had difficulty identifying any national interest in the Balkans.

But this leaves them with the paradox that European states ultimately behaved in a manner that is best explained by institutionalism, without the development of the necessary institutions. The United States eventually did commit its resources, including armed forces, despite the domestic political cost and the lack of perceived geo-political benefits. Hegemonic stability theory is also weak in its explanatory power because the major powers saw the Balkan area outside its province. Neo-realist and institutionalist explanations fail because they ignore the importance of norms and values, especially in the post-Cold War order. Try as they might, Western states could not in the end ignore Serb aggression, the persistence of conflict and massive human rights violations. While the institutionalist explanation is weak (given the weakness of the institutions), a constructivist explanation is attractive because it can explain both the behaviour of the West European states and the United States in the absence of either pressing risks to their national security or institutional commitments. The main problem with both neo-realist and institutionalist approaches is that they fail to explain the phenomenon of advancement of international norms and international law as a major basis of international co-operation that seemed to be effective in mitigating the effects of international anarchy. *Constructivism*, is based on the notion that while the international system is inherently anarchic, states can transcend the anarchy by advancing international norms and common interests. It is not inevitable that states will choose to play zero-sum games. Constructivism has three basic elements: First is the view that shared norms and values guide state behaviour. As a consequence the international system is even in the absence of an over-arching authority no longer purely anarchic. Secondly, the structure of conventions, norms and values affect the self-perception of the actors (states) in the international system. There is a process of socialisation which results in the construction of a shared identity among states. Thirdly structures and agents in the international system determine each other, and although structures determine the identity of actors, the actors can also change structures. In contrast to neo-realism, the order in the international system derives not merely from the hierarchy of power, but also from shared norms and international law.[33]

The international system has changed and the requirements for global and European security have changed radically since 1990. The end of the Cold War is something more fundamental than a shift in the balance of power. It constitutes a change in the nature of international relations. While this is recognised in the United States, Europe and Russia, national security policies and international institutions have not fully adapted to the new environment. Russia and the United States have transformed their bitter adversarial relationship into a partnership and are no longer involved in a global politico-military rivalry. But in Russia the notion of the West as a potential adversary still has some residual political impact, as seen in the debates over NATO enlargement and the reaction to the Kosovo intervention. In the United States likewise a possible adversarial relationship with Russia still has some influence in the political process, even though it has been abandoned by the US government. In other words, Russia and the United States have only partially adapted their relationship to the post-Cold War environment. The same applies to Europe, where, as we have seen, the central dilemma of European security remains unresolved.

The failure by the political élites of the major states in the global system to come to grips with the meaning of the collapse of Communism and the globalisation and demilitarization of security has the result that in Europe and beyond the institutional infra-structure of global security has not been fully reconstructed. It still retains some features and functions that stem from the Cold War period, while new elements that would be required have not yet come into existence. This is what one might call the *strategic paradox* of the post-Cold war era. The particular feature that this book is seeking to address is the strategic nuclear relationship between the United States and Russia.

Options for a post-Cold War strategic environment

The *strategic paradox* of nuclear arms policy has a somewhat different meaning than the central dilemma of European security. The latter is about the failure to construct a new security regime, whereas the former is about the failure to dismantle the old security infrastructure. There was no conceptual guide to the future structure of strategic nuclear relations after the bilateral confrontation. The only thing the political leaders knew to do was to continue with existing arms control frameworks, leaving the central structure of the arsenals intact, albeit at substantially reduced levels, and make sure that there was only one nuclear successor state to the USSR. This has left strategic arms policy in a condition of profound ambiguity. If Russia is no longer the enemy, and US weapons are longer targeted at Russia, then what considerations guide the strategic force posture? What range of threats are the weapons supposed to deter, and what and how many weapons of what kind are required for this task? There is, as yet, no clear answer to this question. Meanwhile strategic nuclear forces remain on a low level of alert, but still ready to be launched at very short notice.

The argument pursued in this book is that even if during the Cold War period nuclear weapons represented a source of stability and contributed to the prevention of war between the United States and the Soviet Union, they now constitute a threat to international security. The objective of arms control should be to contain and eventually eliminate this threat. This will require that the United States and Russia as the major nuclear powers develop a close relationship characterized by strategic co-operation instead of confrontation. In the place of strategic stability, nuclear safety should be the principal criterion of arms control which now be understood as a process of 'co-operative denuclearization'.

The concept of 'co-operative denuclearization' has been proposed by scholars participating in the Co-operative Security/Post Cold War Reconstruction Project at the Center for Science and International Affairs (CSIA) at Harvard University's John F. Kennedy School of Government.[34] It is defined as the elimination of tactical nuclear weapons, the elimination of the bulk of strategic nuclear weapons and the establishment of international norms which push nuclear weapons to the fringe of international life.[35] I will follow this definition here, except that when the term is used it is taken to imply that the placing of a small nuclear weapons force under international control (with all other nuclear weapons having been eliminated) is seen as the endpoint of the process.

The book will discuss the evolution of strategic arms policy in the United States and Russia since 1991. Although neither Russia nor the United States adopted to the objectives of 'co-operative denuclearization', there was a concerted effort to deal with issues of nuclear safety in Russia through the Co-operative Threat Reduction programme, reduce the number of weapons deployed dramatically by means of strategic arms control and inhibit the development of new nuclear weapons through a comprehensive test ban and fissile materials production ban. The book will show how these various elements are conceptually and practically interrelated, and why the major objective of reducing the risks from the Russian nuclear weapons complex has not been achieved so far. As Alexei Arbatov has said, it remains to be seen whether the world will survive the collapse of a nuclear superpower.[36]

Notes

1. John J. Mearsheimer, 'Back to the Future', *International Security*, Vol.15, No.1, Summer 1990, pp.5-56; Kenneth N. Waltz, *Theory of International Politics*, Reading, MA: Addison-Wesley 1979; Kenneth N. Waltz, *The Spread of Nuclear Weapons: More May Be Better*, Adelphi Paper No.171, London: IISS 1981.
2. Hans J. Morgenthau, *Politics Among Nations: The Struggle for Power and Peace*, New York: Knopf 1973; Kenneth N. Waltz (1979), ibid.

3. John Lewis Gaddis, 'The Long Peace: Elements of Stability in the Postwar International System', *International Security*, Vol.10, No.4, Spring 1986, pp.99-142.
4. Mearsheimer, op.cit., p.38.
5. For an analysis of these ideas, see Fred Halliday, 'Cold War as Inter-Systemic Conflict: Initial Theses', in Mike Bowker and Robin Brown (eds.), *From Cold War to collapse: theory and world politics in the 1980s*, Cambridge: Cambridge University Press 1993, pp.21-34.
6. This criticism can be extended to other approaches to International Relations theory; see John Lewis Gaddis, 'International Relations Theory and the End of the Cold War', *International Security*, Vol.17, No.3, Winter 1992/93, pp.5-58.
7. See Fred Chernoff, 'Ending the Cold War: The Soviet Retreat and the US Military Buildup', *International Affairs*, Vol.67, 1991, pp.11-126; Friedrich Kratochwil, 'The Embarrassment of Changes', *Review of International Studies*, Vol.119, No.1, January 1993, pp.63-80.
8. See, for example, the substantial analysis of the domestic political and economic difficulties of the Soviet Union written in the first year of the Gorbachev period which predicted the continued pursuit of expansionist ambitions by the Soviet leadership despite internal weakness by Seweryn Bialer, *The Soviet Paradox*, London: I.B. Tauris 1986.
9. David Easton, *A Framework for Political Analysis*, Englewood Cliffs: Prentice-Hall 1965, p.50; see also Robert Gilpin, *War and Change in World Politics*, Cambridge: Cambridge University Press 1980; J. David Singer, *A General Systems Taxonomy for Political Science*, New York: General Learning Press 1971; Ekkehardt Krippendorf, 'Ist Außenpolitik?', *Politische Vierteljahres-Schrift*, Vol.4, 1963, pp.243-265; Peter Gourevitch, 'The Second Image Reversed: The International Sources of Domestic Policies', *International Organization*, Vol.32, No.4, Autumn 1978, pp.881-911; Graham T. Allison, *Essence of Decision*, Boston: Little Brown and Company 1971; Thomas Risse-Kappen, *Die Krise der Sicherheitspolitik,* München: Christian Kaiser Verlag 1988; Fareed Zalaria, 'Realism and Domestic Politics', *International Security*, Vol.17, No.1, Summer 1992, pp.177-198.
10. For a detailed discussion of this argument see Christoph Bluth, *Soviet Strategic Arms Policy Before SALT*, Cambridge: Cambridge University Press 1992.
11. For an early, path-breaking analysis of New Political Thinking see Stephen Shenfield, *The Nuclear Predicament*, London: Routledge & Kegan Paul 1987; see also Christoph Bluth, *New Thinking in Soviet Military Policy*,

London: Pinter 1990; Michael MccGwire, *Perestroika and Soviet National Security*, Washington DC: Brookings Institution 1991; Peter Shearman, 'New political thinking reassessed', *Review of International Studies*, Vol.19, No.2, April 1993, pp.139-158; see also Mikhail Gorbachev, *Perestroika*, London: Collins 1987 and Eduard Shevardnadze, *Moi vybor*, Moscow: Novosti 1991.

12. This has been interpreted as being a consequence of Soviet weakness and the desire for Western economic support. However, there seems to be no reason to disbelieve Shevardnadze's repeated assertion that the Soviet stance was motivated by their condemnation of Saddam Hussein's actions. Conversations with Soviet political experts close to the Ministry of Foreign Affairs at the time had the 'return to the civilised world' as a recurrent theme. See Shevardnadze, op.cit., pp.179-189.
13. The potential disputes between various Central European States (e.g. Hungary and Rumania) do not seem to result in arms races or military confrontations and are nowhere near crisis point. For more detailed analysis, and support for the argument that such conflicts are likely to be of a political and economic rather than military nature, see Jan Zielonka, *Security in Central Europe*, Adelphi Paper No.272, London: Brassey's 1992.
14. The theoretical issues arising from this statement and its empirical basis cannot be discussed here. The statement that liberal democracies do not go to war to each other seems to be well-founded empirically. For a discussion of the theoretical issues, see Robert Latham, 'Democracy and War-Making: Locating the International Liberal Context', *Millenium*, Vol.22, No.2, Summer 1993, pp.139-164; Randall L. Schweller, 'Domestic Structure and Preventive War: Are Democracies More Pacific?', *World Politics*, Vol.44, No.2, January 1992, pp.235-269; for an opposing view see Mearsheimer, op.cit., pp. 49-51; for an analysis of the empirical evidence, see Alex Mintz and Nehemia Geva, 'Why Don't Democracies Fight Each Other? An Experimental Study', *Journal of Conflict Resolution*, Vol.37, No.3, September 1993, pp.484-503; Z. Maoz and B. Russett, 'Alliance, contiguity, wealth and political stability: Is the lack of conflict among democracies a statistical artifact?', *International Interactions*, Vol.17, No.3, 1992, pp.245-267.
15. Northern Ireland is an example of the political instability generated by a territorial status that is not accepted by a substantial portion of the population.
16. For more detail see Lawrence Freedman and Efraim Karsh, *The Gulf Conflict 1990-1991*, London: Faber & Faber 1993.

17. For a more detailed exploration of these factors, see Alexei C. Arbatov, 'Russia's Foreign Policy Alternatives', *International Security*, vol. 18, no. 2, Fall 1993, pp. 5-43.
18. This can be taken as a fundamental premise of Russian foreign policy, despite the prevalence of anti-Western sentiments in parts of the bureaucracy and political élite which has come to the fore in the debate over the expansion of NATO (see below). See Alexei G. Arbatov, 'Russian National Interests', in Robert D. Blackwill and Sergei Karaganov, eds., *Damage Limitation or Crisis?* (London: Brassey's, 1994), pp. 55-76; see also chapter 1.
19. Alexander A. Pikayev, 'The Russian Domestic debate on Policy Towards the Near Abroad', in Cliff Archer and Lena Jonson (eds), *Peacekeeping and the Role of Russia in Eurasia*, Boulder, CO: Westview Press 1996, pp 33-50.
20. The extent of deindustrialization in Russia is documented and discussed in Roland Götz, 'Rußland auf dem Weg zur De-industrialisierung?', in BIOst, *Zwischen Krise und Konsolidierung* (Munich: Carl Hanser Verlag, 1995) pp. 247- 256.
21. Hannes Adomeit, 'Russia as a Great Power', *International Affairs*, vol. 71, no. 1, January 1995, pp. 35-68.
22. The decline of the Russian economy may have bottomed out and GDP is expected rise from 1997, but this does not affect this point.
23. Abraham S. Becker, 'Russia and Economic Integration in the CIS', *Survival*, vol. 38, no. 4, Winter 1996-7, pp. 117-36.
24. Mearsheimer, op.cit.; Waltz (1979) op.cit.; Waltz (1981) op.cit.
25. Michael Quinlan, 'The future of nuclear weapons: policy for Western possessors', *International Affairs*, Vol.69, No.3, July 1993, pp.485-496.
26. The Cuban Missile Crisis of 1962 and the Berlin Crises 1958-62 are obvious examples. It has recently been claimed by General Anatoli Gribkov that Soviet troops in Cuba had pre-delegated authority to use tactical nuclear weapons in the event of a US attack on Cuba. See Raymond L. Garthoff, 'The Havana Conference On the Cuban Missile Crisis', *Cold War International History Project Bulletin*, No.1, Spring 1992, pp.2-4.
27. The concept of 'launch-under-attack' refers to a SIOP option designed during the tenure of Harold Brown as Defence Secretary to enable the rapid launch of Minuteman forces to prevent their destruction under attack. In this paper the term is used as synonymous with 'launch-on-warning'. See Bruce Blair, *The Logic of Accidental Nuclear War*, Washington DC: Brookings 1993, p.186.

28. This is the central thesis of the book by Bruce Blair, op.cit.
29. For more detail see Alexei Arbatov, *Iadernoe Vooruzheniia i respublikanskiy suverenitet*, Moscow: Mezhdunarodnye otnosheniia 1992; Kurt M. Campbell, Ashton B. Carter, Steven E. Miller, Charles A. Zraket, *Soviet Nuclear Fission*, CSIA Studies in International Security No.1, Cambridge, MA, Harvard University 1991; Graham Allison, Ashton Carter, Steven E. Miller, Philip Zelikow (eds.), *Co-operative Denuclearization*, CSIA Studies in International Security No.2, Cambridge, MA, Harvard University 1993; Steven E. Miller, 'Western diplomacy and the Soviet nuclear legacy', *Survival*,Vol.34, No.3, Autumn 1992, pp.3-27; Christoph Bluth, 'Out of Control? The Future of the Soviet Nuclear Arsenal', *Bulletin of Arms Control*, No.5, pp.2-6, February 1992; Christoph Bluth, 'What do you do with a nuclear arsenal', *New Scientist*, Vol.135, No.1830, pp.26-30, 18 July 1992.
30. For a discussion of the concept of 'co-operative denuclearization', see Christoph Bluth, 'Strategic Nuclear Weapons and US-Russian Relations: From Confrontation to Co-operative Denuclearization', *Contemporary Security Policy*, published in Vol.15, No.1, April 1994.
31. This does not preclude some adjustments to allow Russia to deploy forces in crisis regions, in particular the Caucasus. For an analysis of the current debate, see Jane M.O. Sharp, 'CFE Treaty Under Threat as Russia Requests Revisions', *Bulletin of Arms Control, No.12, November 1993*, pp.2-4.
32. Russia did, of course, have its own brief 'war of dissolution' against Chechnya.
33. Max Otte and Willaim Grimes, *Germany and Japan: Civilian Power, Traditional Power or Institutional Constraints*, unpublished paper 1999, p.3.
34. See Graham Allison, Ashton B. Carter, Steven E. Miller and Philip Zelikow, 'Co-operative Denuclearization: An International Agenda', in Allison, Carter, Miller, Zelikow (eds.), *Co-operative Denuclearization*, pp. 1-24.
35. Allison et al. (1993), p.1.
36. Alexei C Arbatov, 'Russia's Foreign Policy Alternatives', *International Security*, vol.18, no.2, 1993, pp.5-43.

2 The United States: A Strategic Nuclear Power in the 21st Century?

Since the end of World War II, when the United States detonated two atomic bombs over the Japanese cities of Hiroshima and Nagasaki, nuclear weapons have been an essential element of US military power. As the Soviet Union was soon recognized as America's major future potential future adversary, the main role of nuclear weapons was to deter Soviet aggression. The requirements for deterrence were based on the principles of strategic bombing as applied during World War II, except that nuclear weapons were much more powerful and provided a realistic prospect on inflicting 'unacceptable damage' to the enemy. Early strategic plans envisaged the use of 133 warheads against 70 Soviet cities. The strategic calculus of deterrence changed as the Soviet Union detonated its first nuclear weapon in 1949 and began to emulate the United States in other advanced technologies, such as jet and rocket propulsion. The international security environment of the 1950s exhibited two major trends: The increasing perception of the vulnerability of the continental United States to Soviet nuclear attack (dramatically enhanced by the launch of Sputnik in 1957) and the consolidation of the two blocs in Europe, accompanied by the deployment of substantial military forces had an important effect on the thinking about nuclear strategy. From the mid-1950s the defence posture of the United States orientated itself to two major threat scenarios: A strategic surprise attack by the Soviet Union on the United States, and a massive invasion of Western Europe, or a combination of both. The first of these threats demanded a rapid increase in the number of nuclear warheads and the development of diverse delivery vehicles, including land-based and sea-based missiles. At the same time the perceived inferiority of NATO in the European theatre resulted in the deployment of theatre nuclear weapons to deter Soviet aggression. The policy was called ‘massive retaliation’ and threatened large-scale nuclear strikes in the event of even limited Soviet attacks. As Soviet capabilities to target the United States increased this doctrine was replaced by notions called ‘flexible response’ (which allowed for a conventional response in the event of war in Europe until the use of nuclear weapons was deemed necessary) and limited options. The deterrence relationship between the United States and the Soviet Union came to be defined by ‘mutual assured destruction’ as both sides generated a huge stockpile of nuclear weapons (the United States had 30,000 nuclear warheads by the early 1960s, whereas the Soviet Union produced 45,000 by the mid-1980s), delivery vehicles to deliver enough weapons to destroy all the infrastructure and population of the other side several times over and both sides chose to restrict the development of defensive systems.

The basic elements of the strategic triad, as it came to be called, were strategic bombers with nuclear gravity bombs; land-based missiles of intercontinental range (ICBMs) and missiles based on submarines (SLBMs). During the 1970s ICBMs and SLBMs began to be equipped with multiple warheads (so-called MIRVs). This allowed a rapid expansion of the number of warheads without increasing the number of delivery vehicles. At the same time the accuracy of nuclear weapons delivery increased significantly. These technological developments had important strategic consequences. The ‘holy grail’ of missile design is the ability to target and destroy enemy missiles in hardened cement silos. Modern levels of accuracy give planners confidence that they can be certain to destroy a silo with two nuclear warheads. This means that in order to achieve a plausible first-strike capability, the number of warheads must exceed the number of ICBMs deployed by the other side by two-to-one at least, and preferably by three-to-one. The emerging vulnerability of land-based ICBMs became one of the central issues of the strategic debate in the United States in the 1970s and 1980s. This became known as the ‘window of vulnerability’. However, the United States had only one third of its strategic nuclear force based on ICBMs, and about 45 per cent at sea, where it was for all intents and purposes invulnerable. The vulnerability of strategic bombers was reduced by arming them with air-launched cruise missiles instead of gravity bombs, thereby allowing them to attack targets without exposure to the air defences of the enemy. For both sides the risks of a first strike remained prohibitive. By the mid-1980s both the US and the USSR had deployed about 10,000 warheads each on delivery systems of strategic range.

The backbone of the US ICBM force is the Minuteman III missile with a re-entry vehicle (RV) carrying three independently targetable warheads, thus enabling the force to cover 1,500 separate targets. In 1991, there were also 450 Minuteman II single-warhead missiles and 50 *Peacekeeper* ICBM with 10 warheads each. The sea-based force deployed a total of 5,760, with 750 on the highly accurate Trident D5 missile. The strategic bomber force carried 2,665 warheads in the form of gravity bombs and ALCMs.[1]

The question of when and how the United States would employ nuclear weapons in response to a warning of nuclear attack remained politically contentious. In principle the options were launch-on-warning, launch-under-attack (after detonation of the first hostile warheads) and riding out a nuclear attack by the other side. The entire infrastructure of the nuclear command and control system (NC2) was designed to enable the implementation of a launch-on-warning policy. This involved a network of satellites for the early detection of missile launches, the detection of nuclear detonations, long-range radar systems and terminal phase radar systems. The system relied on an elaborate system for the interpretation of strategic and tactical warning. Strategic warning, which was derived from the state of the international system generally and relations with the Soviet Union specifically, was an indication of the degree of international tension and the likelihood of conflict. It was translated into an elaborate system of levels of alert known as the 'Defence Condition' (DefCon) ranging from DefCon 5 (the lowest level of alert) to DefCon 1 (the highest level of combat readiness in anticipation of imminent war). Tactical warnings of an impending attack or an attack in progress were provided the early warning network. The system was designed to enable the rapid launch of the bulk of strategic nuclear weapons as soon as authorization was given by the national command authority (i.e. the President of the United States). The dangers inherent in such a 'hair trigger' posture have already been elaborated upon in Chapter 1. While under ideal circumstances the system was in principle able to perform its fundamental function, this would only be the case if some important factors were ignored. The first was the possibility that an attack could occur without any strategic or tactical warning. This would be the case if attacks were launched out-of-the-blue from submarines with a flight-time of four to ten minutes. In this event the reaction time would essentially be zero. While the absence of strategic warning was very unlikely and SLBMs could not be used to target all US land-based missiles, nevertheless they could devastate the country and attack command and control centres. In other words, under unfavourable conditions the system would be unable to respond rapidly enough. The second factor was the human factor - it was never clear that in the event the national command authority would in fact give the order to launch and the decision time would be excruciatingly short - at most 15 minutes, but, by the time the warnings had been confirmed and the information passed to the NCA it could be a matter of five minutes or less. The contradictions inherent in a launch-on-warning posture given the technical infrastructure available were never resolved and were perhaps irresolvable in principle.

The employment of nuclear weapons in the event of war would be based on the Single Integrated Operational Plan (SIOP) which was developed on the basis on a Joint Strategic Planning Document (JSPD) and the joint strategic capabilities plans (JSCP). Political direction for military planning was given through the policy guidance for the employment of nuclear weapons (NUWEP). It appears that political guidance, however, was very general. Civilian leaders were not well informed about the details of SIOP and the sheer number of strategic nuclear weapons deployed resulted in a situation where many targets were given multiple coverage and the coherence of the entire plan was in doubt. Attempts by higher civilian authorities to develop options for limited nuclear strikes were in conflict with the central defining theme of the SIOP, namely the rapid, centralized execution of a massive nuclear strike in the event of tactical warning to prevent the large-scale loss of nuclear assets. Consequently they did not begin to affect strategic planning until the 1980s and even then only in a limited fashion.

Until the 1980s arms control treaties had been designed to limit the further expansion of arsenals, or the development of technologies that were seen as destabilising. The concept of actual reductions in nuclear weapons was introduced into the arms control dialogue in the 1980s. At first this was a ploy by the Reagan administration to prevent arms control and at the same time blame the other side, but things changed when Gorbachev became leader of the Soviet Union in 1985. From the very outset he pursued nuclear disarmament, and on 15 January 1986 he proposed the total elimination of all nuclear weapons by the year 2000.[2] This was generally interpreted as a utopian vision not to be taken seriously. There was general surprise therefore when at the Reykjavik summit in 1986 Presidents Reagan and Gorbachev came very close to an agreement on a drastic reduction in strategic nuclear forces (which in some versions discussed during the summit could have involved the total elimination of strategic nuclear delivery vehicles (SNDV) within 10 years). At the same time, Gorbachev indicated his preparedness to accept the 'zero option' for Intermediate Nuclear Forces (INF) stationed in Europe. For the Europeans, the Reykjavik meeting was a shock even though the summit ended without agreement. This was because Gorbachev made an agreement conditional on the abandonment or curtailment of SDI. This was an area in which President Reagan was unwilling to compromise.[3] For the Europeans the fact that they even discussed such wide-ranging proposals, however, conjured up the spectre of an US-Soviet condominium. In the European's view, the most threatening aspect of the military confrontation was the conventional threat in Central

Europe. For decades one of the principal objectives of the Europeans in relations with the United States had been to secure the protection of US strategic nuclear forces as the ultimate guarantee against Warsaw Pact aggression. The reaction of the European Allies to the Reykjavik summit indicated therefore that nuclear arms control was linked with broader military and political détente in Europe and elsewhere and could not be pursued in isolation.[4]

Although the Reykjavik proposals as such were never implemented, the summit redefined the agenda of the START (Strategic Arms Reduction Treaty) and the INF negotiations which had been initiated during the first Reagan administration but stalled without progress in 1983. The INF negotiations resulted in the INF Treaty, which banned a whole class of weapons (INF with a range greater than 500 km) entirely.[5] The START negotiations can be interpreted as an effort to implement the first phase of Reykjavik, albeit with somewhat more modest targets (i.e. reductions by about 35 per cent in the number of warheads).[6] These negotiations were plagued by political and technical complexities and thus dragged out beyond the lifetime of the Reagan administration and throughout most of the Bush presidency.

After the INF Treaty political developments in Europe seemed to race ahead of arms control negotiations as the Warsaw Pact and with it the division of Europe began to dissolve. A major revision of the SIOP was undertaken in 1988 to allow for much greater flexibility in nuclear operations, and the pressure of political changes and arms control prompted President Bush's Defence Secretary Richard Cheney to conduct a major review of SIOP. The briefings Cheney and Chairman of the Joint Chiefs of Staff Colin Powell received revealed a disturbing structural incoherence and a detachment from political objectives. The plan had been assembled by teams from the Joint Strategic Planning Staff and refined over the years to adapt it to new targets, weapons systems and computerised planning methods, without any clear conception of the overall impact and purpose of the military actions it involved and without the separate teams necessarily knowing what the others were doing. Some cities, such as Moscow, contained a large number targets and thus were covered by an absurdly high number of weapons. Kiev, for example, was to be hit by almost 40 weapons, each with many times the explosive power of the atomic bomb that destroyed Hiroshima. Soft targets less then a mile apart were covered by separate weapons. Cheney and Powell were truly appalled the total lack of coherence of political and military operational objectives uncovered by their review. The result was a revision of the SIOP with the elimination of many non-military targets. Moreover, the planning process was streamlined and in 1991 the Strategic Air Command (SAC) was abolished and replaced by a unified strategic command called STRATCOM.[7]

While there was an awareness of the changes in the international environment and their possible impact on nuclear planning, this did not have a fundamental impact on the Cheney review of the SIOP. Nevertheless the Bush administration was very aware that the changing situation in Europe had implications for nuclear policy. In particular, they began to worry about the internal stability of the Soviet Union and the safety and security of Soviet nuclear weapons. With an estimated 27, 000 tactical and strategic nuclear weapons deployed through the territory of the former Soviet Union, parts of which were turning into crisis regions, it became an important objective of US policy to secure this arsenal. The main policy instrument was the START I treaty, which finally was signed in May 1991 and envisaged a dramatic reduction in the number of strategic warheads deployed, from over 10,000 to a maximum of 6,000 on each side. This in itself was going to have only a very peripheral effect on the issues of safety and security, but it helped to create a climate and an institutional basis in which nuclear co-operation became easier American anxieties were heightened dramatically by the coup in August 1991. This prompted a series of unilateral measures by President Bush such as the elimination of all ground-based missiles with nuclear warheads in Europe, the withdrawal of all tactical nuclear weapons from naval vessels, taking the strategic bomber force off alert and likewise all ICBMs that were to be dismantled under START I, and finally the cancellation of US ICBM development and modernization programmes, including the *Peacekeeper*, the single-warhead *Midgetman* and a short range system known a *S-RAM.* The Soviet reciprocated with similar measures (nuclear weapons were being withdrawn from Central Europe in any event because of the Soviet military withdrawal from former Warsaw Pact countries).

The events of August 1991 also prompted a reaction from the US Senate, partly in response to the publication by the Center for Science and International Affairs at Harvard University of a study of the safety and security risks of nuclear weapons in the Soviet Union entitled *Soviet Nuclear Fission* under the direction for Ashton Carter.[8] The Harvard study delivered a stark message: The destiny of the nuclear weapons in the Soviet was a paramount concern of the times and one without precedence that required action without delay. It discerned three separate sets of concerns: The dispersal of nuclear command authority to new political structures at the republican level (assuming the possible disintegration of the Soviet Union), the loss of control over weapons which could fall into the hands of unauthorised persons, and finally the proliferation of nuclear materials and knowledge about nuclear weapons design to nations and terrorists beyond the borders of the Soviet Union. The study crystallised the concerns that Senator Sam Nunn and Les Aspin, then Chair of the House Armed Services Committee, had felt about the risks to nuclear safety as a result of political breakdown and the social and economic dislocation in the former Soviet Union.

Senators Richard Lugar and Sam Nunn organised a briefing given by Ashton Carter and subsequently collaborated in bringing forward legislation in the Senate designed to provide support for co-operative measures to secure the Soviet nuclear arsenal. The Nunn-Lugar amendment, later called the Nunn-Lugar Co-operative Threat Reduction programme, was signed into law by President Bush in December 1991. It provided $ 400 million for nuclear safety in the (former) Soviet Union.[9]

Arms Control after the Soviet collapse

The dissolution of the Soviet Union had important and perplexing ramifications for arms control. The immediate question that raised itself was whether there would be several nuclear successor states and if so what this would mean for arms control agreements that had been concluded with the Soviet Union. A consensus developed very soon between Russia and the United States that there should be only one nuclear successor state to the USSR, namely the Russian Federation. Strategic nuclear weapons were located in Russia, Belarus, Ukraine and Kazakhstan. At a protocol to the START agreement signed in Lisbon it was agreed that those four countries would undertake to fulfil the obligations the Soviet Union had assumed when it signed START. The so-called Lisbon protocol required all states other than Russia to eliminate its nuclear weapons and join the nuclear non-proliferation Treaty as non-nuclear states. In this way the START I agreement became an instrument of non-proliferation in the former Soviet space. Under the pressure of some resistance to denuclearization and in the atmosphere of the new US-Russian partnership Presidents Yeltsin and Bush moved very quickly to negotiate and sign a follow-on agreement. START II was a bi-lateral US-Russian treaty and envisaged further drastic reductions in strategic nuclear forces, including the complete elimination of land-based missiles with multiple warheads. The outgoing Bush administration thus left with a very substantial agenda in US-Russian strategic relations and arms control in place.

The Nuclear Posture Review

The Clinton administration came into office with US-Russian relations and nuclear non-proliferation as top foreign policy priorities. To restructure relations with the principal successor state to the former global adversary was considered an essential element in the construction of New World Order after the Cold War. The twin objectives were closely linked in that the most pressing and serious dangers of nuclear proliferation arose from the territory of the former Soviet Union, which needed close and unprecedented co-operation from Moscow in order to be addressed. The priority which US-Russian relations was given in US policy soon became know as the 'Russia first' policy. The veteran Russia special Strobe Talbott, a well-known journalist from Time magazine and a specialist in arms control, was first appointed as Clinton's expert on Russia and later promoted to Deputy Secretary of State.

Les Aspin was appointed to be Secretary of Defence, and two major figures from Harvard (Graham Allison and Ashton Carter) who had been instrumental in alerting politicians to the dangers of the nuclear arsenal in the FSU and who were also proponents of radical approaches to co-operative denuclearization were drafted into the Defence Department. All these circumstances favoured a new and radical approach to US defence policy in general and strategic arms policy in particular.

A fundamental review of the basic assumptions and objectives of defence policy and the associated programmes was initiated in 1993 called the bottom-up review. It initially concentrated on conventional forces with the aim to establish a consensus for a strategy that would adapt the armed forces to the security requirements of the post-Cold War world in the context of increasing budgetary constraints. The results did not fulfil the expectations of those who were looking for a decisive shift in policy and a sizeable peace dividend. Indeed, the review was a parade example of bureaucratic politics.

Defence Secretary Aspin had gone on record that he supported a reduced role for nuclear weapons and expressed the view that a non-nuclear world would be favourable for the United States. The concept of co-operative denuclearization, which was advanced by the Harvard Project on Co-operative Denuclearization in their path-breaking study early 1993 was driven by threat of nuclear chaos in the former Soviet Union and was extremely vague about the larger strategic issues.[10]

The study proposed a programme for action with the following objectives:

1. Maintain safe, secure and unitary control over the nuclear arsenal of the former Soviet Union
2. Eliminate most of the nuclear weapons currently in US and Russian stockpiles in a safe and secure manner

3. Prevent proliferation of nuclear weapons capability to countries not recognized as nuclear weapons states.[11]

The endpoint of 'co-operative denuclearization' thus remained undefined. In their introduction, the editors of the study expressed the view that it was now possible to 'establish new international norms that push nuclear weapons to the fringe of international life'.[12]

The Clinton administration failed to adopt a clear set of objectives for its strategic arms policy, primarily because the President rarely addressed nuclear weapons issues. The extent to which the concepts of 'co-operative denuclearization' and Les Aspin's perspective informed US policy is questionable.

The Nuclear Posture Review began formally in the autumn of 1993. It was billed by Aspin as a fundamental review that would emphasize the political character of deterrence and the reduced importance of strategic nuclear forces in the new security environment. It was supposed to be incorporate strategic force planning, nuclear safety and security and arms control in one overarching framework It promised genuine and far-reaching reform, and was to overseen by Deputy Defence Secretary William Perry, an arms control expert from the Centre for International Security and Arms Control at Stanford University.

Les Aspin resigned in January 1994 and the Nuclear Posture Review became the purview of Perry's successor John Deutch who had no interest in it after he realized that no significant savings in defence expenditure were going to result from it (William Perry succeeded Aspin as Defence Secretary). Operational responsibility for the review was assigned to Ashton Carter, the assistant secretary of defence for nuclear security and counterproliferation (later retitled assistant secretary of defence for international security policy) and Lieutenant General McCaffrey (soon replaced by Lieutenant General Wesley Clark). Ash Carter's seriousness and sense of urgency and his relationship to Defence Secretary Perry injected the process with considerable momentum.

Carter established six working groups including military and civilian staff to conduct closed door hearings at the Pentagon. Everything was on the table, he wanted them to brake free from the constraints of Cold War thinking and fashion a new nuclear strategy. The new strategic environment was characterised by two serious threats to US security, which emanated not from the hostile intentions of another power, but from the presence of nuclear weapons, their manner of deployment and command and control. The first was the 'hair trigger alert status' of strategic nuclear forces configured to enable launch-on-warning. This had been perhaps the most dangerous aspect of the Cold War. It remained dangerous as forces were still on alert, while the command and control and early warning infrastructure in Russia had deteriorated considerably. Carter was interested therefore in looking at those elements in the nuclear force posture that contributed to this posture, such as land-based missiles. The second was the problem of safety and security of nuclear weapons in Russia. One element in a strategy to deal with this problem was the notion of eliminating as many nuclear warheads as possible and reducing the size of the arsenal such that the remaining weapons could be kept at safe and secure locations under Russian government control. This was only likely to happen if the United States also engaged in deep reductions.

The idea of the elimination of all land-based missiles was clearly radical stuff and was likely to meet very substantial resistance both from the armed services (especially the United States Air Force) and many other elements of the national security bureaucracy, as well as Congress. The strategic planning community in particular had already resented the changes brought about by General Colin Powell and former Defence Secretary Cheney and was unhappy about what they saw as the interference by the Clinton officials.

This raises the important question as to what extent the political system was capable of generating such a radical review of the nuclear defence posture. The strategic planners were looking at nuclear force planning as a virtually autonomous process, to be conducted by experts, and with little influence by the political threat assessments. A radical review required a consensus about the nature of the new security environment and the most appropriate strategy to deal with the range of potential threats identified. While there was a consensus that there was a real threat of 'loose nukes' in Russia, there was no consensus that the United States should completely abandon its alert posture. Frank Miller, the most knowledgeable Pentagon official on nuclear planning who had served under four administrations and who was the essential link between Carter and the strategic planning officers, did not see any urgent need for radical changes beyond those instigated under Cheney.

Janne Nolan has characterized the distinction between Carter's and Miller's approach as follows: Miller thought the review should develop a new posture of deterrence. This would involve a review of the potential risks and threats, and the requirements to deter them. There was no reason why this would involve any change in the general principles of nuclear targeting or the nuclear force structure beyond the requirements imposed by arms control. Miller's view, that the United States required sufficient nuclear forces at high alert to be able to hold at risk nuclear forces held by potential adversaries, was shared through much of the national security establishment in the United States. On this level, despite the changes in US-Russian relations, nothing had changed since the end of the Cold War.[13]

The Carter vision of 'mutual assured safety' to be achieved by moving away from prompt nuclear response postures and co-operative denuclearization was fundamentally at odds with the views in the military establishment which emphasized adherence to classic deterrence.

The review was conducted by establishing a range of working groups with specific aspects of the agenda such as force structure and infrastructure, operations, command and control, counterproliferation, contingencies, missions and capabilities. Carter arranged for the groups to receive a range of briefing materials, including academic articles and papers presenting the case for significant measures to reduce nuclear dangers, such as de-alerting, no-first-use policies and the like. In addition various briefings with outside analysts took place.

The deep division between Carter's objectives (supported in principle by Defence Secretary Perry) and the prevailing consensus in the bureaucracy dominated the process of the review. The controversy went to the very core of strategic arms policy and force posture. For decades the design of the entire infrastructure had been orientated towards achieving a launch-on-warning capability. There was a paradox at the heart of the system. The one thing which it strove to accomplish, namely to provide the option for a time-urgent response to an attack was so unlikely that no one in the bureaucracy believed that it would ever occur. The President of the United States had the option to respond with an all-out nuclear strike given two independent indications of an impending attack. But given the shortage of time for a decision and the enormity of it, it was expected by the Strategic Air Command that no launch order would be issued until at least some enemy weapons had detonated on US territory. As a former air force chief of staff stated in an interview with Janne Nolan, there was a deliberate absence of policy. The formal position was that the United States was prepared to launch on warning, while the expectation by the military establishment was that this would not happen in practice. However, concomitantly it was expected that no President would leave a nuclear attack without response and that once nuclear detonations had occurred significant retaliation would be initiated, most likely in the form of an all-out strategic nuclear strike. The possibility that a President would fully 'ride out' a nuclear attack was considered unlikely.[14]

There are two important issues here that came to the fore. One is that the principal scenario which drove strategic force planning was one that was considered to be extremely remote. The second is that there was a deliberate lack of clarification of policy. Such ambiguity was considered to be conducive to deterrence, denying the adversary the possibility of calculating precisely how the United States would react to given contingencies. It also meant that the national command of the United States itself was uncertain about its response in the event of imminent nuclear war.

Carter took the view that the principal requirement was for a survivable second-strike force. Submarine based forces were ideal because they were virtually invulnerable, while not designed for a co-ordinated massive prompt response. Deterrence would be enhanced since the adversary was unable to launch a co-ordinated attack on US strategic nuclear forces. Land-based missiles (ICBMs) on the other hand were vulnerable, they encouraged the deployment of forces able to target them, and constituted at the same a powerful reason to maintain a prompt response posture (because otherwise they might be lost in a first strike) and the means to execute it.

Such views were contrary to a long established strategic culture in the US nuclear planning community. The essence of their thinking was that deterrence is best served by the ability to wage war credibly. The need to be able to hold at risk the adversary's prime military assets was considered to be paramount. Moreover, a strategy based on retaliation against the adversary's population was considered to be morally questionable, politically dubious and lacking in credibility. Credibility, however, is the cornerstone of deterrence. The concept of the elimination of ICBMs therefore met fierce resistance by the military, especially STRATCOM.

The working groups proved to be a disaster for the simple reason that they persistently ignored Carter's demand to come up with new options. To Carter's intense frustration, what they came back with were plans based on the existing force posture, scaled down slightly. In order to rescue the process Carter decided to by-pass the working groups and hired two outsiders, Steve Fetter from the University of Maryland and Lieutenant Commander Leo Mackay, a naval officer who had been Carter's Ph.D. student and was now his military assistant, to develop the next briefings for the Nuclear Posture Review. Despite resistance from the planning staff, Fetter and Mackay developed a briefing for John Deutch which focused on a range of new options, including the status quo, but also the elimination of land-based missiles and reductions to very low minimum deterrent levels.

At the core of the analysis were two propositions: The first was that the requirements for launch-on-warning (or prompt response) were far greater than the requirements for deterrence in post-Cold war era. It undermined the public position that nuclear weapons were no longer targeted, that Russia was no longer considered an adversary and that nuclear weapons would be used against Russia only in retaliation. The second was that co-operation with Russia to deal with the threats to nuclear safety and security in the country would be put at risk if the US strategic posture were perceived to remain in Cold-War mode. The United States had to shift from a prompt launch to a ride-out posture.

The content of the briefings set alarm bells ringing in the Pentagon and a letter was sent from the deputy chiefs of operations and plans of each of the services to the joint staff director, Vice Admiral Richard Macke, objecting to Carter's briefings on the grounds that they violated the terms of the review by ignoring the representatives of the Joint Chiefs of Staff and were put forward without adequate consultation. The letter was leaked to Congress and mobilised political support against the review. Strom Thurmond, a Republican Senator from South Carolina, asked the commander of US strategic forces Admiral Henry Chiles if he supported the elimination of land-based strategic missiles. Chiles went on record that in his view ICBMs are a necessary element of future US strategic forces, and that the elimination of land-based missiles had not been seriously considered by the review working groups. Four senators subsequently wrote to President Clinton, criticizing Carter and his views, describing the dangers to the United States resulting from the elimination of ICBMs because of the potential of a surprise nuclear attack by Russia, China or some rogue nation.

There was no political will on the part of Deutch or Perry to override the determined assault on Carter's exploration of a radical new force posture. The attempts to move away from the launch-on-warning posture, either by eliminating ICBMs or else by de-alerting measures such as storing warheads separately from ICBMs, were rebuffed; there was to be no change in US operational policies. Reductions in US force levels would go no lower than those specified by the START II agreement. Nuclear weapons in Europe would be maintained at current levels. Instead of Les Aspin's original goal to look at where US strategic nuclear policy would go after START II, the review simply became in exercise in working out precisely how the United States would configure its forces under the constraints of START.

The Nuclear Posture Review and the structure of US strategic nuclear forces

Under START II, strategic nuclear forces have to be reduced to a level of at most 3,500 warheads and land-based missiles can only have one warhead. The implications for US strategic forces are as follows: All 450 Minuteman II ICBMs were taken off alert and taken out of service. Modernisation of weapons has virtually ceased; the *Midgetman* will not be developed, the most modern ICBM (the MX *Peacekeeper)* will be scrapped and when the elimination of

MIRVed ICBM envisaged by START II goes ahead there will be a kind of reverse modernisation, with the abandonment of technological advance and a partial reliance on older missile systems (i.e. Minuteman III, down-loaded to a single-warhead configuration). Production of the high-yield W88 warhead has ceased at an estimated level of 400 rather than the projected 3500.

The *Lafayette* class SSBNs with Poseidon (C3) missiles and Trident I (C4) missiles have been decommissioned; the missiles and their warheads are to be dismantled.[15] Under START II the Trident II (D5) missiles will carry, on average, four rather than eight warheads, assuming that the projected number of SLBMs will be deployed on *Ohio* class SSBNs. However, the Clinton administration is considering taking the first eight *Ohio* boats out service in the next few years (thus cutting the total number from 18 to 10), reducing the number of missile tubes on the SSBNs from 24 to 12 and thereby cut the total number of Trident II missiles to be procured.

The United States will cut its bomber force substantially. The B1 bomber has been converted to conventional use, although in return for allowing Russia to retain some SS-19 missiles the US is allowed to use B1 bombers as a nuclear weapons platform as some of the older B 52s are taken out of service.[16] The B-2 Stealth Bomber programme has been curtailed dramatically and the B-2 will only be deployed in token numbers (a total of 20). As a result of an agreement with Russia concluded in January 1994 that the two countries would no longer target each other with strategic nuclear weapons, the previously existing primary target sets for the ICBMs and SLBMs have been changed, but this is a purely symbolic gesture since it is completely non-verifiable and the old target data can be reprogrammed at very short notice.

Having said all this, the United States is likely to retain weapons capabilities on a scale more or less equal to those of Russia. This is easily achievable in the context of currently agreed arms reductions.

As far as US nuclear forces in Europe are concerned, they currently consist of 490 nuclear gravity bombs and the NPR envisaged they should be maintained as this level. No nuclear weapons are to be deployed in the territories of new members of NATO that formerly belonged to the Warsaw Pact. The United States will not deploy nuclear weapons on its navy surface vessels, but retain nuclear cruise missile capabilities on submarines.

The Nuclear Posture Review was adopted as policy in the form of Presidential Decision Directive, PDD-31, by President Clinton in September 1994.

Notes

1. These figures are based on the counting rules used for the START I agreement.
2. For a detailed examination of this proposal, see Stephen Shenfield, *Entering the Third Millennium Nuclear-Free: Reflections on the Soviet Proposal To Eliminate Nuclear Weapons by the Year 2000*, Paper presented at a meeting of the British International Studies Association, King's College London, 17 July 1987.
3. See Chapter 5 for a more detailed analysis of SDI.
4. For an analysis of the Reykjavik summit from the Soviet perspective, see MccGwire, op. cit., pp.198-203; the European response is discussed in Ivo H. Daalder, *The Nature and Practice of Flexible Response*, New York: Columbia University Press 1991.
5. For an account of the history of the INF negotiations see Jonathan Haslam, *The Soviet Union and the Politics of Nuclear Weapons in Europe, 1969-87*, London: Macmillan 1989.
6. For more detail, see Christoph Bluth, *New Thinking in Soviet Military Policy*, London: Pinter 1990, pp. 47f.
7. This account is based on Janne E. Nolan, *An Elusive Consensus*, Washington DC: Brookings 1999, Chapter 2, where more detail can be found.
8. Kurt Campbell, Ashton B. Carter, Steven E. Miller and Charles A. Zraket, *Soviet Nuclear Fission: Control of the Nuclear Arsenal in a Disintegrating Soviet Union*, Cambridge, MA: CSIA 1991.
9. For an account of the origins of the Nunn-Lugar programme, see Sam Nunn, 'Foreword: Changing Threats in the Post-Cold War World', in John M. Shields and William C. Potter (eds.), *Dismantling the Cold War*, Cambridge, MA. MIT Press 1997, pp.ix-xx.
10. Graham Allison, Ashton B. Carter, Steven E. Miller and Philip Zelikow (eds.), *Co-operative Denuclearization*, Cambridge, MA: CSIA 1993.
11. Allison et al., op.cit., p.280.
12. Allison et al., op.cit., p.1.
13. Nolan, op.cit., Chapter 3.
14. Nolan op.cit., p.48. This author carried out interviews with a range of members of the national security community in the United States and came to similar conclusions.
15. Trident I (C4) missiles are still deployed on more modern *Ohio* class SSBNs.

16. Much of this analysis is based on *The Military Balance*, op.cit., pp.222-229, which was published before the signing of START II but after the Bush-Yeltsin agreement. Considerably less reliable are figures cited in newspaper reports of the START II accord; see *Financial Times*, 30 December 1992; *The Independent*, 30 December 1992 and 4 January 1993; *The Times*, 4 January 1993.

3 Russian Strategic Arms Policy after the Cold War

The national security policy of a state, which involves elements of foreign policy as well as military policy, can generally be understood to be designed to safeguard vital national interests and protect the state from external political and military threats. Russia inherited a vast military establishment from the Soviet Union which was largely designed to engage in high-intensity warfare with the West or China. This included the bulk of the Soviet strategic nuclear arsenal. At the same time the General Staff in Moscow lost control over substantial military assets that had been forward deployed in other republics. The task for the Russian military leadership was to restructure the country's military forces on the basis of this inheritance in a radically different geopolitical environment. This required that the Russian Federation would come to terms with being an independent state and define its national interests and foreign and security policy objectives.

The principal reality that defines the new frame of reference for Moscow is the disintegration of the Warsaw Pact and the Soviet Union itself. For 40 years, most of the territories controlled by Moscow were adjacent to territories protected by the United States or to China. The Russian Federation is now virtually surrounded by former Soviet republics, all of which experience deep political, social and economic problems, and some of which are highly unstable and subject to violent civil conflicts. The territory of the Russian Federation itself, about 75 per cent of the territory of the former USSR with about 60 per cent of its population, is still not properly defined, given that significant sections of the borders are purely notional, and the degree of control that Moscow can exercise over the entire Federation is uncertain.[1]

The external and domestic environment faced by Moscow's policymakers has been transformed. Russia has emerged from a tremendous global conflict with the highly industrialised countries of the West which endured for over 40 years, and an even longer period of totalitarianism and mismanagement of all aspects of government. In this context, Russia, as the largest and by any measure most powerful of the Soviet successor states, has to deal with the many issues arising from the loss of empire - the relations with the former Soviet states and Eastern Europe, policy towards the former adversaries of the Soviet Union and the extent of any remaining global role that Russia might play. More fundamental and important is how the Russian people, having been defeated in the struggle with the West and betrayed by the totalitarian misrule of their own leaders, and having rejected the most basic values on which their society had supposedly been based, redefine their own national identity and how this determines their relations with the rest of the world.[2]

The domestic political process of defining the national interests and the foreign policy agenda suffers from the fact that although the old decision-making structures of the Communist system have disintegrated, the transition to a liberal democratic state is far from complete. Indeed, with the loss of power of the CPSU and the disintegration of the union Russia became a territory that lacked many fundamental institutions of state and the process of state-building is still on-going, without any certainty as to its end.[3]

The difficulties in achieving a domestic consensus on foreign policy is exacerbated by the fact that Russia is passing through a profound economic and social crisis. Neither the end of this crisis nor the direction of Russia's future socio-political development are yet in sight. The need to convert a huge industrial complex which is primarily geared to military production to the requirements of an efficient high technology economy that is competitive at world level and based on market principles requires an extensive period of economic transformation at a gigantic scale. So far this has been exceedingly poorly managed. The consequence is a substantial decline in industrial production, an enormous budget deficit and a growth in foreign indebtedness. It is unclear how Russia is going to extricate itself from this situation.[4] What can be said is that it has become greatly dependent on the leading industrialised nations (the G7 - with Russia referred to as G8). This in turn means that Russia has a great incentive to maintain good relations with the West. In this context, it is likely that Russia's powerful industry leaders will strongly oppose the attempt by any government to return to a foreign policy that puts Russia so much at odds with the West that the emerging efforts to enter the world economy are put at risk and Russia is cut off once again both from Western investments and world markets.[5]

The lack of consensus on Russian security policy and more broadly, on what constitutes Russia's national interest has the result that Russian voices on strategic arms policy and nuclear arms control are confused and contradictory. One of the few issues, however, on which there *is* a relatively broad consensus in Russia is that Russia should remain a nuclear power for the foreseeable future. The reasons for this are complex and deep-rooted. They are based on general political considerations, as well as economic and military ones.

Remaining a nuclear power: political considerations

From a *political* perspective, it is believed by most members of the political élite that strategic nuclear weapons are the last remaining symbol of Russia's Great Power status. Sergei Karaganov warns of the 'Versailles syndrome' currently experienced by the Russian people. He states:

> It is in the nuclear field where the hardening of positions is almost inevitable and where, if by pressure or negotiating tactics the United States or the West as a whole tries to cut back weapon holdings much further than presently envisaged, a backlash is almost inevitable...[6]

There is also an underlying assumption rarely mentioned in public: in times of extreme societal, economic, political and military weakness, Russia is interested in a heavier rather than a lighter political reliance on its possession of nuclear weapons.

There is a perception that the principal reason why the West and the United States in particular is paying so much attention to Russia is because Russia remains a strategic nuclear power. The idea that Russia should maintain some claim to a Great Power status does not mean that Russia should rebuild a global role. It is rather based on the fear that Russia may become marginalised, and the current political leadership seeks to avoid this at all costs in order to retain and increase the potential for international economic co-operation and aid. These are perceived as essential for Russia to reverse its sharp political and economic decline and achieve a successful transition to modern democratic state with a strong economy based on market principles. Moreover, they are essential for the preservation of the wealth of the country's élites. There is a deep paradox inherent the maintenance of a substantial arsenal of strategic nuclear weapons on the basis of such considerations. It results from the fact that Russia's strategic nuclear weapons are technically the principal military threat to the United States. This produces a plethora of political efforts to reduce or eliminate the nuclear weapons as a factor in relations with the West. On the other hand, a residual threat based on the mere possession of a substantial arsenal is required to ensure that the West takes Russian concerns seriously.

The political considerations which underlie the preservation of strategic nuclear forces, as Karaganov points out, are both important in terms of Russian foreign policy and domestic politics. Russia has absorbed relatively peacefully the enormous shift in the geostrategic balance, which has resulted in the loss of its influence in a sizeable part of the Third World, the collapse of the Warsaw Pact and thus the loss of Russian dominance in Eastern Europe and the dissolution of the Soviet Union itself. There is a fear in Russia that without its nuclear status it will lose its last vestige of international influence and respect, given the collapse of the domestic economy which at least in the short-term deprives Russia of other indicators of power and influence.

Economic reasons for remaining a nuclear power

It is a commonplace argument that conventional weapons are more expensive than nuclear weapons. The perception in Moscow is that the nuclear deterrent, even though the entire nuclear weapons complex is very expensive to sustain, is still cost- effective since it dissuades potential aggressors in a way that conventional forces could not. Some analysts believe that Russia may not be able to sustain an adequate mix of nuclear and conventional forces into the next century and that as the military-industrial complex contracts hard choices will need to be made between reliance on an adequate conventional forces and nuclear forces.

The overall GDP of the Russian Federation can be taken as a measure of the resource base that limits the options for the development of the armed forces. When the Soviet Union was dissolved, Russia accounted for 61 per cent of the GDP of the former Soviet Union. This has fallen precipitously, and by the end of 1995 Russian GDP amounted to only 36 per cent of the last figure for the Soviet Union. The maintenance of military forces and capabilities on anything approaching the scale of those of the former Soviet Union on such a reduced and falling resource base is clearly an untenable position. Since 1992, the GDP of the Russian Federation has fallen relentlessly.[7] The most optimistic forecasts predicted that during the period 1997-2000 Russia would experience economic growth of the order of 5 per cent per annum. This forecast already looked too optimistic for 1997 and was completely thrown off course by the economic crisis in 1998 which resulted in a dramatic collapse of the ruble. The hope that Russia would have increased resources in the near future has well and truly disappeared.[8]

Year	1992	1993	1994	1995	1996	1997	1998
%Change	-14.5	-8.7	-12.6	-4.0	-6.0	0.8	-4.6

The key question is, of course, what share of the national income the political élite is willing to allocate to the military. There have been vigorous internal debates in Russia about the appropriate share of resources for the military so that it can adequately provide for the security of the state. Former defence minister Pavel Grachev and his deputy Andrei Kokoshin fought hard to maximize the resources allocated to the military. On the whole, it must be said that Grachev and Kokoshin were not very successful, Despite very vigorous lobbying of parliament, almost to the point of blackmail, military spending has steadily declined as a percentage of GDP. According to IMF estimates, Russian defence expenditure in 1992-5 amounted to between 4.4 and 5 per cent (compared with at least 15 per cent for the Soviet era). In 1996 it fell further to 3.6 per cent of GDP, and in 1998 the figure was 2.5 per cent. These figures underestimate true defence expenditure because of peculiar accounting practices, barter transactions that are not recorded etc. and the IISS estimates that the true figure is about 5 per cent of GDP.[9] It is quite clear all the same that there has been a severe contraction of military spending, and there has been a consensus in the legislature since 1992 that military spending should not exceed 5 per cent of GDP despite the predominance of Communists and nationalists in the Duma.

This can be explained by the competing political influences on government spending. The defence budget is drawn up by the ministry of defence, but has to be approved by the government in the first instance. It is evident that the ministry of finance has the backing of the president and the prime minister in imposing severe limits on all government spending, including military expenditures, in order to keep inflation in check and satisfy the IMF that Russia is moving towards a sound financial policy. The draft state budget is subsequently submitted to parliament. The Duma imposes a limit on the overall budget deficit, thereby further reducing the scope for lobbying by special interests. Moreover, here military industry has to compete with other important interest groups, such as the gas and oil industries and the agricultural lobby.

Another important aspect of Russian budgetary politics is the underfulfilment of public spending plans. Even when the military can persuade the Duma to agree to a higher military budget, this does not mean that the monies authorized will also be available. The persistent shortfall between projected tax receipts and actual revenues means that military expenditure tends to be a good deal less than is budgeted for. This shortfall is added to the arrears from previous years, which spills over into the next federal budget. As a consequence the government debt to the armed services and defence industries increases, while actual expenditures amount to only about half the amount that the military leadership considers to be the bare minimum. Indeed, at the end of the year the Duma typically makes additional emergency appropriations of the order of 2-3 trillion roubles to prevent mass starvation in the armed forces.[10]

The defence budget for 1996 reflected the priorities of the political élite. Defence spending was reduced from 21.3 per cent to 17.0 per cent of the federal budget. This implied a reduction from 5.5 per cent to 3.8 per cent of GDP. Social costs (salaries, pensions, housing, etc.) accounted for most of the budget; a mere 10 per cent was to be spent on procurement. In view of the large sums required by the ministry of defence to pay off its debts to military enterprises, this meant that actual procurement was virtually reduced to zero.

For the 1997 budget, the military had to go around the same loop again. The request for minimum sufficient financing exceeded the government draft figure by 40-50 per cent. The 1997 federal budget submitted by the government allocated about 104.3 trillion rubles for the item 'national defence'. This amounts to 19 per cent of the entire federal budget for 1997, or 3.7 per cent of the forecast GDP of Russia. This total amount represented an increase over the 1996 allocation equal to the rate of inflation. A closer analysis of the defence budget (as close as the limited information published permits) shows that again most of it went on the maintenance of the armed forces. Procurement of weapons and military equipment and, even more importantly, research and development were to get even fewer resources than in the previous year. As a consequence, Aleksei Arbatov has painted a vision of the Russian army in ten years' time, facing new military threats on Russia's geostrategic borders without a modern military, without state-of-the art weapons technology and without a mobilization base.[11]

Plans for military reform continue to be hampered by a lack of clear direction at the highest level about Russia's security interests and force requirements. In order to provide a more unified approach to policy on the armed forces, a Defence Council (an institution which previously existed in the Soviet Union) was established with Yuri Baturin as secretary. Soon a power struggle between the Ministry of Defence and the Defence Council. In the absence of clear guidance from the President, no progress was made on any of these issues and indeed in the first five months of 1997 the Defence Council did not meet.

When Yeltsin had seemingly recovered sufficiently from the consequences of his multiple heart by-pass operation and other medical problems, a meeting of the Defence Council was held on 22 May 1997. Two days before Defence Minister Rodionov submitted a report to the President which projected constant military expenditures at R 160,000 billion for the next ten years. This apparent unwillingness to take on board the fiscal realities, and moreover the failure to make any progress with regards to military reform as well as the criticism of the decision to establish the Defence Council as an institution angered Yeltsin. At the meeting of the Defence Council on 22 May 1997, Yeltsin berated the high military command and Rodionov personally for their obstructive behaviour. He expressed the view that military expenditure at a level of 5 per cent of GDP was unsustainable and higher than the military expenditure anywhere in the 'civilised world'. He set a target of 3-3.5 per cent of GDP for defence expenditure in the future.[12] Yeltsin's intent to bring the leadership of the armed forces into line was dramatically demonstrated by the dismissal of both Rodinov and Chief of the General Staff Viktor Samsonov from their posts. Igor Sergeev Commander of the Strategic Rocket Forces, was named Defence Minister, and Anatoli Kvashinin, commander of the North Caucasus military district was appointed Chief of the General Staff. Vladimir Yakovlev became Commander of the SRF.[13]

During the Soviet period, even in the age of *perestroika*, there was virtually no information on the detailed line items of the defence budget. Since the independence of the Russian Federation the official budget has contained general separate headings but the information is still not very detailed. Moreover, it is clear that the defence budget is based to some extent on smoke and mirrors and that more is spent on personnel than is apparent from the official figures. Nevertheless, some reasonable estimates can be made of the overall proportion of resources spent on the nuclear weapons complex. The 1998 defence budget amounted to 81.765 billion roubles, of which according to official figures more than half (44.527 billion roubles) was allocated to personnel, and 2.095 billion roubles (2.6 per cent) to the nuclear complex. By comparison, the United States spends about $50 billion annually to maintain its strategic nuclear forces. In August 1998 the Russian State Duma Defence Committee stated that roubles 70 billion ($38.7 billion) would be required to maintain Russia's nuclear arsenal at START I levels (5,000 warheads) until 2007-2010. The Commander of the Strategic Rocket Forces Yakovlev has stated that to maintain Russian strategic forces at a level of 6,000 warheads (the maximum permitted under START I) will cost 40 billion roubles per year, whereas at a level of 1,500 warheads (a possible outcome of START III) modernization and deployment costs would be about 6 billion roubles per year.[14] Although the publicly declared figures remain confusing, the sheer costs of maintaining the arsenal is such that it is likely that even in the absence of arms control quantitative reductions will take place.[15] Moreover, the funds for procurement are very tightly constrained and while new systems are being developed, it remains unclear to what extend funding will be available to build and deploy them. In March 1999 the State Duma approved the draft law on funding for strategic nuclear forces. It determines the level of funding until the year 2010. This funding is ring-fenced and cannot be appropriated for other purposes. It is a measure of the determination to preserve a leaner, but modern strategic nuclear force in the face of the collapse of virtually everything else.[16]

The poor state of Russia's conventional armed forces is a major factor that underpins the maintenance of Russia's nuclear status. The situation in the armed forces is critical as the dissolution of the Soviet Union and the lack of resources has degraded the fighting capability of the conventional forces to such an extent that they are scarcely capable of dealing with small local conflicts. Rebuilding Russia's armed forces will required the sustained deployment of substantial resources over years and remains an unlikely prospect in the foreseeable future. Modest strategic force modernization may therefore remain the only financially viable way in which Russia can maintain a military force that is capable of deterring major external threats.

At present no-one seems to believe that Russia will have to give up nuclear weapons altogether; the economic costs of maintaining a nuclear arsenal are balanced by the costs of arms control, dismantling nuclear weapons and verification regimes. However, there is a strong belief in government circles that the present size of the nuclear arsenal is unsustainable and that the level of strategic nuclear forces in particular will have to be cut substantially, at a minimum in line with established arms control agreements.

Implications for strategy, force posture and arms control

All of this adds up to the conclusion that Russia will remain a nuclear power for the time being. However, given the consensus that the Cold War is over, there is a range of views on nuclear strategy and force posture. These differences have important implications on the role and the future of strategic nuclear arms control agreements.

In the wake of the break-up of the Soviet Union, the concept of 'co-operative de-nuclearization' was proposed by scholars participating in the Co-operative Security/Post Cold War Reconstruction Project at the Center for Science and International Affairs (CSIA) at Harvard University's John F. Kennedy School of Government.[17] It is defined as the elimination of tactical nuclear weapons, the elimination of the bulk of strategic nuclear weapons and the establishment of international norms which push nuclear weapons to the fringe of international life.[18] This concept arose as part of a major effort to draw the attention of the political leaders in the US to the risks emanating from the declining safety and security of the nuclear arsenal of the former Soviet Union. This effort gave rise to the Co-operative Threat Reduction programme (CTR, also known as the Nunn-Lugar programme) to provide for the safety and security of nuclear weapons in the Newly Independent States.

At the other end of the spectrum of views on the role of nuclear weapons in the present era is the concept of 'residual deterrence' which in the view of the Russian General Staff defines the future of the strategic relationship. In this view, while at the political level Russia and the United States no longer consider each other enemies, they still continue to deploy nuclear weapons as deterrent forces. This means that Russian strategic arms policy must be formulated with the purpose of maintaining strategic parity with the United States.

The concept of 'co-operative de-nuclearization', as we have seen, was never fully adopted by the US administration even though some of its proponents were appointed to influential positions in the government. It also found no support in Russia either at official or unofficial levels, for reasons explained above. Nevertheless, elements of it have found their way both in official statements and actions to an extent which makes it legitimate to use it to define the boundary of the spectrum of different views on the future role of nuclear weapons. Thus although Yeltsin and his government have remained within the consensus in favour of retaining a residual strategic nuclear force, the approach of the government has been in the direction of substantially building down nuclear forces and eliminate the strategic competition with the United States. One symbolic measure to take nuclear weapons out of the US-Russia relationship consists in the so-called de-targeting of strategic nuclear weapons. The first step in this direction was the announcement by Yeltsin on ABC television on 25 January 1992 to the effect that ICBMs under the strategic command of the *Commonwealth of Independent States* were no longer targeted at the United States. This was clearly designed to underscore his statement that the United States and Russia were no longer enemies. According to a television interview with the Commander of the CIS strategic forces Shaposhnikov on 22 February 1992 this meant that they had been assigned a 'zero mission', i.e. no target information was programmed.[19] There have been conflicting reports about whether indeed the entire CIS arsenal has been taken off alert without specific target information, but Western experts are generally sceptical.[20] In October 1992 Russia's defence minister Pavel Grachev claimed that the missiles stationed outside Russia had been 'taken off alert' and 'withdrawn to reserve'. Even those missiles still on alert had no 'specific targets'. This latter statement was qualified by the phrase 'the bearings have been issued', which may mean that the target information could be programmed quickly in a crisis.[21]

Interviews with a range of experts in Russia, Ukraine and the United States revealed that the consensus of the expert communities in all three countries is that these were purely political declarations and that nothing actually changed on the ground, except that the missiles outside Russia were most likely stripped of all target information.[22] However the concept of de-targeting strategic nuclear forces was revived during the Moscow summit in January 1994 when US President Clinton and Russia's President Yeltsin signed an agreement not to target nuclear weapons at each other. Strategic bombers had already been taken off alert and their nuclear munitions put into storage on the basis of an agreement between Presidents Bush and Gorbachev in October 1991. The United States began to replace the primary targets sets in its ICBMs with the co-ordinates of points somewhere in the world's oceans in April 1994. According to statements by the Commander of Russia's *Strategic Rocket Forces*, all land-based missiles in Russia have been stripped of the target data. It is assumed that SLBMs will likewise be de-targeted. This agreement remains a symbolic one, however, for two reasons. The first is that the targeting of missiles is not observable by national technical means (i.e. satellite surveillance) and the agreement has no provisions for verification. The second is that both the United States and Russia have developed extensive target sets on each other's territories which can be reprogrammed into the guidance systems in a matter of minutes. Russian ICBMs have three different target co-ordinates, so that even if the primary set has been changed or deleted, it is possible to quickly switch to the reserve sets. Even if the systems contain no target sets whatsoever, they can be easily and quickly programmed. A more concrete step in the direction of dismantling the strategic nuclear stand-off would be to take the warheads of the missiles and store them separately.[23] Neither the United States nor Russia have shown any interest in doing this. In the case of Russia, one argument against such a step would be the lack of storage space for warheads and the safety implications of storing a very large number of warheads in this manner. One significant step was taken towards the end of 1999 when Russian military officers were invited into the NORAD Command Centre and US officers likewise into the Russian early warning centre to exchange real-time early warning data as a precaution against accidental war during the changeover to the new millennium. If continued this is a significant confidence-building measure that reduces the threat of accidental nuclear war.

Other important symbols of de-nuclearization are two major arms control agreements, the Comprehensive Test Ban Treaty and the Fissile Materials Production ban. Although described primarily as measures of preventing the spread of nuclear weapons capabilities, in the long run these agreements would inhibit the capacity of the main nuclear powers to maintain their large arsenals.

At the time of writing, these agreements have not passed through all the required procedures in order to enter into force. Moreover, in 1999 the US Senate rejected the CTBT, thus dealing a substantial blow to the entire network of interlocking arms control agreements.

The debate and the agreement about de-targeting strategic nuclear forces illustrates the prevailing attitudes about the disposition of these forces after the Cold War. The current political leaders want to remove the last vestiges of the global confrontation between the United States and Russia. The translation of this desire into concrete reality however is hampered by a variety of factors described above, such as ambiguity of the strategic environment and the role of nuclear forces, the unwillingness by important sections of the political élite and the military establishment to give up Russia's most important remaining claim to global importance, and the sheer technical difficulties in even substantially reducing the existing arsenal of strategic nuclear forces.

Nuclear weapons and military security

Are there still sound military reasons for Russia to retain a strategic nuclear arsenal after the Cold War? In order to assess how this question is answered by the decision-making élite in Russia, a brief analysis of the development of military policy since the end of the Cold War is in order. After the end of the Soviet Union, the traditional perceptions of the international security environment that dominated the Cold War period were abandoned surprisingly quickly by the political élite. The military was somewhat slow to follow along a similar path. By mid-1992 the relevance of the 'defence of the Western Perimeter was seriously questioned',[24] but traditional thinking still pervaded the debate until well into 1993. By the time a new military doctrine was approved in November 1993, a radical re-evaluation of the security threats facing Russia had been adopted by the Russian military.[25] The military and arms control policies of Russia since then reflect the perceptions of the security environment after the Cold War. There was widespread acceptance among the military leadership and the political élite that the security relationship with the West had changed and that the principal military threats come from the southern periphery of the Russian Federation and from Third World countries that are acquiring weapons of mass destruction and ballistic missiles. In line with a general restructuring of the Russian military to rapid reaction and crisis intervention roles, there was a fundamental change in thinking about the role of nuclear weapons to meet the new range of threats. The utility of strategic nuclear weapons in this environment was perceived to have declined fundamentally, although the need for a strategic deterrent force remained. Tactical nuclear weapons were withdrawn from eastern Europe and the non-Russian newly independent states.

As far as the role of nuclear weapons is concerned, the emphasis was placed squarely on nuclear deterrence. The aim of the Russian Federation's policy in the sphere of nuclear weapons according to the 1993 doctrine was to eliminate the danger of nuclear war by deterring any aggression against the Russian Federation and its allies.[26] This committed Russia to a policy of extended deterrence against threats to the security of its (unspecified) allies. There was a policy of no nuclear use against non-nuclear states that acceded to the NPT, but there was no longer such a policy *vis-à-vis* nuclear weapons states or non-nuclear states which enjoy a nuclear guarantee by nuclear weapons states. This constituted an abandonment of the pledge not to use nuclear weapons first which had been a central element of Soviet declaratory policy since 1981. Some Western commentators found this alarming. But it should be pointed out that the 'no first use' pledge was made in the context of the confrontation in central Europe, where the Soviet Union was determined to avoid escalation to the nuclear level in any conflict. The new doctrine was more in line with the notion of a deterrent as a last resort in the kinds of conflicts for which Russia was preparing. It could also be interpreted as a warning to Turkey against any involvement in the conflict between Armenia and Azerbaijan, or to Ukraine as it considered the fate of nuclear weapons on its territory.[27] However, as the capabilities of the Russian armed forces decline, one can detect an increasing emphasis on nuclear forces to compensate for weakness at the conventional level. At present, tactical weapons are not forward deployed and therefore Russia lacks the instrument to implement a policy of regional nuclear deterrence in any operational sense. There have been suggestions, however, that Russia might redeploy tactical nuclear weapons if NATO expands to include countries of the former Warsaw Pact.[28] However, no countermeasures were undertaken following the *Founding Act on Mutual Relations, Co-operation and Security between NATO and the Russian Federation* signed at the NATO Summit on 27 May 1997 as NATO declared its intention not to deploy nuclear weapons in the new member states except in a crisis.

The use of the armed forces in international peacekeeping operations, their deployment outside the national territory and the conduct of peacekeeping operations on the territories of the former Soviet republics together perhaps constituted the most important new element in Russian military doctrine. The doctrine also stated that the units of the armed forces could be used in *internal* conflicts to support the forces of the interior ministry of the Russian Federation to localize and blockade the conflict region, to suppress armed clashes and to separate the conflicting parties as well as to defend the strategically important objects.[29] This part of the military doctrine was in conflict with the law on defence, which prohibited the use of regular armed forces inside the Russian Federation. The use of nuclear weapons, obviously, was not contemplated under such circumstances.

The military doctrine asserted that Russia did not consider 'any state as its enemy' and will not use its armed forces or other armed formations against any state for any purposes other than individual or collective self-defence in the case of an armed attack on the Russian Federation, its citizens, territory, armed forces or the other Russian armed formations, or its allies.[30]

The potential sources of a military threat towards the Russian from outside include, according the 1993 military doctrine:

- territorial claims to the Russian Federation from the other post-Soviet states;
- existing and potential sources of local wars and armed conflicts, primarily those in direct proximity to the Russian borders;
- proliferation of nuclear and other weapons of mass destruction, the means of delivery and modern military technologies;
- the oppression of the rights, freedoms and legitimate interests of the citizens of the Russian Federation abroad;
- the enlargement of military blocs and alliances (e.g. NATO) in such a way as to violate the military security interests of the Russian Federation.

According to the document, the greatest threat to Russia arose from armed conflicts caused by aggressive nationalism and religious intolerance. The main objective of the organizational development of the Russian Federation armed forces and other troops was to create and develop forces capable of defending the independence, sovereignty and territorial integrity of the country, the security of the citizens, and the other vitally important interests of society and state in line with the military-political and strategic situation in the world.[31] In view of the absence of an agreed concept of the national security of Russia it is unclear, however, what the vital interests of the Russian Federation were considered to be. Such statements in the military doctrine therefore remained open to interpretation.

The military part of Russia's new military doctrine set out a view of the possible character of future conflicts. Under conditions in which the danger of global war (both nuclear and conventional) was reduced substantially, though not completely eliminated, local wars and armed conflicts represented the main threat to stability and peace. Their probability in some regions was considered to be increasing.[32]

The doctrine went on to note that combat action in local war and armed conflicts could be waged by the groups of forces deployed in the region of conflict in peacetime. If necessary, these groups of forces could be reinforced by units re-deployed from other regions. The Russian Federation needed to maintain the combat potential of the groups of forces deployed in peacetime at a level sufficient to repulse aggression on a local (regional) scale. The term 'aggression on a local (regional) scale', however, remained vague and open to a variety of interpretations.

Local wars and armed conflicts were perceived as the most likely source of military threats to Russia. The military doctrine assumed that a wide variety of forces could be engaged in these operations, from a small number of armed units up to operational-strategic groups of forces, along with the use of all types of weapons, from small arms to modern precision-guided 'smart' weapons. The priority was the development of the Russian Federation armed forces and other troops intended for deterrence against aggression, as well as the mobile forces of the Russian Federation Armed Forces and other troops able to re-deploy within a short period and to mount and conduct manoeuvre operations in any sector (region) where a threat to the security of the Russian Federation could arise.[33] Furthermore, Russian armed forces could be deployed outside the national territory to safeguard the security of either the Russian Federation or other former Soviet republics.[34]

The document on military doctrine reflected a basic contradiction in the way in which force requirements are defined. On the one hand, local wars and armed conflicts were clearly presented as the principal security threat. On the other hand, the operational strategic concepts and the remarks on practical implementation had the appearance of a guide for the preparation of military operations around the globe, based on the acquisition of sea- and airlift capabilities on a global scale. This was also in contradiction to the intention asserted by the Soviet Union in the period of 'new political thinking' of liquidating the capabilities to launch surprise attacks or large-scale offensive operations. The emphasis on the defensive nature of the military-technical aspects of military doctrine thus appears to have been lost.

One possible interpretation is that the military doctrine was designed not only to define the military contingencies with which Russia will most probably have to deal, but also to provide a rationale for the ambitious force goals of the military establishment, which sought to preserve something as close as possible to the military capabilities of the former Soviet Union. This probably also applied to strategic nuclear weapons, which have no role to play in any of the conflicts or potential conflicts that Russia is involved with.

The 1997 national security concept reaffirmed the concept of 'first use' introduced in the 1993 military doctrine, and the same is true for the new military doctrine which was developed in 1998, although its approval was postponed. The provisions on first-use remained the same, even though there had been some attempts to remove some of the restrictions with regard to non-nuclear countries.[35] The war in Kosovo had also considerable impact as Russia took the threat of NATO intervention in the former Soviet Union more seriously and once again strengthened the emphasis on nuclear deterrence, including tactical nuclear weapons. A special meeting of the Security Council in April 1999 decided to put in a place a programme on the development and deployment of tactical nuclear weapons, including new low-yield nuclear warheads. It was also reported that a redeployment of tactical nuclear warheads to land-based short range missiles and artillery was proposed, thereby ending the unilateral arms control measures put in place by Presidents Bush and Gorbachev in 1991. Large-scale exercises called *Zapad* conducted in June and July 1999 during the Kosovo crisis were based on the scenario of a NATO attack from Poland against Kaliningrad, involving the simulated use of nuclear weapons when Russian forces were in difficulty.[36]

Despite the safety and security concerns, and despite far-reaching arms control agreements, Russia has placed renewed emphasis on the nuclear arsenal because of the virtual collapse of its conventional military capabilities and the instability and conflicts on the territory of the former Soviet Union. However, the military doctrine, while renouncing the pledge not to use nuclear weapons first, does not specify targets or circumstances under which nuclear weapons might be used. The possibility that Russia might redeploy tactical nuclear weapons to compensate for the lack of conventional military power is occasionally mooted. This is troublesome because the kind of conflicts Russia is or might become involved in, such as in Chechnya or Tajikistan, are not susceptible to nuclear deterrence. In other words, a nuclear threat might result in nuclear use. President Yeltsin and his successor, Vladimir Putin, have resisted notions of nuclear peacekeeping, but it cannot be taken for granted that in extreme situations the nuclear option will not be reconsidered if the condition of the Russian armed forces continues to deteriorate. On the other hand, if such fears are unwarranted, it means that nuclear weapons have no role in the kinds of conflicts Russia is most likely to be involved in, either in terms of deterrence or military action. In other words, where nuclear weapons are effective, there is no threat in any event, and where there is a threat, they are not effective. This is a fundamental contradiction in the new emphasis on nuclear weapons in military doctrine that remains unresolved.

There is a strong perception in Russia that nuclear weapons are vital to its security. It could even be argued that because nuclear weapons provide Russia with security, they obviate the need for conventional rearmament and thereby release political, economic and financial resources for reform and development. There is some truth to this argument, but at the same time it should not be overstated, because, as we have seen, there are no threats to Russian security that require or are susceptible to nuclear deterrence, whereas there are real military threats where nuclear weapons have no role. In other words, the security nuclear weapons provide for Russia in the present is psychological and not military. This leaves Russia still with the need to find military means to address its actual security risks. Moreover the nuclear weapons complex itself poses a substantial risk to Russia's national security. While a nuclear emphasis in the face of conventional weakness is understandable, it is unclear that the military doctrine as it is evolving represents the most appropriate response to the national security dilemmas that Russia faces.

Strategic force planning

Military doctrine does not provide any clear guidance for strategic force planning. The end of the Cold War and the end of US-Soviet rivalry has had no effect on strategic analysis in the general staff which is still based on the relationship between US and Russian strategic nuclear forces. The objective of strategic arms policy remains that of nuclear strategic parity, or, if that is not possible, sufficiency *vis-á-vis* the United States. There is, of course, an awareness that third-country nuclear arsenals, such as those of Britain, France and China, remain in place and (in the case of China) are even augmented. For Russian strategic planners, the future relationship with China, in an environment where the military-strategic balance and the two countries' relative economic potential are changing substantially, remains potentially the most troublesome. For all these reasons, they perceive the need to guard against nuclear attack or nuclear blackmail in the future. Nevertheless, force requirements are still defined on the basis of US capabilities. In this sense, the US-Russian strategic relationship has not yet adapted to the new global political environment.

Russian military planners do not base their objectives on the notion of a 'minimum deterrent', such as has been advocated by civilian analysts.[37] For them, strategic parity presupposes the qualitative equality of the strategic capabilities of both sides in their ability to conduct effective operations against each other's strategic offensive forces. It also means that Russia must be sure to maintain, as a minimum, an adequate second-strike countervalue reserve force *vis-à-vis* the United States.[38] Indeed, the latter seems to be now the main guiding principle of strategic force planning and modernization.

The Soviet strategic deterrent as it had been developed by the early 1980s was based on a time-urgent counterforce capability configured to a launch-on-warning posture. In other words, land-based missiles with highly accurate warheads targeted at American missile silos and other hardened military assets were ready to be launched at a moment's notice. This was based on the assumption that in the age of highly accurate counterforce systems even hardened systems could not survive a determined, large-scale first strike. Early warning and command and control systems were designed to enable such a posture to be operationalised. However, it is clear that the General Staff was acutely aware of the technical problems involved in accurately assessing a large-scale nuclear surprise attack and the very short decision-times. Although substantial resources and planning were directed towards achieving the capability for launch-on-warning (known as *otvetno-vstrechii udar* - a retaliatory meeting-strike), the confidence that such a response could be successfully carried out in a manner which would allow the bulk of Soviet counterforce-capable strategic nuclear forces to be launched was not very high. Thus an aide to the former first deputy-defence minister A Kokoshin, Michael I. Gerasev, stated at a conference organised by the Russian Institute for Strategic Studies in Moscow in 1993 that because of the time constraints and the technical problems involved the threat of the *otvetno-vstrechii udar* during the Soviet period was unsound.[39] Soviet military planners were acutely aware of the vulnerability of land-based ICBMs. Given that 70 per cent of Soviet strategic nuclear forces were in this category. The determined development and continuous improvements of a launch-on-warning capability was clearly one indication of this. This including advances in missile technology to allow rapid launch and the development and deployment of ground and space-based early warning systems.

Another indication was the Soviet preoccupation with the security of command and control facilities. A vast network of underground command posts, some as deep as 1,000 feet below the ground, was designed to complicate US attempts to destroy Soviet command and control in a first strike. The sheer scale of the Soviet effort, and the maintenance of a ballistic missile defence system around Moscow, bore witness to the importance attached to this objective.

The third was the nature and direction of their fifth generation ICBM developments. Both the SS-24 and SS-25 were to be deployed in a mobile mode. This would allow the maintenance of a second strike reserve force equivalent to the sea-based force of the United States. However, by the time the USSR was dissolved, the deployment of mobile ICBMs was far from complete.

The deployment and role of mobile missiles is one of the elements of the current debate about the future of Russia's strategic nuclear forces.

There are a variety of possible future lines of development for Russia's strategic nuclear forces, assuming that at least some forces will be maintained. At one end of the spectrum would be the preservation of a deterrent of last resort on the scale of British and French forces. The deployment of large-scale counterforce capabilities and configured to an integrated launch-on-warning mode would be given up in favour of a small-scale residual second-strike deterrent. This option does have active supporters in the Russian political and military élite. At the other end of the spectrum would the retention of the existing capabilities (which require extensive modernisation by the turn of the century) and the continuation of previous trend in force deployments (i.e. the increased development and deployment of mobile ICBMs and sea-based systems with multiple warheads).[40] While this option is also favoured by some, in the Russian élite it is generally believed that such a policy would not be in conformity with the new international situation or Russia's strategic interests. It would also be extremely difficult to implement given the economic problems Russia faces and the consequences of the disintegration of the Soviet Union which has resulted in major missile construction facilities remaining located outside Russia. An intermediate option would be a policy to maintain parity *vis-a-vis* the United States in the context of large-scale reductions as envisaged by the START treaties. This is currently official policy, but the fundamental questions regarding nuclear strategy and the details of the future force posture have remained largely unresolved. In order to get a better understanding of the various options currently under discussion; it is useful to consider the various elements of the strategic nuclear force separately.

Strategic bombers

In the final years of the Soviet Union, the strategic bomber force appeared to be finally emerging as a genuine third leg of a 'strategic triad'. However, this branch of the strategic forces was most severely affected by the break-up of the Soviet Union. A substantial portion of the strategic bomber fleet was lost to Ukraine, including most of the modern TU-160 *Blackjack*. Several *Blackjack* were flown back to Russia in July 1992 by dissident pilots, but the bulk of the fleet remains in Ukraine.[41] The *Bear H* bomber force has likewise been severely fragmented by the break-up of the Soviet Union; out of 88 bombers 40 were based in Kazakhstan and 26 in Ukraine, including five at the only repair facility for the *Bear* at Belaia Tserkov in Ukraine. The only Il-78 *Midas* strategic tanker aircraft is also in Ukraine. The government of Kazakhstan has proven more amenable to returning at least some of the aircraft to the Russian Air Force.[42]

Currently Russia has 63 Tu-95MS heavy bombers, which date back to the 1950s but were modernised in 1980 in order to be able to carry air-launched cruise missiles (ALCMs). The bombers exist in two variants - 28 that can carry six ALCMs and 35 that carry 16 ALCMS. There are six Tu-160 in Russia, carrying 12 ALCMs each. Russia was willing to by back the 19 Tu-160 based in Ukraine, but gave up in 1997 after five years of negotiations over the price. However, in the aftermath of the Kosovo crisis the Security Council decided in April 1999 to purchase the only serviceable strategic aircraft still in Ukraine (eight TU-160 and three TU-95MS) as payment for some Ukraine's energy debt. An agreement was finally reached and a number of aircraft were returned to Ukraine in early 2000.

Nevertheless, any expansion of the bomber force as part of a restructuring of Russian strategic forces under START appears unlikely, not least because of the cost. Production lines for strategic bombers were closed down in 1992 and are unlikely to be re-opened.[43] Interviews with Russian military experts confirm that there is no substantial interest in rebuilding a strategic nuclear bomber force, even though some have voiced an interest in reviving the project for a 'Stealth Bomber' abandoned in the early 1980s to match the American B-2. The Commander of the Strategic Rocket Forces, Vladimir Yakovlev, has come out in support for the triad and the need for a heavy bomber force, possibly in response to US plans to deploy a National Missile Defence. There is also a project for a new supersonic ALCM, the Kh-101, which can be deployed as a nuclear and conventional missile, thus possibly giving bombers new military role. However, the TU-95MS and even the TU-160 are becoming obsolete, and there seems little prospect for a properly funded programme to develop a new strategic bomber.

In conclusion, the most likely scenario is that despite the fact that START I favours deployment of bombers, this leg of the strategic nuclear deterrent force will be abandoned by Russia or at best maintained at a minimal level.

ICBMs

The ICBM force which Russia inherited from the Soviet Union is a mix of the fourth and fifth generation of Soviet strategic missiles. The fourth generation of Soviet ICBMs, consisting mostly of the highly accurate SS-19 with six warheads (360 missiles deployed) and the heavy SS-18 (308 missiles, mostly deployed in an eight to ten warhead configuration)[44] gave the Soviet Union a substantial counterforce capability against the United States and thus radically transformed the Soviet strategic nuclear force posture. Key advances were made in fuel technology (allowing the SS-17 and SS-18 to be cold-launched), guidance systems (putting ICBM silos in the continental USA in reach of the SS-18 and SS-19), and the development of missiles with multiple, independently targetable warheads (MIRVs), which allowed a large expansion of the number of warheads deployed while keeping the number of launchers fixed as provided for by the 1972 SALT I agreement.[45]

The SS-18 (RS-20), codenamed *Satan* by NATO, is a very heavy missile and a successor to the SS-9. As its designation might indicate, this missile was perceived by Western analysts as the most threatening element of the Soviet strategic arsenal and is still considered the most potent weapon in the Russian ICBM force. In 1974 it was deployed with a single 24 megaton warhead and an estimated accuracy of 0.24 nautical miles. By the late seventies, the fourth modification of the SS-18 was carrying 10 MIRVed 0.55 megaton warheads while the accuracy had improved to 0.14 nautical miles. By 1980 308 SS-18 were therefore in principle capable of delivering 3,080 warheads on the continental United States.

The SS-19 (RS-18), a hot-launched liquid fuel missile developed by the Chelomei design bureau, is capable of carrying 60.55 megaton MIRVed warheads or a 4.3 megaton single warhead. 350, mostly of the MIRVed modification 3 were ultimately deployed in 4 silo fields. The SS-19, like the SS-11 (RS-10) is a missile of variable range and it has been estimated that 120 were deployed as regional weapons in the European and Far Eastern theatres, rather than in an ICBM mode. During the Soviet period the SS-18 and the SS-19 were seen by Western analysts as the principal counterforce elements threatening the US Minuteman ICBM force.

The structure of the Soviet fourth generation ICBM force (including the surviving elements of the third generation, the SS-11 and the SS-13) was such that it provided a versatile capability against a whole range of targets, including civilian and economic targets. It is quite evident nonetheless that the SS-18 and SS-19 force was clearly designed to provide the capability to attack Minuteman silos. American analysts have taken the view based on the available information about the hardening of the Minuteman silos and the accuracy of the Soviet missiles that at least two warheads would need to be targeted on a Minuteman silo to achieve a good probability of destruction. Apart from Minuteman silos, hardened command and control centres were also likely targets for this force. Important soft targets in the continental United States, such as strategic bomber fields, military headquarters and countervalue targets[46] could be handled by single-warhead SS-17 and SS-19 missiles. The SS-11 and the SS-18 were also suitable for attacking long-range naval targets.

The fifth generation of Soviet ICBMs which emerged in the 1980s constitutes an important step forward towards a truly modern missile force measured by the standards of American technology. The first successful solid-fueled missile deployed by the Soviet Union was the intermediate range SS-20. Both the SS-24 (RS-22) and SS-25 (RS-12M) are solid-fueled, thus enabling the quick alert rate and mobility which can only be achieved with the use of solid fuels. It is also clear that the Soviets had made important advances in inertial guidance systems. The accuracy of the SS-24 and SS-25 is given by the IISS at 200 metres CEP (circular error probable) - slightly better than that of the most accurate Minuteman III (220 m CEP), but not in the same class as the American MX *Peacekeeper* missile (100 m CEP).[47] The SS-24 was essentially the Soviet answer to the MX. Its throw-weight is estimated to be slightly higher than that of the MX, and like the MX it carries 10 MIRVed warheads. The yield of the warheads is given for the SS-24 by the IISS as 100 kt. It was deployed both in silos, and in a rail-mobile mode in line with the current Soviet view to ensure invulnerability through mobility. The SS-25 is a single-warhead missile deployed in silos or in a road-mobile mode. Deployment began in 1985.

The dissolution of the Soviet Union and the START process have thrown into focus some existing and some new weaknesses in the structure of the ICBM force that Russia has inherited. The break-up of the Soviet Union generated doubt about Russia's ability to maintain heavy MIRVed missiles in the future. The fourth generation ICBMs reached the end of their service life by the end of the century and need to be modernised. By the end of the decade the SS-18 in particular was due for replacement, and extensions of its service life (using a variety of means, including the purchase of spare parts and missiles that were manufactured recently and not yet deployed) cannot prolong its deployment indefinitely. Thus it is projected that the entire SS-18 force would have to be retired by 2006 irrespective of arms control agreements. Production of this missile which was manufactured at the Yuzhny engineering works in Dnepropetrovsk in Ukraine has ceased and is unlikely to be resumed in the current climate of relations between Russia and Ukraine. The design documentation and intellectual property rights associated with the design are in the possession of the Yuzhnoe design bureau. It has therefore become difficult to provide for the technical safety of these missiles and their modernisation would require a substantial investment in missile technology and production facilities in Russia. This is true more generally for the production of MIRVed ICBMs. Russia is unwilling to rely on design bureaux and missile production facilities outside the Russian Federation and therefore has deliberately cut its ties with *Yuzhnoe* and other missile design and production centres.[48] The first victim of this attitude was the *Courier*, a small mobile ICBM that was being developed by *Yuzhnoe* in the 1980s.[49]

The SS-24 faces similar problems since it also was assembled in Ukraine. Only the guidance systems for the SS-24 were manufactured in Russia. In 1992 plans had been made to develop and deploy a follow-on to the SS-24 in silos and in a rail-mobile mode to replace all the SS-18 and SS-24 after the year 2005. After the signing of START II and in view of the break-down in the links with Ukraine these plans have been quietly shelved.

There were also severe safety problems associated with the deployment of the SS-24 in a rail-mobile mode. Large parts of the Russian rail system were simply inadequate to permit the secure transportation of the missiles. This meant that if the trains were out on patrol they occupied sections of the rail network for a considerable period of time that were required for civilian use. Even then there remained a substantial risks of accidents; in one incident the missile train caught fire. The highly toxic fuel burned with an intensity that made it impossible for some time for fire-fighters to approach the scene of the accident. As a consequence of these problems, the concept of rail mobility has now been all but abandoned. The existing SS-24 missiles are all deployed at fixed points (i.e. in silos) and no rail patrols are taking place. In view of these problems there is no significant opposition to scrapping the SS-24 by way of the implementation of strategic arms control agreements. The SS-24 will be taken out of service by 2010 if not before. Likewise, the SS-19 will have to be retired by 2009 at the latest, and even the SS-25 (*Topol*) will reach the end of its service life by 2005 (although it can be extended by five years). This means that Russia has one decade to complete replace its existing ICBM force with new missiles.[50]

The problem is that there is now only one design bureau in Russia that is involved in missile design (the Moscow Institute of Thermal Technology - MIT); all the others have reverted to civilian projects, such as space launchers. This design bureau is therefore solely responsible for the new generation of ICBMs. The only missile it has produced is the *Topol-M*, a follow-on to the SS-25 that is now commonly designated the SS-27 (although previously referred to as variant 2 of the SS-25).

It is important to recognize that the abandonment of MIRVed ICBMs, although to some extent forced by the break-up of the Soviet Union, is a matter of policy. The main requirements for the modern Russian ICBM force are survivability and penetration capability. This means a low number of warheads per missile (most likely one), deployment in hard silos or in road-mobile form, a hardened missile body, protection against electromagnetic pulse and other defence penetration capabilities, including an unusually low boost trajectory to confound space-based defences.

Technically Russia has the option to continue to deploy MIRVed missiles, either by putting three warheads onto the *Topol M* or by deploying a new MIRVed SLBM as an *ersatz* ICBM in silos.[51] The concept which is currently considered most actively by Russian military planners and has the support of some political analysts, including for example Alexei Arbatov, is the deployment a new type of uniform missile to be deployed both as an SLBM and as an ICBM on land. The option favoured by Arbatov is a missile with characteristics similar to the SS-27 (with a launch-weight of 40 tons), with 3-4 warheads. The land-based version would be developed to carry three warheads (down-loaded to a single warhead configuration to conform with START II) in a road-mobile mode. The sea-based version could be deployed with four warheads. The buses (devices that enable the independent deployment of several warheads on one missile) for the MIRVed system for the land-based version would be stored, together with the warheads, to provide a recovery potential of up to 2000 warheads in the event of a break-out from the treaty regime by the United States.[52] This approaches the estimated recovery potential of the United States as a consequence of the downloading of Minuteman III ICBMs. In the event of the deployment of National Missile Defence system by the United States, there may be a lot of pressure in Russia to deploy MIRVed ICBMs.

The principal consequence for Russian military planners is that under START II the land-based force has to consist of single-warhead ICBMs. Except for 109 downloaded SS-19s, these will all be SS-25 and SS-27. After the retirement of older missiles, the ICBM will consist only of SS-27 and a new dual ICBM/SLBM follow-on to the SS-27 (with one warhead if land-based), provided the plans to develop such a missile are successful (see below). Under START II ceilings Russia intends to deploy ultimately 690 SS-25/27.

The SS-25 is deployed in silos and a road-mobile mode. Mobility, while strategically desirable, inevitably introduces safety risks. Much of the Russian road network is in poor condition, especially in the country-side where the SS-25 patrols take place in order to avoid detection. There have been a number of accidents with mobile launchers which have toppled over. Road-deployment also makes the missiles more vulnerable to attacks by terrorists or (in the event of war) foreign agents.[53]

Russian military planners remain convinced of the desirability of mobility for ICBMs nonetheless. The sustained but largely fruitless effort to locate and destroy mobile missile launchers in Iraq during the Gulf War of 1991 demonstrated that mobility provides some protection even against modern space-based reconnaissance systems and vastly complicates any first strike plans. For this reason most of the SS-27 will also be deployed in road-mobile mode, although all the SS-27 in service so far are in silos.[54]

The decision to begin production of the *Topol-M* was made by President Yeltsin in February 1993 after design work which began in the 1980s. The first test flight was in December 1994. In 1997 the missile was officially adopted for deployment, but initially only two missiles were deployed in 'evaluative mode'. The first group of *Topol-M* was deployed with great fanfare at the end of 1998 at the Tatishchevo missile base in the Saratov region.[55] The annual rate of deployment is projected to be 30 to 40 per year, although funding problems might reduce it that number considerably. Thus by 2010 Russia may have deployed 500 missiles, but with funding at a level of only 48 per cent of what is required the production rate may be much lower. To be consistent with START II levels the ultimate number of *Topol-M* must not exceed 800.

Given the ratification of START II, the principal focus of Russia's strategic nuclear force posture will be a single-warhead force deployed to provide a secure second strike force with low vulnerability. Its manner of deployment will preclude a launch-on-warning posture, but the mobility of the forces and the fact that the United states will also no longer deploy land-based missiles with multiple warheads means that this will no longer seen to be necessary.

Political and economic circumstances suggest that the most likely future of Russia's ICBM force is its consolidation to a single-warhead mobile land-based second strike force. However other options are under consideration and may be pursued more actively if relations with the United States should deteriorate and the economy remains sufficiently stable to allow the pursuit of a strategic challenge to the United States.

The sea-based deterrent

The Russian leadership seems to recognize that the naval component of the strategic nuclear triad will become more important as a result of START. Russia could maintain virtually all of its most modern missile-carrying submarines, the Delta III, Delta IV and Typhoon and remain under the limit of 1,750 SLBM warheads imposed by the second phase of START II by downloading some of its MIRVed SLBMs under the agreed rules. Currently about 30 per cent of Russia's long-range ballistic missiles are deployed on submarines; under START this could increase to over 50 per cent without any new nuclear submarines having to be built or missiles to be manufactured.[56] Russia's sea-based forces, however, cannot be used to execute the kind of co-ordinated attack on time-urgent hard targets as the currently deployed land-based force and such a shift would therefore require a completely different strategic doctrine and operational plans. The Russian submarine force is also plagued by communications problems which hinder effective command control in situations of crisis. It is also vulnerable to American antisubmarine warfare (ASW).

The problem is that Russia's ballistic missile submarine fleet is currently in poor condition. There are increasing concerns about safety problems associated with the older SSBNs, and currently there are very few patrols even of the most modern boats. Ten *Yankee* class submarines have been decommissioned since START I was signed. The more modern boats can remain in service for another decade or so; by 2006 even the *Delta IV* (Russian designation *Delphin*) and *Typhoon* (Russian designation *Akula*) need to be decommissioned. To maintain its sea-based force Russia will therefore have to design and deploy a follow-on system to enter service shortly after the envisaged implementation of START II. Given that military ship-building in Russia has almost come to a complete halt and the entire industry is in a state of decay, this requires substantial investments. The construction of a new submarine called the *Borey* began in November 1996 at the Severodvinsk shipyward. The *Borey* could also be called the *Delta V* because it is essentially a modernization of that SSBN class. It marks a shift away from the larger boats of the *Typhoon* class. Due to funding shortages it is envisaged that by 2010 Russia will have one and at most two operational *Borey*.[57] The *Borey* will carry 12 SLBMs.The missile apparently intended for the *Borey* was a project called 'Bark', a follow-on to the SS-N-20. This was a missile with a throw weight of 3.05 tons designed to carry 10 warheads. The development of this missile continued until 1997 when it was cancelled after three failed test-flights. On 3 July 1998, at the meeting of the Security Council which adopted a strategic forces development programme until 2010, a decision was made to procure a new solid-fueled SLBM to be jointly developed by the MIT and Miass (SLBM) design bureaux. This new missile, which is to be deployed both as an ICBM and SLBM, will be called *Bulava* and is essentially going to be a derivative of the *Topol-M.* In its SLBM configuration the *Bulava* would carry three or four warheads; each *Borey* submarine would be able to deliver either 48 or 64 warheads as a result (assuming an increase in the number of missile tubes from 12 to 16). Nikolai Sokov points out that there are option for liquid-fueled follow-on designs based on existing SLBMs which could be deployed on the *Borey* if the *Bulava* is delayed or fails to materialise, with six warheads per missile.[58] As a consquence the precise configuration of warheads based on sea in the future is quite difficult to predict, but it is clear that if current plans are implemented the share of warheads based on sea in the Russian arsenal will increase from 30 to 50 per cent within the next two decades with about 800 to 900 warheads deployed at sea. The *caveat* is funding; while the number of warheads based on land will certainly decrease, the ability of Russia to increase their sea-based arsenal depends on financial resources. It is expected that ultimately seven *Borey* will be deployed. These may not be forthcoming if the economic crisis in Russia deepens during the next decade. Moreover, Russia's surface navy which has a key role in protecting SSBNs would require substantial rejuvenation, thus raising the cost of rebuilding and expanding the sea-based strategic nuclear forces. The strategic plans of the Russian navy thus may turn out to be unrealisable.

Conclusion

As the Cold War ended, there were calls for a commitment to co-operative denuclearization as the most important objective in the US-Russian strategic relationship. In many respects this would be a logical consequence of the change in the political relationship between the two main protagonists of the Cold War.

Although both sides are taking faltering steps in the direction of dismantling the strategic nuclear confrontation of the Cold War, the political commitment to co-operative denuclearization has diminished. The strategic withdrawal from Central and Eastern Europe, the dissolution of the Soviet Union and the concomitant disintegration of the Soviet military, the implementation of conventional arms control agreements and the economic collapse are factors which have resulted in the virtual disintegration of Russian military capabilities. As a consequence, there has been a definite shift towards greater reliance on nuclear weapons, both tactical and strategic. Strategic force modernization has been undertaken with great determination. Its direction is the creation of a strategic nuclear force that will be different in structure from that which emerged in the Soviet period. The destabilizing accumulation of missiles with multiple warheads will be reversed with the deployment of survivable, mobile single warhead systems. But it will still be a substantial force, configured to provide a reliable second-strike deterrent against US, Chinese and any other forces. The direction of strategic force modernization does reflect Russia's circumstances, but it is not in accordance with the development of the international environment. The adaptation of nuclear weapons policies to Russia's post-Cold War relations with the West has yet to begin.

Notes

1 For a more detailed exploration of these factors, see Alexei C. Arbatov, 'Russia's Foreign Policy Alternatives', *International Security*, Vol.18, No.2, Fall 1993, pp.5-43.
2 Sergei A. Karaganov, *Russia: The New Foreign Policy and Security Agenda*, London: Brassey's 1992.
3 Ole Diehl, 'Eastern Europe as a Challenge for Future European Security', in Mark Curtis, Ole Diehl, Jérôme Paolini, Alexis Seydoux and Reinhard Wolf, *Challenges and Responses to Future European Security: British, French and German Perspectives*, London: European Strategy Group 1993, pp.15-68.
4 Alan Smith, *Russia and the World Economy*, London: Routledge 1993; Julian Cooper, The Conversion of the Former Soviet Defence Industry, London: RIIA 1993.
5 This issue is discussed by Kimberly Zisk, 'The Foreign Policy Preferences of Russian Defense Industrialists: Integration or Isolation', unpublished manuscript (December 1993).
6 Karaganov, op.cit, p.24 and p.25; it should be added that Karaganov supports the scrapping of all tactical nuclear warheads and some reductions in strategic nuclear forces.
7 Economist Intelligence Unit, *Country Profile Russia 1997-98*, London: EIU 1997 p.41.
8 Dmitri Trenin, 'Russia's Military Resources', paper presented at a conference of the Federal Institute for International and East European Studies, Cologne, November 1995.
9 IISS Military Balance 1999-2000. Oxford; Oxford University Press 1999, pp. 110-112
10 Aleksei Arbatov, Obshchaia Gazeta, 31 October 1996.
11 Ibid.; see also 'Russia's Military: The Politics of Reform', *Strategic Comments*, vol. 2, no. 2, October 1996.
12 'Russia' TV Channel, cited from Lynch., op.cit.
13 *Nezavisimaia Gazeta*, 23 May 1997.
14 Nikolai Sokov, *Russian Strategic Modernization*, Oxford: Rowman & Littlefield Publishers 2000, p.122.
15 Pavel Podvig (ed.), *Strategicheskoe Iadernoe Vooruzhenie Rossii*, Moscow: IzdAt 1998.
16 Sokov, op.cit., p.122.
17 See Graham Allison, Ashton B. Carter, Steven E. Miller and Philip Zelikow, 'Co-operative Denuclearization: An International Agenda', in

Allison, Carter, Miller, Zelikow (eds.), *Co-operative Denuclearization*, pp. 1-24.

18 Allison et al. (1993), p.1.

19 This contrasts, however, with a statement by Foreign Minister Kozyrev to the effect that although such a decision had been taken, it had not yet been implemented (Izvestiia, 13 February 1992).

20 Based on conversations with experts at the FCO in London and the Ministry of Defence in Bonn.

21 Interview with Grachev in *Rossiskaia Gazeta*, 21 October 1992, p.2; see also *Izvestiia*, 15 October 1992.

22 Interviews in Kiev (July 1993), Moscow (November 1993 and May 1994) and Washington DC. (April 1994).

23 This measure was also advocated by the CSIA Report.

24 Ibid., p. 28.

25 *Izvestiia*, 18 November 1993, p. 4.

26 *Voennaia mysl'*, Special issue, May 1992. 'Osnovnye polozheniia voennoy doktriny Rossyskoi Federatsii', pp. 3B23 at p. 5. Note that only a description of the basic provisions of the military doctrine of the Russian Federation has been published. Any reference to the military doctrine in this chapter is to that description as published in *Voennaia mysl'*.

27 For analysis see Charles Dick, '*The Military Doctrine of the Russian Federation*', Jane's Intelligence Review, special report no. 1, January 1994.

28 Interviews in Moscow, April 1996.

29 *Voennaia Mysl'*, p. 16.

30 Ibid., p. 4.

31 Ibid., p.16.

32 Ibid., p. 12.

33 Ibid., pp. 17&18.

34 Ibid., p. 18.

35 Anatoli Klimenko and Alexander Koltukov, 'Osnovnoi Dokument Voennogo Stroitelstva', *Nezavisimoe Voennoe Obozrenie*, 13 February 1998, p.4 This contains much of the draft text of the new military doctrine.

36 *Nezavisimaia gazeta*, 30 June 1999, p.2; *Segodnia*, 2 July 1999, p.1.

37 See Committee of Soviet Scientists for Peace, Against the Nuclear Threat, *Strategic Stability under the Conditions of Radical Nuclear Arms Reductions* (Moscow: Novosti, 1987); Alexei Arbatov, 'Strategic Equilibrium and Stability', in Yevgeny Primakov, ed., *Disarmament and Security 1987 Yearbook*, Moscow: Novosti, 1988, pp. 239-63.

38 This means that even in the event of the worst case of a first strike by the United States, Russia would still retain sufficient nuclear weapons for use against soft targets (cities and industry) to be able to inflict what is called 'unacceptable damage' to the United States.
39 Interviews with various experts in Moscow in May 1994.
40 Anton Surikov, 'Daite Start Tiazhelym Raketam', *Pravda*, 6 September 1997, for example.
41 Douglas L. Clarke, '*The Impact of START-2 on the Russian Strategic Forces*', *RFE/RL Research Report*, Vol.2, No.8, 19 February 1993, pp.65-70, p.70; Russian commentators often give the impression that all of the *Blackjack* bombers are still in Ukraine, but this is not the case. See *Pravda*, 23 February 1993, p.3.
42 Clarke, ibid.
43 Production of the *Blackjack* and the *Bear H* was stopped, according to an announcement by President Yeltsin on 29 January 1992.
44 International Institute for Strategic Studies, *The Military Balance 1988/89*, London: Jane's Defence Publishers 1988; see also Robert P. Berman and John C. Baker, *Soviet Strategic Forces*, Washington: Brookings 1982, p.105.
45 Robbin F. Laird and Dale R. Herspring, *The Soviet Union and Strategic Arms*, Boulder: Westview Press 1984.
46 Analysts distinguish between counterforce, countermilitary and countervalue targets. These refer respectively to the enemy strike forces (in particular nuclear missiles and aircraft), military installations and equipment, and civilian targets (cities, industrial centres).
47 IISS Military Balance 1988/89.
48 For more detail, see Dean Wilkening, *The Evolution of Russia's Strategic Nuclear Force*, Palo Alto, CA: CSAC Stanford 1998
49 Nikolai Sokov, op.cit., p.73
50 Podvig, op.cit.; Wilkening, op.cit.
51 Based on interviews with Russian experts. However, the activities of the so-called 'Ukrainian lobby' in Moscow (led by representatives from the missile production complex in Ukraine) are directed against START because of the implications for heavy missiles produced in Ukraine.
52 Wilkening calculates the US ballistic missile upload capability at 2,700 warheads under START II and at about 2,000 warheads under START III. This takes into account downloaded ICBMs as well as downloaded C-4 and D-5 SLBMs (the latter from eight to four warheads). See Wilkening, op.cit., p.38

53 Petr Belov in *Rossiskaia Gazeta*, 3 November 1992, p.4; this author is scathingly critical of the SS-25 for these reasons.

54 During the Gulf War of 1991 the destruction of mobile missile launchers even in conditions of complete air superiority turned out to be a much more difficult task than anticipated. See Martin Navias, *Saddam's Scud War and Ballistic Missile Proliferation*, London: Brassey's 1991, pp.28-35; Lawrence Freedman and Efraim Karsh, *The Gulf Conflict 1990-1991*, London: Faber&Faber 1993, pp.307-309. Russian criticisms about the supposed 'invulnerability' of mobile missiles is discussed below.

55 'Russia Inaugurates 21st Century Missiles', *Reuters News Service*, 27 December 1998.

56 Alexei Arbatov, '*START II, Red Ink and Boris Yeltsin*', Bulletin of the Atomic Scientists, April 1993, pp.16-21, p.20.

57 See the article by Yuri Maslyukov at www.rus.ru/forums/zagran; see also Sokov, op.cit., p.135.

58 See Sokov, op.cit., p.139.

4 Strategic Nuclear Weapons of the former Soviet Union outside Russia

During the period of the Cold War confrontation both the United States and the Soviet Union saw tight central control over nuclear weapons as essential. With large arsenals deployed in such a manner that any nuclear detonation or confirmed missile launch on one side could trigger a massive nuclear exchange, the possibility of unauthorised use had to be completely excluded. The disintegration of a major nuclear weapons state was, from this point of view, a complete nightmare.

In late 1990 Western and Soviet academics were already discussing the consequences of social and political disintegration in the Soviet Union for nuclear weapons safety.[1] During the second half of 1991 deep concerns about the security and safety of nuclear weapons in the Soviet Union began to surface publicly in the United States. These concerns fell into broadly three categories:

- the integrity of command and control (e.g. the prevention of the unauthorised use of nuclear weapons)
- the physical security of weapons and nuclear materials
- the proliferation of nuclear materials and nuclear engineering expertise.

Some of these issues will be discussed in later chapters. What is of interest here is the attitude adopted by the United States and later Russia about the presence of nuclear weapons in non-Russian republics and the political consequences that flowed from them.

Nuclear weapons outside Russia

Before addressing the conceptual issues, it might be useful to recall the disposition of the Soviet nuclear arsenal at the time when the Soviet Union was dissolved. Tactical nuclear weapons (TNF) were deployed widely throughout the Soviet Union. Russia, Ukraine, Belarus, Kazakhstan, Turkmenistan, Uzbekistan, Moldova, Kyrgyzstan and Tajikistan all had TNF on their territories.

Strategic nuclear forces based on land consisted of ICBMs in fixed silos, road- and rail-mobile ICBMs and long-range aircraft. The bulk of these forces were based in Russia, but some were in three other former Soviet republics, Belarus, Ukraine and Kazakhstan.

Table 4.1: Soviet Strategic Nuclear Weapons Outside Russia

State	*System*	*Number*	*Warheads*
Ukraine	SS-24	46	460
	SS-19	130	780
	Bear H	21	168
	Blackjack	13	156
Kazakhstan	SS-18	104	1040
	Bear H	40	380
Belarus	SS-25	54	54

Note: These data reflect the situation in mid-1991, just before the Soviet Union was dissolved[2]

The dissolution of the Soviet Union raised the issue of the ownership and disposition of these forces. The withdrawal of all tactical weapons to Russian territory prior to the break-up of the country was technically feasible but did not occur as the military high command believed that it would be able to remain in control of all military assets even if the Soviet Union formally was dissolved. The relocation of strategic nuclear forces, especially missiles in fixed silos, was a different matter altogether. The uncertainty about the nature of the government in the states that emerged from the ashes of the Soviet Union and the possibility that some regions might not have any stable government at all raised considerable anxiety about the fate of nuclear weapons and the potential for unauthorised use.

The dangers of unauthorised use

In assessing the risks of unauthorised use, a distinction needs to be made between tactical and strategic nuclear weapons. Tactical nuclear weapons are based on delivery systems that have a relatively short range.[3] They are considered to be very much less secure than strategic nuclear weapons. ICBMs are mostly based in silos and it would take a very large military force to secure physical access. Even then it would not be possible to launch the weapons; any modifications necessary to by-pass the launch control mechanisms would take months to put in place, would a great deal of technical expertise and technical infrastructure. The unauthorised use of strategic nuclear weapons could be virtually excluded; only the military high command of Russia or (in the immediate aftermath of the dissolution of the USSR) some of the successor states (especially Ukraine) were capable of using these weapons without authorisation by the Russian president. Strategic nuclear warheads are equipped with environmental sensing devices which require the warhead to experience a certain degree of acceleration before it can be armed. Therefore, even if an unauthorised group of persons managed to penetrate a missile base and acquire warheads, they would be unable to use them as nuclear weapons without also obtaining missiles to launch them on trajectories that fall within certain parameters.

The risks are considerably higher with regard to tactical nuclear weapons. First of all there is a greater risk that unauthorised persons could come into possession of tactical nuclear warheads. This was particularly the case in the early post-Soviet period since these weapons were dispersed over a large number of bases throughout the Soviet Union, some of which were located in what are now crisis regions. Although even tactical nuclear warheads require substantial transport facilities, it is nevertheless conceivable that a warhead would be stolen and hidden. Thus physically tactical nuclear weapons are less secure than strategic nuclear forces.

Furthermore tactical nuclear weapons largely lack the electronic locks (PALs - permissive action links) and other security systems that prevent the unauthorised use of strategic nuclear weapons. In the case of tactical nuclear weapons Soviet-style PALs in any event merely delay and do not ultimately prevent the arming of the weapon.[4]

Finally it is unclear to what extent an adequate inventory of all tactical nuclear warheads was kept. Although there are some reports that each nuclear warhead has a serial number, it remains uncertain that the precise number and location of each warhead was known by the Soviet military leadership.[5]

The combination of all these factors leads to the conclusion that this dispersal of tactical warheads throughout the territory of the Soviet Union was dangerous. The United States and Russia both concluded that the only way to make these weapons safe was to withdraw them to secure depots in Russia.

Approaches to dealing with the Soviet nuclear legacy

In principle, several different approaches to dealing with the Soviet nuclear legacy were conceivable. The simplest one would have been to apply the same principle that pertained with regard to most other assets of the former Soviet Union - whatever happened to be located on the territory of a republic when the Soviet Union was dissolved belonged to the new state that emerged from it. Another option was to limit nuclear weapons status to those republics that had ICBMs deployed on their territory. At the other end of the spectrum was the idea that there should be only one nuclear successor state to the Soviet Union, namely Russia, and that all weapons should be removed from the territories of the former non-Russian Soviet republics.

Both the United States and Russia adopted the last of these options as their firm policy with regard to the nuclear legacy.

In the case of the United States, some of the main reasons were as follows:

- In terms of US security interests, the most favourable outcome of the dissolution of the Soviet Union would be for there to be no nuclear successor state. But given that the nuclear weapons existed in large numbers and would not disappear over night, the next preferable option was that there should be one.
- The international environment would remain predictable. Dealing with more than one nuclear successor state would render the strategic nuclear relationship much more complex and uncertain, in a manner that was perceived to have most likely a negative impact on US national security. Russian leaders inherited experience in dealing with a nuclear deterrent relationship over many decades and the United States had reasonable confidence that the nuclear arsenal would be safest under Russian control.
- The nature of the political leadership in the various post-Soviet states was very uncertain. There were conflicts raging on the territories of some of the former republics or between them. In situations of civil unrest, ethnic conflict or irrational and unpredictable political leaderships the presence of nuclear weapons was considered to be an extremely dangerous element. The perceived dangers ranged from the unauthorised acquisition of nuclear

weapons by armed participants in civil conflicts to the use of nuclear weapons by one newly independent state against another, or even against the United States.

- The presence of a very large number of nuclear weapons on a large territory that is subject to political instability and intense civil conflict raised strong concerns about the safety and security of nuclear weapons. It was judged that the best way to assure the security of the weapons would be it there was one nuclear successor state. This should be a state with experience in managing a large technical and military infrastructure that could keep the weapons secure.

With regard to strategic nuclear weapons, the principal security concern was the integrity of command and control. If the command and control system established during Soviet times, which American experts judged to be essentially sound, were to be dismantled, then the strategic nuclear weapons which were outside whatever command and control system remained in Russia had to be judged insecure and a threat to the Untied States. There was no confidence that the other successor states would be able to establish a similarly secure command and control system.

As regards tactical nuclear weapons, the primary concern was unauthorised access to weapons dispersed over the territory over the former Soviet Union.

In the judgement of the United States government, the only way to address the problems of both the strategic weapons and the tactical weapons was to make sure all weapons were removed from non-Russian territories. Only Russia was judged to posses the technical expertise, the facilities, the infrastructure and the resources to manage a large nuclear arsenal safely.

- The emergence of a number of nuclear successor states was considered a bad precedent in terms of nuclear nonproliferation. Furthermore, poorer nation in the Commonwealth of Independent States might decide to become active proliferators to deal with their acute economic problems by selling nuclear materials, weapons components or even complete warheads. The drive towards the denuclearization of all former Soviet republics except Russia thus was fuelled by proliferation concerns.

Although such considerations informed US policy, they were not unanimously supported by the expert community. One counter-argument was that since the principal security concern was about tactical weapons, the United States should not get involved since US security interests would not be affected by the nuclearisation of civil conflicts in the former Soviet Union. Needless to say, this rather cynical view had few adherents. Another argument that found wider echo in the expert community was that the possession of nuclear weapons by several former Soviet republics might be a good thing. This was discussed with particular vigour in relation to Ukraine. It was based on the notion of a deterrent effect resulting from the possession of nuclear weapons. Conventional conflicts would become considerably less likely if Russia was not the only state to possess nuclear weapons. A third argument, which was advanced by some Western experts and also quite vigorously by many in Ukraine was that it was an erroneous assumption that Russia should be considered the principal successor state to the USSR and that the other successor states had a right to control whatever assets of the former Soviet Union were on their territory, including nuclear weapons. It was by no means obvious by what right Russia was assumed to be the only legitimate nuclear successor state to the USSR. Furthermore, it could not be taken for granted that Russia was inherently more trustworthy or democratic than other states, such as Ukraine or Belarus. Indeed, as voices in the Russian political élite demanding a dominant position in the former Soviet space began to grow, it was increasingly pointed out that non-Russian republics like Ukraine faced a real security threat from Russia and they had a right to protect themselves. Nuclear weapons appeared to be quite effective for this purpose.

All of these arguments will be reconsidered when discussing the policies of the individual post-Soviet states. The following section will discuss how the issue of nuclear control was handled in the period following the dissolution of the Soviet Union.

The command and control of nuclear weapons in the CIS

When the Soviet Union was finally dissolved and the CIS was established at the end of 1991, a separate agreement on strategic forces was signed on 31 December 1991 in Minsk which specified that all nuclear weapons would remain under a joint command based in Moscow. The decision to use strategic nuclear weapons (wherever based) would be made by the Russian President in agreement with the leaders of Belarus, Kazakhstan and Ukraine and after consultation with the leaders of the other independent states.

The situation with regard to command and control in the immediate aftermath of the dissolution of the Soviet Union could consequently be summarised as follows:

- Political control over nuclear weapons was exercised jointly by the leaders of Russia, Belarus, Ukraine and Kazakhstan.
- The Commander of the forces of the CIS was Marshal Evgeny Shaposhnikov. Operational control of nuclear weapons was in the hands of Marshal Shaposhnikov and President Yeltsin who were each in possession of a so-called 'football' (i.e. a briefcase which contains the 'Kazbek' terminals that allow the authorisation codes to necessary to launch nuclear weapons to be transmitted). The commander of the Strategic Rocket Forces of the Soviet Union, General Yuri Maksimov, became the commander of the SRF of the CIS. The entire command and control system was managed by the Russian General Staff, just as it had been managed by the Soviet General Staff. The political leaders of Belarus, Ukraine and Kazakhstan had a political veto, but could not physically prevent the launch of weapons.[6] The transition from the Soviet command structure to that of the Commonwealth of Independent States left the existing command and control system intact.

Although the immediate concerns of the disruption of the existing command and control system which contained stringent safeguards against unauthorised use proved unfounded, the new situation was far from satisfactory. First of all there was the wider concern that the traditional structures of political control in the Soviet Union (the party organisations and the KGB) which assured civilian control over the military were no longer functional. At the same time, although Yeltsin assumed control over the launch of nuclear weapons, there was no functioning formal political authority within the CIS that could be said to exercise *effective* political control over the armed forces. While Yeltsin was the President of Russia, he had no supreme command authority in the CIS as such. Shaposhnikov was technically responsible to the Council of the Heads of State of the CIS which was not a body with any decision-making capacity. As a consequence there was a potential for the armed forces to become a quasi-independent institution within the CIS, controlling a large arsenal of strategic nuclear weapons.

The creation of the CIS strategic command was designed to have a wider purpose than merely the control over nuclear weapons. It was supposed to preserve the integrity of the former Soviet military as a whole. The implication was that there would be a central command for all nuclear and non-nuclear 'strategic' forces. The newly independent states would only create territorial defence forces under their own command, whereas central command over the bulk of the former Soviet conventional forces would be preserved intact. This was evidently unacceptable to the non-Russian states and consequently the CIS strategic command remained an institution without any role except for the control of nuclear forces while these remained dispersed throughout several of the Newly Independent States.

The first step towards the denuclearization of the non-Russian Newly Independent States was the removal of all tactical nuclear weapons. There was some resistance to this initially from Ukraine, but eventually it was agreed that the removal of these weapons would be permitted. In an extraordinary military operation, which effectively monopolised much of the Russian rail network for a number of months, all tactical nuclear weapons from the former Soviet republics were moved to Russian territory was by 6 May 1992.[7] This process allayed Western fears very considerably. In a protocol to the START Treaty originally concluded between the United States and the Soviet Union (the Lisbon protocol, signed on 23 May 1992), Russia, Belarus, Kazakhstan and Ukraine agreed to assume the obligations of the USSR under the treaty. Furthermore Belarus, Kazakhstan and Ukraine agreed to adhere to the non-nuclear proliferation treaty (NPT) as non-nuclear weapons states.[8] The signing of the Lisbon Protocol, however, did not settle the matter. On the contrary, it only marked the beginning of a protracted political struggle as it was revealed that the attitude to denuclearization differed marked in the various former Soviet republics, with the outright opposition coming from Ukraine. What follows is a brief review of how this issue developed in the three non-Russian states.

Belarus

Belarus can be described as an 'accidental country', which acquired sovereignty at the end of 1991 by virtue of being a Soviet republic and as one of the three main participants in the meeting that resulted in the agreement to dissolve the USSR and establish the Commonwealth of Independent State, but (unlike in Ukraine) there was no great yearning for independence either in the country or the political élite. This is borne out by the sustained efforts in recent years to recreate a union with Russia. As the Soviet state was disintegrating, parliaments in the various Soviet republics issued declarations of sovereignty, and Belorussia (as it was then called) was no exception. Article 10 of the declaration adopted on 27 July 1990 set the unprecedent goal of establishing Belarus as a neutral state whose territory would be a nuclear-free zone.

This aspect of the declaration was politically charged as it implicitly denounced both the political control of the central government of the Soviet Union and the place of Belarus in the Soviet military system.

The Belorussian SSR, like Ukraine, had very substantial Soviet military forces and facilities on its territory given that it was on the Western attack corridor. About 10 per cent of the territory of the republic were occupied by military and nuclear facilities.

Strategic nuclear forces deployed in Belarus consisted of two bases for SS-25 (RS-12M) *Topol* missiles at Mosur and Lida. There were 54 missiles deployed altogether on 27 mobile launchers at each base, with one nuclear warhead per missile. There were an estimated 1,120 tactical nuclear warheads deployed on the territory of Belarus, 270 for the army, 125 for air defence, 575 for the air force and 150 for the navy.

The reality of independent statehood induced in all of the former Soviet states a change in attitude towards all foreign and security policy issues, and this was true to a limited extent for Belarus as well. Two important questions were raised by the newly appointed defence minister, Piotr Chaus with regard to the nuclear weapons issue:

1. The division of the USSR into separate states also represented a division of economic assets. Such assets included nuclear weapons and therefore the transfer of nuclear weapons from the territory of Belarus should not take place until the matter of the division of property was settled.
2. Belarus still adhered to the objective of becoming a nuclear-free state, but nuclear disarmament should also occur in the neighbouring states with nuclear weapons. There should be no unilateral disarmament.[9]

This indicates that while Belarus itself had no nuclear ambitions, there were questions of the national interest at stake. However, the perception of the government of Belarus of the national interest began to centre more and more on the relationship with Russia. The consequence was a policy of general compliance with Russia. The chairman of the Supreme Soviet, Stanislau Shushkevich, stated that:

> nuclear weapons on the territory of Belarus are Russian, they are under Russian jurisdiction, and the problem of our nuclear disarmament is to repatriate them onto the territory of Russia[10]

In October 1992 the Council of Ministers of the Republic of Belarus adopted a decree according to which Belarus would accede to the NPT. On 4 February 1993 the Parliament of Belarus ratified both START I and the Lisbon Protocol without any preconditions. By way of implementing its obligations, it also endorsed a decision to accede to the NPT as a non-nuclear state. On 22 July 1993 accession to the nuclear nonproliferation treaty was completed. Thus Belarus became the first state with a nuclear arsenal to renounce its nuclear weapons status voluntarily.[11] Another important step was the ratification by he parliaments of Belarus and Russia of a Treaty on the Coordination of Activities in the Military Sphere and the Agreement on the Strategic Forces Temporarily Stationed on the Territory of Belarus. These agreements codified the withdrawal of strategic nuclear forces, Russian military forces (comprising a unit of 35,000) and the turning over of military bases to Belarus (after dealing with the environmental caused by military activities).

Even before these agreements were signed in September 1993, the withdrawal of SS-25s and the associated military contingents had already begun. By 1996 the withdrawal was complete.

The election of the first President of the Republic of Belarus in 1994, Alexander Lukashenka, did not result in any significant changes of policy with regard to nuclear weapons. Negotiations began on a number of issues, among the most important for Russia being an agreement to lease the early-warning radar near Baranovichi and the Vileika naval communications centre.

Although Belarus had not made any attempt to use the presence of nuclear weapons on its territory as a means to obtain political or financial concessions, it did become involve in discussions over compensation for the transfer of nuclear warheads which were undertaken largely as a result of Ukraine's recalcitrance with regard to its nuclear status. Russia initially questioned the right of Belarus, Ukraine and Kazakhstan for compensation and even assuming such a right, the estimates of the quantity of fissile materials involved were disputed. An agreement reached between Russia and Ukraine acted as a precedent for the other non-Russian states. Compensation for nuclear warheads (tactical and strategic) transferred to Russia was linked explicitly to a US-Russian agreement to purchase $12 billion worth of highly enriched uranium from Soviet warheads. Belarus also received substantial assistance through the Nunn-Lugar co-operative threat reduction programme.[12]

Belarus was the only one of the four 'nuclear successor states' of the Soviet Union that was unambiguously committed to denuclearization throughout the entire process. The most important reason for this was probably its relationship with Russia. Whereas Ukraine pursued a path of radical independence that resulted in a general unwillingness to co-operate with Russia, especially (but not exclusively) in the military sphere, and Kazakhstan had, like other Central Asian states, are rather complex relationship with Russia, Belarus saw itself closely connected with Russia. There was also the realization the Belarus did not have any resources to sustain a nuclear weapons complex; it had no deposits of uranium ore and no facilities for uranium enrichment or plutonium production - indeed no nuclear reactors of any kind. Other elements of a nuclear weapons infrastructure, including command and control centres and an integrated early warning capability were also lacking. For these reasons, no attempt to develop a nuclear status, or even use the presence of nuclear weapons on Belarus territory as a bargaining tool for political or economic concessions of some kind was ever made.

Ukraine

Ukrainian attitudes towards nuclear weapons underwent a curious evolution. During the final year of the Soviet Union and in the initial period of its existence as an independent state Ukraine seemed to be firmly on course to become a non-nuclear state. In mid-July 1990 the Ukrainian parliament threw down the gauntlet to the central authorities in Moscow and adopted a *Declaration of the State Sovereignty of Ukraine.* As a consequence, it also asserted the right of Ukraine to establish and control its own security and military forces. Then, an even more radical proposal by Ivan Drach, the leader of the Ukrainian Popular Movement for Restructuring *(Rukh)* was adopted whereby Ukraine declared its intention to become a neutral state that does not participate in military blocs and that adheres to three non-nuclear principles: not to maintain, produce or acquire nuclear weapons.[13] These principles were accepted and incorporated in the final version of the Declaration of Sovereignty adopted on 16 July 1990.

The non-nuclear position at the time commanded general support both in Parliament and the population.[14] Two principal reasons can be discerned. The first is the general anti-nuclear mood resulting from the experience of the accident at the Chernobyl power plant in April 1986. This event, which resulted in large-scale radioactive contamination in parts of Ukraine and Belarus, including the Ukrainian capital Kiev, was a traumatic experience for the population and had sparked of active antinuclear and environmental campaigns. The second is that the rejection of the presence of the nuclear weapons struck at the most potent symbol of the power of the Soviet regime. The claim that Ukraine had the right to become an international actor in its own right, create its own military forces and the assertion that Ukraine intended to become and neutral and non-nuclear state were perceived as additional ways to exert pressure for independence from Moscow.

Western reactions to Ukrainian attempts to develop some form of independent foreign policy were unexpected and, for the supporters of an independent, neutral and non-nuclear Ukraine disappointing. The United States and Britain made it quite clear that they preferred the Soviet Union to remain intact. During a visit to Kiev at the beginning of August 1991, President Bush made a speech to the Ukrainian parliament in which he praised the achievements of Soviet President Gorbachev and stated:

> Freedom is not the same as independence. Americans will not support those who seek independence in order to replace a far-off tyranny with a local despotism. They will not aid those who promote a suicidal nationalism based on ethnic hatred.[15]

This speech, which was dubbed the 'Chicken Kiev' speech by columnist William Safire, resulted in much criticism of a one-sided policy of support for Gorbachev.

As the Cold War was winding down and the Warsaw Pact had been disbanded, the West began to fear the prospect of an uncontrolled disintegration of the Soviet Union, with unpredictable consequences. Among the spectrum of conceivable developments were widespread civil conflict, or the reassertion of am authoritarian and anti-Western government in Moscow. Indeed, one of the fears was that the pressure for independence coming from various republics would provoke an authoritarian coup against Gorbachev. This fear was soon to be proven justified when the Moscow Coup took place at the end of August 1991, even though it failed within a few days. Until then, Western policy was directed towards dampening down the pressure for independence from the republics and supporting Gorbachev against his Communist opponents. The view that the continued existence of the Soviet Union was required for the stability of Europe after the Cold War was widely shared in the academic community, particularly those international relations specialists from the neo-realist tradition. They feared an unstable Europe, driven by ethnic violence and inter-state conflicts in the absence of the ordering effect of Great Power rivalry.[16] John Lewis Gaddis summarised this attitude in his book on the end of the Cold War:

> Despite the fact that the Cold War did end as the result of asymmetrical decline, and despite the surprise that his happened peacefully, I am still prepared to argue that the stability of post-Cold War international relations requires the continued survival in some form - not necessarily its present form - of the Soviet Union.[17]

The prospect of a violent disintegration of the Soviet Union was extremely alarming to Western policymakers partly because of the large numbers of nuclear weapons on the territory of the Soviet Union.

In Ukraine Western concerns about nuclear weapons were interpreted as the result of Moscow's imperial policy to instil fear about the emergence of 15 new nuclear powers in order to obtain support for the preservation of the Soviet Union as a single state. Serhii Holovaty, a leading members of *Rukh* and a member of the Ukrainian parliamentary Commission on Foreign Affairs stated at a conference in Germany that the source of the threat to peace and security in Europe was not the break-up of the Soviet Union, but rather the continued existence of the 'only remaining totalitarian empire', i.e. the USSR. He went on to argue that other nations did not have a right to safeguard their own security at the expense of the self-determination and independence of other nations.[18]

The precarious state of Ukraine's movement towards independence was highlighted by the Coup in August 1991. The Chief of the Ground Forces, General Varennikov, threatened Ukrainian leaders that unless they supported the State Committee for the State of Emergency in the USSR the army would intervene in Ukraine. The sense of powerlessness against this threat explains the rather vacillating attitude of Leonid Kravchuk, then chairman of the Ukrainian Supreme Council. After the defeat of the coup the control over the armed forces on its territories became a top priority for the Ukrainian leadership. The nuclear weapons issue already gained political salience in the context of the coup and its immediate aftermath. One question that received a certain amount of public attention was the command and control over nuclear weapons during the days of the coup itself. Apparently Gorbachev was separated from the equipment (the 'football') that would allow him to initiate the launch of nuclear weapons. The system was disabled and the communication lines severed. The 'footballs' assigned to the Minister of Defence and the Chief of the General Staff also went dead when the President's system was down.[19] Even if this is a correct reconstruction of events the Emergency Committee could have gained control of nuclear weapons provided that the senior command of the Strategic Rocket Forces fully co-operated. Thus, although the nuclear weapons played no role in the crisis as such, it created an awareness of the dangers of uncertain command and control of nuclear weapons in a situation of political crisis or civil conflict. On 26 August Russian Vice-President Rutskoi suggested that the presence of nuclear weapons in various Soviet republics was a compelling reason for them to sign a Union Treaty (something which Ukraine was reluctant to do even prior to the coup) because otherwise there would be a new Russian empire given that only Russia could properly keep strategic nuclear weapons.[20] More importantly, on 28 August 1991 Russian President Yeltsin announced that nuclear weapons based on Ukrainian territory would be transferred to Russia since Ukraine had declared its intention to become a non-nuclear state.[21] This was a unilateral statement issued without any prior consultation with Ukrainian leaders. During the following days contradictory statements were issued; the Ukrainian ambassador to the United Nations, Gennaddii Oudovenko confirmed Ukraine's commitment to a non-nuclear states and that nuclear weapons in Ukraine would be placed under central control, even though Ukraine intended to create its own armed force and its own ministry of defence. Viacheslav Chornovil claimed in an interview with the *Washington Post* that the Soviet military was already removing nuclear weapons Ukrainian soil to Russia on orders from Moscow.[22]

The democratic leaders in Russia whose political status was transformed as a consequence of the August Coup were not necessarily favourably inclined towards Ukrainian independence or the terms under which Ukraine leaders sought to achieve it. Both public comments about nuclear weapons in Ukraine and possible boundary revisions were ominous from a Ukrainian point of view. On 28 August there was a meeting between high-level delegations from Moscow (including representatives of the Supreme Soviet of the USSR and the Russian government) and Kiev to discuss the future relations between Russia and Ukraine. A joint Russian-Ukrainian communiqué signed by Kravchuk and Rutskoi affirmed the 'inalienable right' of Russia and Ukraine to independent statehood. Two other important features of the communiqué deserve to be mentioned. The first is that it reaffirmed a bilateral treaty signed by Kravchuk and Yeltsin in November 1990 in which Russia and Ukraine recognised each other's borders and territorial integrity. The second is that the special significance of military-strategic problems and the need for a system of collective security were recognised. It was also agreed that there should be no unilateral decisions on military-strategic issues. Even more importantly, it affirmed that both states would adhere to commitments by the USSR in international relations, including agreements on arms reduction and arms control.[23]

Ukrainian independence and nuclear weapons after the Soviet Union

In the months following the August Coup, as the dissolution of the Soviet Union was approaching and the independence of the former Soviet republics was coming closer to being a reality, Ukrainian attitudes to the future of nuclear weapons based on their territory began to change. While a commitment to neutrality and a non-nuclear status were useful instruments to oppose the central regime in Moscow, the emergence of an independent Russia which demanded control over the principal military resources of the former Soviet Union and began to portray itself as the successor to the Soviet Union in the international sphere gave rise to a reconsideration of Ukraine's national interests. In addition, for the first time, the sheer size of the nuclear arsenal based in Ukraine (comprising 1,240 warheads on strategic nuclear missiles and 3,000 tactical warheads) became public knowledge. The most articulate presentation of the reasons for the change of mood which affected large segments of the Ukrainian political élite came from Chornovil, *Rukh* Candidate in the Ukrainian presidential election scheduled for December 1991. First of all, he rejected the idea the Ukraine should hand over all its nuclear weapons to Russia. Indeed, he considered the very idea that one state should transfer its nuclear arsenal to another 'strange'. This became an important theme in the nuclear weapons issue later on, when in the West and Russia Ukrainian nuclear disarmament came to be seen as requiring the transfer of weapons to Russia, whereas Ukrainian politicians separated those two questions. This led Chornovil onto another point which was to play a key role in the whole issue, namely that Ukraine, like the other former Soviet republics was a rightful heir to all the material and technical resources, including weapons, of the former Soviet Union.[24]

However, he did not suggest that Ukraine should give up its objective of becoming a non-nuclear state; quite to the contrary. His argument was that all the issues related to nuclear weapons in the former Soviet republics needed to be decided through agreements between the various states and that in the context of such agreements the gradual and complete elimination of nuclear arsenals could be achieved. The most important practical consequence of this argument was that weapons should not be transferred to Russia and the nuclear disarmament might take a considerable period of time.

Other contributions to this debate, which have been analysed in some greater detail by Bohdan Nahaylo, made similar points. There was a spectrum of views of what precisely should happen to the weapons. Some thought it would be 'normal' for weapons to remain in Ukraine, some suggested a joint command with Russia on the basis of the former Soviet strategic command, some suggested that Ukraine should become non-nuclear quickly and that the weapons should be destroyed on Ukrainian territory. There was virtually unanimous agreement on one point, namely that weapons should not be transferred to Russia.[25]

An official position of sorts emerged by late September/early October 1991 and was expounded by Kravchuk to Western audiences. A very similar position was taken by Parliament in a statement on the status of nuclear weapons in Ukraine on 24 October 1991. The principal elements of this position were as follows:

- Ukraine did not want to become a nuclear state and the presence of nuclear weapons on Ukrainian territory was temporary.

- Ukraine would join the Nuclear-Non Proliferation Treaty (NPT) as a non-nuclear power.
- Ukraine would co-operate in the implementation of the START Treaty but would demand the right to participate on all future negotiations on nuclear disarmament, and the elimination of weapons in Ukraine would be negotiated in such an international forum involving the other nuclear successor states of the USSR.
- Command and Control over nuclear weapons was currently exercised by the appropriate structures of the former USSR. Ukraine would seek the establishment of a joint command involving the former Soviet republics on the basis that it would have a veto over the use of nuclear forces based on its territory (for example, by means of a 'dual key' system).

There are several issues here that deserve consideration. Was it feasible for Ukraine to become a nuclear power? How would Ukraine have operationalised nuclear weapons and how would they contribute to the security of Ukraine? Where would this have left START I, the Lisbon protocol and the NPT?

Could Ukraine have become a nuclear power?

In the course of the public debate on this issue, it was frequently been asserted that Ukraine had the technical capabilities to maintain a strategic nuclear weapons complex. The existence of the largest missile factory in the world near Dnepropetrovsk (Yuzhmash) where the SS-18 missiles were manufactured and the SS-24 were assembled (some of which were stationed in Ukraine) was cited as evidence, as well as the research centres in Kharkov which specialised in missile guidance, targeting and control.[26]

It is true that Ukraine could in principle have become a nuclear weapons state, but the costs of building a nuclear weapons establishment to maintain the weapons and create early warning and command control facilities were prohibitive.[27] For example, Ukraine lacked the capabilities to build and maintain nuclear warheads. The essential facilities were all located in Russia. The production of nuclear weapons is a very complex process. It would have required a major commitment of industrial resources to develop a functioning nuclear weapons production complex. Even assuming that Ukraine had been able to harness some of the expertise of the former Soviet Union to this end, it was very unlikely, in the light of the existing economic problems, that it coold have been able to commit the resources required.

Partly as a result of the disagreements between Russia and Ukraine there was a breakdown in the operational procedures for the maintenance of the weapons systems. By transferring the administrative command of the Strategic Nuclear Forces in Ukraine to the leadership of the Armed Forces of Ukraine, the country assumed the financial burden of servicing the missiles and keeping them safe, but evidently lacked the resources to fulfil its commitments. The disregard for safety procedures for the maintenance and storage of nuclear weapons in Ukraine was such that there was an increasing likelihood of a major nuclear accident.

The first area of concern about the safety of nuclear weapons in Ukraine related to the maintenance of the missile warheads. Warheads require a certain amount of routine maintenance, but warheads of American design have quite an extensive shelf life. Warheads of Soviet manufacture appear to have greater long-term maintenance requirements in addition to regular routine maintenance.

One of these requirements common to all thermonuclear warheads of whatever design arose from the fact that the tritium which boosts the nuclear fission in thermonuclear warheads decays quite rapidly (half-life - 12.6 years) and must therefore be renewed. The only heavy water reactors that can serve as a source of tritium are located in Russia. This requirement is not critical; the absence of tritium merely results in a much reduced yield.

Other components of nuclear warheads also need attention, including the plutonium. Weapons grade plutonium consists of at least 93 per cent Pu-239, but also contains other isotopes such as Pu-240, Pu-241 and Pu-242. Pu-241 decays into americium which needs to be removed on a regular basis. The americium has a large neutron capture cross section and the accumulation of americium in a warhead will inhibit nuclear fission and thus render it unusable. Weapons-grade plutonium of Soviet manufacture seems to be less pure than that to be found in American warheads, where americium accumulation and the accumulation of other impurities resulting from spontaneous fission does not appear to be a problem. It has recently emerged from discussions between Western and Russian experts that the way in which the Russians deal with this problem is by simply diluting the plutonium in the warheads with fresh plutonium on a regular basis. One of the reasons given for the continued production of weapons grade plutonium in Russia is that it is required to maintain the warheads. Apparently, major maintenance takes place every three to six years, when the plutonium pit, the conventional high-explosive and the tritium are replaced. The plutonium pits removed are transported to nuclear warhead production facilities for reprocessing. Currently all such facilities from the former Soviet Union are in Russia and Ukraine would have had to create them on its own territory.

Another problem was reported by Viktor Litovkin in an article in *Izvestiia*:

> ... 446 strategic missile warhead assemblies and 162 cruise missile warheads did not have the necessary chemical components guaranteeing their total nuclear safety changed during 1992 and the first three months of 1993. Nuclear specialists describe these components as absorbents, which act as filters to neutralize the gases given off by the nuclear charges during protracted storage, impede the formation of combustible compounds in them, and thus prevent emergencies from arising.[28]

The emission of gamma radiation by the fissile materials in the warhead causes the entire warhead assembly to heat up. Although nuclear charges are cooled, the temperature gradient between the central part of the plutonium pit and the surface of the warhead is typically 80°C. These effects result in the gradual chemical decomposition of the conventional explosive which is designed to trigger the nuclear fission of the plutonium. Among the products of these chemical processes is hydrogen, which builds up inside the warhead and will form an explosive mixture with oxygen if it reaches a certain level of concentration. It also interacts with zirconium, one of the materials used in the construction of the warhead, forming zirconium hydride which ignites on contact with air.[29] In order to prevent the accumulation of dangerous concentrations of hydrogen, the warheads are fitted with hydrogen absorbers. They are designed to keep the hydrogen content to a level below 2 per cent. These absorbers get saturated and need to be replaced at regular intervals. Although Ukraine was capable of manufacturing hydrogen absorbers, this was not done and routine maintenance did not take place. In one case, a build-up of hydrogen close to the ignition threshold was detected. Overall 162 cruise missile warheads and over 400 ballistic missile warheads were said to have deviated from standard specifications.[30]

The administrative and financial problems involved had the effect that warhead storage depots in Ukraine contained an excessive number of warheads (in at least one case about five times the norm). The storage depots became so full that the Ukrainian military started to stockpile the warheads at the missile bases themselves. Storage depots (so-called 'Objects S') had been designed on the principle that a minimum distance is maintained between the stored nuclear charges. The congestion at nuclear warhead storage sites in Ukraine resulted in the systematic breach of these regulations and warheads were being stored at a much closer physical distance from each other than is permissible.[31] The consequence appeared to be that warheads were subject to a higher than specified neutron flux from other warheads and increased gamma radiation.

This it was said could produce a range of unintended effects. One which became apparent was that it caused the temperature of some warheads to rise quite alarmingly. Such temperature increases will accelerate the decomposition of the high explosives and the undesirable build-up of hydrogen in the weapons. Another result was an alarming rise in the level of radiation in the depots (up to 1 million Roentgen per hour).[32] Eventually, it was decided by the commanders in charge of the weapons to remove warheads that appear to have become unsafe and simply ship them back to Russia as quickly as possible. This was done without political approval.

It was considered unlikely that an accidental nuclear detonation would occur, given that the explosion that triggers a full-scale fission of the plutonium has to produce a shockwave of a precise geometrical shape. But there must have been a real possibility that an accident occurs, which could have resulted in the large-scale dispersal of fissile materials and contamination of the environment.

There were also disturbing reports about the breakdown in routine maintenance of ICBMs. The SS-19 missiles contain a liquid fuel called heptyl, a modified form of a rocket fuel called hydrazine. It must be kept in sealed containers under pressure and constantly cooled. It is highly volatile and toxic and if mixed with air spontaneous combustion may result. The oxidiser, nitrogen tetroxide, is highly corrosive and if left in the missiles indefinitely will begin to leak. Under normal circumstances, two thirds of the missiles in an SS-19 field will be on alert, while the remaining third are drained of fuel and undergo maintenance. This process was interrupted in 1992 as maintenance of missiles off alert ceased. This was in part due to the downturn in Ukrainian-Russian relations. But it has been observed that the weakening of central administrative control and the chronic shortage of supplies and funds everywhere in the former Soviet Union has resulted in a general decline in maintenance standards even with regard to strategic nuclear weapons. Thus liquid-fuelled ICBMs in Russia (especially the SS-18) are considered to be at risk. As far as Ukraine is concerned, there were fears that the liquid fuel in the SS-19 missiles would begin to leak or that the oxidiser and the fuel might come into contact as a result of corrosion or inadequate handling, resulting in a massive explosion. If fuel leaks from the missiles, toxic chemicals will contaminate the silos which will have to be declared unsafe. The missiles might also have exploded and scattered fissile materials from the warheads into the environment.

The SS-24 missiles contain solid fuel which does not involve the same kind of risks. But the lack of maintenance threatened to render them also inoperable. The information about the operational status and the safety of nuclear weapons in Ukraine was not surprisingly very sketchy. But two conclusions can be drawn. The first is that there were enough indications of serious breaches of routine safety procedures that there was a risk of major accidents. The second is that for Ukraine to maintain a strategic nuclear weapons force would have required the build-up of a sophisticated industrial infrastructure that would have been prohibitively expensive, particularly given the catastrophic state of Ukraine's economy.

The missiles deployed on Ukrainian soil were not suitable instruments of Ukrainian security policy. They were long-range missiles with a minimum range that inhibited their use against Moscow or targets in most of European Russia.[33] However, researchers in Dnepropetrovsk started work to reduce the range of the SS-24 by altering its trajectory in the form of a so-called 'loop-manoeuvre' whereby all the fuel would be burned up and the missile then could reach its target in Russia. Plans to transform the three-stage SS-24 ICBM to a two-stage intermediate range ballistic missile (IRBM) with either nuclear warheads or single 15-ton radiological or bio-chemical warhead also existed. Clearly, serious thinking about how to operationalise the weapons went on in Ukraine.

There were intensive research efforts in Kharkov for two years regarding technical options for re-targeting of missiles, breaking down the 'go-codes' installed in the Soviet period from Moscow and the creation of a national combat control system. The Russians believed that the Ukrainians would eventually succeed in their efforts. As a result Ukraine could have acquired the technical capability to put ICBMs on the Ukrainian soil under Kiev's operational control.

Ukraine could have used the bombers deployed on its territory, but apparently they did not intend to make the bombers operational. Part of the reason may have been that Ukraine was unable to maintain the *Blackjacks*. There was also a shortage of qualified pilots. Flight plans and navigational equipment had been transferred to Russia. The problems are illustrated by the fact that during the whole year of 1993 the *Blackjacks* in Ukraine were only flown twice, most of the planes ceased to be serviceablePart of the reason why the Ukrainians had no interest in using the bombers as nuclear weapons platforms may also have been the knowledge that the bombers would be highly vulnerable to Russian air defences. Ukraine therefore decided to sell the *Blackjacks* back to Russia.[34]

Ukraine also decided to dismantle the SS-19 which were perceived as more of liability than an asset, which means that it would have kept the SS-24 only. To develop an effective nuclear capability thus the existing delivery vehicles would have had to be substantially modified or new delivery vehicles developed and deployed. In addition, a fully functioning strategic force requires early warning systems (satellites and large-scale radar complexes), and command and control facilities. The best Ukraine could hope for on the basis their existing assets was a very crude, limited capability for political purposes.

There were fears in Russia and the West that radiological weapons created by modifying nuclear warheads could be deployed in Ukraine. Work on such weapons was done in Kiev and some other places without the Ukrainian parliament's sanction. Radiological weapons of this kind are rather simple in technical terms. Thermonuclear charges extracted from nuclear weapons are used. A thermonuclear warhead consists of a so-called 'spherical charge' (atomic trigger) and a thermonuclear unit, both of which contain Plutonium-239 and/or Uranium-235. One can place explosive charges on a thermonuclear device in such a manner that their detonation will destroy it. y. As a consequence fissile materials will be thrown into air leading to radioactive contamination of Chernobyl-type. One should bear in mind that one gramme of highly dispersed plutonium can render the territory of 1 sq km uninhabitable and modern thermonuclear warheads contain between 2.5 to 4 kg plutonium. (It is useful to remember that estimates of the amount of plutonium released from the RBMK-1000 reactor in the Chernobyl nuclear disaster were of a similar order of magnitude.) The Russians were also alarmed by the existence of para-military units in Western Ukraine over which Kiev had no control and the potential for nuclear terrorism.[35]

The costs and political implications of a Ukrainian effort to develop a nuclear arsenal based on its Soviet heritage convinced President Kravchuk that Ukraine must become a non-nuclear state. This however was for some time met with great resistance from the Ukrainian political élite.

Ukrainian efforts to translate the presence of nuclear weapons from the arsenal of the former Soviet Union on its territory into tangible benefits in terms of military and economic security focused on compensation for the fissile materials in the weapons and support for the costs of dismantlement as well as a demand for some unspecified security guarantees. These efforts were initially relatively unsuccessful. Western and Russian experts were sceptical about Ukrainian notions about strategic nuclear weapons as an economic asset. The cost of dismantling well exceeded the value of fissile materials on an already over-supplied market.[36] Ukrainian demands of US $3 billion for the dismantlement of nuclear weapons in Ukraine proved to be not only economically but also politically unacceptable to the West.

The Russian and Western efforts to compel Ukraine to give up the nuclear weapons stationed on its territory contributed much to a change of mood in the Ukrainian political élite on this issue. Resistance to these demands became to some extent a symbol of Ukraine's assertion of its independent statehood.[37] Paradoxically, while overestimating the value of the nuclear weapons as a political bargaining chip, Ukrainian politicians appeared to underestimate the detrimental effect that a refusal to ratify START I and accede to the NPT could have on relations with the West.

At the Massandra summit between Russian President Yeltsin and Ukrainian President Kravchuk in September 1993 realism about Ukraine's economic predicament appeared to have prevailed. An agreement was made to settle another issue about the division of military assets, namely the question of the Black Sea fleet, and to transfer all nuclear weapons to Russia. In return, Ukraine would receive the fissile materials from the warheads for use in nuclear power stations, and Ukraine's mounting debt to Russia (primarily due to energy imports) would be cancelled. However this agreement met with determined political resistance in Kiev and was therefore difficult to implement.[38]

The United States subsequently made an effort to put US-Ukrainian relations on a more constructive footing and promote Ukrainian nuclear disarmament. US Secretary of State, during a visit to Kiev in October 1993, promised US $155 million of aid in addition to US $175 million for nuclear disarmament, and promised US support for international business to invest in Ukraine to a level of at least several billion dollars.[39] This did not have much effect on political opinion in Ukraine. In defiance of the President and the international community, the *Rada* voted on 18 November 1993 by a wide margin (254 to 9 out of 440 members) to ratify the START I Treaty and the Lisbon protocol, with reservations and conditions. The reservations relate to Article 5 of the Lisbon protocol; the *Rada* voted that Ukraine would *not* join the NPT as a non-nuclear state. Among the conditions were: Ukraine must get compensation for the tactical nuclear warheads withdrawn, there must be financial assistance for nuclear disarmament, binding security guarantees and the recognition of Ukraine's territorial integrity.[40] The vote was severely criticized by the United States and Russia. President Kravchuk also found this vote unacceptable and promised to resubmit the START I Treaty to a new parliament after elections in March 1994.

Apart from economic problems, what drove Ukraine finally to give up the weapons on its territory may have been its increasing inability to assure their safety. Statements by Russian Foreign Minister Kozyrev warning of impending disaster if Ukraine did not give up its nuclear weapons could be interpreted as an attempt to use the nuclear safety issue to compel Ukraine to accept the Lisbon protocol, ratify START I and allow the transfer of the nuclear weapons on its territory to Russia. Political motivations aside however, it was clear that the weapons in Ukraine were deteriorating and there really was an increasing risk of a serious accident. The principal potential threat for the West did not arise from Ukrainian possession of nuclear weapons as such. It arose from the consequences of a major nuclear accident that could well have exceeded the dimensions of the Chernobyl disaster of 1986.

The Moscow agreement of 14 January 1994 represented a renewed attempt by Ukrainian President Kravchuk to deal with the nuclear weapons issue.[41] The trilateral agreement signed by Presidents Clinton, Yeltsin and Kravchuk required the elimination of all nuclear weapons on Ukrainian territory. The key provisions were:

- All nuclear warheads were to be transferred from Ukraine and dismantled in Russia. All the SS-24 ICBMS were to be deactivated within a ten month period. The warheads for the strategic bombers were also to be transferred to Russia, but nothing was said about the future ownership of the aircraft (the *Bear* and *Blackjack*).
- Ukraine was to receive compensation in the form of nuclear fuel and a share in the proceeds of the sale of the fissile material recovered from the warheads.
- Ukraine would be given the standard assurances against nuclear attack given to all non-nuclear signatories to the nuclear nonproliferation treaty (NPT). (These require action of an unspecified nature by the UN Security Council in case a non-nuclear state is subject to an attack with nuclear weapons, or the threat of an attack with nuclear weapons.) In addition Ukraine would be able to strengthen its security through participation in the NATO Partnership for Peace programme and from economic assistance from the US and participation in multilateral organizations.[42]

The security guarantees offered fell far short of the security guarantees previously demanded by many prominent Ukrainian political leaders. The same is true of the financial aspects of the deal. Some Ukrainian politicians opposed giving up nuclear weapons under any circumstances.

President Kravchuk decided not to submit the trilateral agreement itself to parliament. Instead a resolution was submitted to parliament authorizing the exchange of the instruments of ratification of the START I Treaty and the accession to the NPT. The resolution on START was passed on 3 February 1994. This time the previous preconditions were dropped. In particular, the Ukrainian parliament approved Article 5 of the Lisbon protocol which commits Ukraine to accede to the NPT as a non-nuclear state in the shortest possible time. However, the resolution to accede to the NPT failed. The issue as to whether START obliges Ukraine to eliminate all its nuclear weapons also remained without clarification. However the way became clear to move forward with the Moscow agreement, and all its provisions were implemented.

Kazakhstan

Kazakhstan was not a party to the agreement that dissolved the Soviet Union and like all other Central Asian states, Kazakhstan would have preferred the preservation of the Union. As a result of the decision by Russia, Belarus and Ukraine, Kazakhstan faced the problems of creating a state and developing a national identity. The most important Soviet strategic assets on Kazakhstani territory were the ICBM bases with 104 SS-18, the Semipalatinsk nuclear test site, the Baikonur space launch centre, and the ABM radar site. The disposition of these assets raised major difficulties since on the one hand Kazakhstan could not integrate them into its own military forces, on the other hand it had an interest in getting the most out of their presence on its soil. Furthermore President Nazarbayev insisted that all military installations in Kazakhstan were the property of Kazakhstan.

When the Soviet Union was dissolved in December 1991, the armed forces on the territory of Kazakhstan consisted of 440,000 military personnel. About 95 per cent of the officers were from Russia, Ukraine and Belarus. President Nazarbayev expressed a clear preference for the preservation of unified CIS forces when Russian President Yeltsin created the armed forces of the Russian Federation in 1992. After that the process of separating Russian, CIS and Kazakhstani armed forces was undertaken. A Republican guard of 2,500 men to protect the President and the Parliament was created. Initially force planning by the Kazakhstan Ministry of Defence was based on the criterion that troop numbers should be at least 0.5 per cent of the state's population (i.e. about 83,000). This proved to be unrealistic due to the shortage of funds and the inability to enforce conscription consistently. The other serious problem for the Kazakhstani armed forces is the lack of experienced Kazakhstani military leadership personnel. About 6,000 Russian troops from the former Soviet 40th Army remained in Kazakstan to provide military training. According to bilateral agreements with Russia, 500 officers from Kazakhstan are sent to Russian military schools each year. Nevertheless, Kazakhstan still has to rely on ethnic Slavs for most of its officer corps. Kazakhstan has armed forces of about 46,000 men.

Nazarbayev was acutely aware of the geopolitical situation of Kazakhstan. The ethnic mix of the population of the country is unbalanced, with the north being mostly Russian. This gives rise to the fear that Russia may have designs on those parts of Kazakhstani territories where Russians predominate and where the strategic military assets were located. Kazakhstan is also a front-line state with regard to China. Potential security threats for Central Asia come from several directions: The relationship with Russia remains precarious and is perceived as posing a potential security risk to the national interest of Central Asian states. It is true that Russia has not intention of re-assimilating the Central Asian states; Russia does not have the resources to fully support the economies of the Central Asian countries. Nevertheless Russia claims this area as part of her sphere of influence. Relations with China are good, but the instability of China's Xinjiang province and the uncontrolled movement of population from China to Kazakhstan presents a strategic problem. The civil conflicts in Tajikistan and Afghanistan were seen as a potential destabilising factor in the region. The victory of the Taliban in Afghanistan and the peace agreement in Tajikistan have allayed fears to some extent, but Central Asian states still perceive the potential for subversion through Islamic extremism and terrorism or other forms of violence emanating from Afghanistan as a major security problem . The main threat to stability in the region, however, comes from internal problems - the lack of economic development, the steep decline in GDP since the dissolution of the Soviet Union and the resulting social problems, and the internal ethnic and political tensions in states whose identities and institutions have not properly formed since the Soviet collapse. But in view of Kazakhstan's inability to defend itself against external threat, retaining nuclear weapons appeared an attractive option.

After Ukraine staked out its claims, Nazarbayev also asserted Kazakhstan's rights to nuclear weapons based on its geo-political position, and he was much less circumspect than the Ukrainians about pointing out that Russia might be a potential adversary.[43]

Soon after this statement Nazarbayev sent a joint letter from him and Yeltsin to President Bush stating that strategic nuclear weapons should remain in Kazakhstan, under Russian control, as foreign weapons based in Kazakhstan to provide for Kazakhstani security. This proved completely unacceptable to the United States, and although there was widespread support in Russia for this concept, the Russian government later stipulated that the fact that Yeltsin had signed this letter did not mean that its content constituted government policy.[44] The strategic nuclear missiles were stood down as part of the START process and all the nuclear warheads were transferred to Russia as Kazakhstan joined the NPT as a non-nuclear power. The Semipalatinsk site was closed. After much political wrangling, the Baikonur space complex was made available to Russia on the basis of a 20-year, renewable lease.[45]

Conclusion

The withdrawal of strategic nuclear weapons from Belarus, Ukraine and Kazakhstan represents the most visible success of US-Russian co-operation in the field of enhancing the safety and security of nuclear weapons. The strategy chosen by Moscow and Washington, to use the START I Treaty as an instrument of nonproliferation, was effective. Ukraine for some time tried to instrumentalise the nuclear weapons for political and financial gain, but pursued a very confused strategy. Belarus, on the other hand, was co-operative from the start, whereas Kazakhstan alternated between co-operation and occasional obstruction in order to explore the possibilities of enhancing its security. Keeping the nuclear weapons was a theoretical option, especially for Ukraine, but entailed enormous practical difficulties and potential negative reactions from both Russia and the West. In the end a combination of general security assurances and limited financial inducements helped to smooth the passage to an arrangement which the political leaders of the former Soviet states clearly perceived to be in their country's best interests.

Notes

1. For example, a meeting took place in Moscow in 1989 between British experts (under the auspices of the IISS) and Soviet specialists (under the auspices of the Institute of Europe) which discussed the safety of tactical weapons and the fate of strategic nuclear weapons outside Russia.
2. From Alexei Arbatov, *Iadernoe vooruzheniia i respublikanskiy suverenitet*, Moscow: Mezhdunarodnye otnosheniia 1992.
3. Recall that so-called long range theatre nuclear forces capable of reaching Western Europe from the territory of the former Soviet Union were subject to elimination according to the 1987 INF Treaty.
4. Modern PALs designed by the US actually disable the warhead if the wrong code is fed in and the warhead needs to be disassembled to be repaired. Soviet PALs for ICBMs were designed in such a way that if an incorrect code was entered three times the control system would permanently disable the arming mechanism.
5. The issue of the safety and security of nuclear weapons in the former Soviet Union will be discussed in more detail in Chapter 6.
6. 'Ministers Discuss Nuclear Strategy', FBIS-SOV-92-173, 4 September 1992, p.4, citing a report from Moscow ITAR-TASS, 3 September 1992. This was the case even in Ukraine despite the 'administrative control' over the missiles by the Ukrainian Armed Forces, as indicated by President

Kravchuk's recently reiterated demands for technical control to prevent missile launch. See *Krasnaia Zvezda*, 2 February 1993, p.3.

7. The deputy head of the department of nonproliferation at the Ministry of Foreign Affairs of the Russian Federation stated in January 1992 at a conference in the United Kingdom that all warheads had been returned to Russian territory and that they were all accounted for. This appears to be accepted by Western governments, but some degree of scepticism is warranted.
8. Excerpts of the Protocol are reprinted in *Survival*, Vol.34, No.3, Autumn 1992, pp.136-137.
9. *Respublika*, 14 January 1992; see also Vyacheslau Paznyak, 'Belarusian Denuclearization Policy and the Control of Nuclear Weapons, in George Quester (ed.), *The Nuclear Challenge in Russia and the New States of Eurasia*, Armonk N.Y: M.E. Sharpe 1995, pp.153-179.
10. *Nezavisimaia gazeta,* 26 November 1992, p.1, cited in English from Paznyak, op.cit., p.161.
11. This statement could be challenged in so far as the matter of the ownership of the nuclear weapons was never fully tested, and Belarus never acquired control over the weapons, but at least potentially Belarus was a nuclear weapons state until it acceded to the NPT.
12. For more details on the aid Belarus received see chapter 6.
13. Bohdan Nahaylo, 'The Shaping of Ukrainian Attitudes toward Nuclear Arms', *RFE/RL Research Report*, Vol.2, No.8, 19 February 1993, pp.21-41.
14. It was adopted by a margin of 355 to 4; see Nahaylo, ibid.
15. Cited from Michael R. Beschloss and Strobe Talbott, *At the Highest Levels*, London: Little Brown & Company 1993, p.418.
16. The classic contribution to these theme is the paper by John J. Mearsheimer, 'Back to the Future', *International Security*, Vol.15, No.1, Summer 1990, pp.5-56.
17. John Lewis Gaddis, *The United States and the End of the Cold War*, Oxford: Oxford University Press 1992, p.142. This book was completed in July 1991, but not published until 1992, i.e. after the end of the Soviet Union.
18. Sheri Holovaty, 'The Peaceful Disintegration of the USSR as a Guarantee of Security and Freedom in Europe', *Franz Josef Strauss Symposium*, München 1990.
19. For a full analysis of these events, see Bruce Blair, *The Logic of Accidental Nuclear War*, Washington DC.: The Brookings Institution 1993, pp.82-86.
20. Reuters, 26 August 1991.

21. Reuters, 28 August 1991.
22. *The Washington Post*, 30 August 1991.
23. Cited from Nahaylo, op.cit., p.24.
24. *Molod Ukrainy*, 12 September 1991.
25. Nahaylo, op.cit., pp.25-26.
26. The Ukrainian Minister for the Environment and Chief Negotiator with Russia on the status and maintenance of strategic nuclear weapons, Yuri Kostenko, has claimed that Ukraine has the capability to build nuclear weapons. See *Nezavisimaia Gazeta*, 27 April 1993, p.3. Given the facilities located on Ukrainian territory, this is at best a theoretical capability; there are no nuclear warhead production facilities in Ukraine.
27. The need for command and control and early warning facilities to operationalise nuclear weapons is often overlooked. During discussions at Kiev University in July 1993, Ukrainian experts seemed to be acutely aware of this problem.
28. Viktor Litovkin, *Izvestiia*, 7 April 1993, p.5; cited from FBIS-SOV-93-065, 7 April 1993, p.26.
29. Discussions with British specialists in nuclear warhead design indicate other plausible mechanisms for the accumulation of hydrogen, for example by the reaction of water vapour with the fissile material itself. This apparently was a serious problem for earlier generations of American nuclear warheads.
30. Based on interviews in Moscow and Kiev, July and November 1993. See also Igor Sutyagin, 'Can Ukraine Keep Its Nuclear Power Status?', in *Military Journal*, No.8, Postfactum Analytical Series, No.85, 1993, pp.7-12; Igor Sutyagin, 'How Russia Ensures Safety of Its Nuclear Weapons, *Military Journal*, No.7, Postfactum Analytical Series, No.83, 1993, pp.7-12.
31. By 1 September 1993 all Russian personnel had left the 'S' installations in Ukraine and the Ukrainian military took control of them. *Izvestiia*, 22 October 1993.
32. *Izvestiia*, 16 February 1993, p.4; Christoph Bluth, 'What do you do with a nuclear arsenal', *New Scientist*, Vol.135, No.1830, 18 July 1992, pp.31-35.
33. The minimum effective range results from the properties of the guidance and control systems, the maximum reentry angle of the warheads and the time required for warhead separation from the bus of the MIRV.
34. According to interviews in Ukraine in July 1993, which included very highly placed military and political sources.

35. The threat to change a nuclear charge to radiological one and use it at a designated point is much more realistic in technical terms than the threat to explode nuclear power stations made by Ukrainian nationalists. *Sunday Times*, 6 February 1994.
36. For a more detailed discussion, see John W.R. Lepingwell, 'How Much is a Warhead Worth?', *RFE/RL Research Report*, Vol.2, No.8, 19 February 1993, pp.62-64. It is a strange notion of an economic 'asset' that is valued without taking into account the investment required to realize it.
37. For more detail, see Serhij Tolstov, 'Ukraine's nuclear dilemma', *The World Today*, Vol.49, No.6, June 1993, pp.103-105; Bohdan Nahaylo, 'The Shaping of Ukrainian Attitudes toward Nuclear Arms', *RFE/RL Research Report*, Vol.2, No.8, 19 February 1993, pp.21-41.
38. John W.R. Lepingwell, 'Negotiations over Nuclear Weapons: The Past as Prologue?', *RFE/RL Research Report*, Vol.3, No.4, 28 January 1994, pp.1-11; the Massandra agreement superseded by the trilateral Moscow agreement.
39. For detailed reports, see FBIS-SOV-93-205, 26 October 1993, pp.54-56.
40. *RFE/RL Daily Report*, No.222, 19 November 1993, p.1.
41. John W. R. Lepingwell, 'The Trilateral Agreement on Nuclear Weapons', *RFE/RL Research Report*, Vol.3, No.4, 28 January 1994, pp.12-20.
42. For the full text of the trilateral Moscow agreement, see John W. R. Lepingwell, 'The Trilateral Agreement on Nuclear Weapons', *RFE/RL Research Report*, Vol.3, No.4, 28 January 1994, pp.12-20, at pp.14-15.
43. *Washington Post*, 6 May 1993, p.1.
44. Nikolai Sokov, *Russian Strategic Modernization*, Oxford: Rowman & Littlefield Publishers 2000, p.108.
45. For more detail about the nuclear debate in Kazakhstan, see Murat Laumilin, 'Kazakhstan's Nuclear Policy and the Control of Nuclear Weapons', in George Quester (ed.), *The Nuclear Challenge in Russia and the New States of Eurasia,* London: M.E. Sharpe 1995, pp.181-211.

5 Strategic Arms Control after the Cold War

Both during and after the Cold War the primary conduit of US-Russian dialogue on their strategic relations has been strategic arms control. Strategic arms control plays a critical role in the formulation of strategic arms policy and the development of nuclear force postures. It is therefore important to look at the strategic nuclear arms control process after Cold War in greater detail, to see if and how the philosophy and the politics of arms control has changed in the new international security environment, and look at likely future trends and possibilities.

Strategic arms control after the Soviet Union

Strategic arms control negotiations in the form that we have known them during the Cold War are a unique feature of the nuclear age. They began in the late 1960s after the Soviet Union and the United States had both deployed substantial strategic nuclear force arsenals and had reached a certain state of parity.[1] In confidential exchanges in the autumn of 1968 before the SALT (Strategic Arms Limitation Treaty) negotiations got under way, there was agreement that the objective should be a stable mutual strategic deterrence', recognizing an 'integral interrelationship' between offensive systems and strategic defence.[2] At the time, two potential threats to stability were identified - an unrestrained quantitative arms race in strategic offensive systems, and the introduction of anti-ballistic missile systems (ABM). The latter was seen as a potential threat to the principle of 'mutual assured destruction' on which the notion of 'mutual deterrence' was based. The criterion of 'strategic stability' was thus generally taken to be the preservation of an 'assured second strike' capability for both sides. There were wide-ranging debates in the Soviet Union and the United States about the kind of arms control measures that would enhance stability. One that seemed to command most agreement was the abolition of missiles with multiple warheads. Banning MIRVs (multiple independently targetable re-entry vehicles) would effectively make the achievement of a first-strike capability impossible as long as there was more or less parity in the number of launchers on both sides.[3] The most contentious issue was the effect of strategic defences on stability. A total area defence as envisaged by the Strategic Defence Initiative (SDI) would render one side invulnerable and give it a first-strike capability. The attempt to achieve such a protection could trigger an intensive arms race in offensive systems in order to inhibit its realization. The transition from an offensive to a defensive dominated strategic system was also considered by some arms control specialists to be unstable and indeed dangerous. On the other hand, a 'hardpoint' ABM system that would only protect ICBM sites could be considered stabilising in so far as it reduced the first-strike capability of the other side without affecting its capability to launch a second strike.

What should the final objective of the arms control process be? Those arms control experts who wanted to end the East-West strategic competition but were skeptical about the notion of 'putting the nuclear genie back into the bottle' proposed the notion of a stable 'minimum deterrent' on both sides consisting of perhaps 1000 single-warhead missiles. Eventually perhaps all nuclear weapons could be put under international supervision, for instance by the United Nations.

Despite the anti-nuclear rhetoric of the US-Soviet summit at Reykjavik in 1986, where the elimination of all strategic nuclear delivery vehicles within 10 years was seriously discussed, START (Strategic Arms Reductions Treaty) I and II were designed on the basis of 'stability' criteria which assume the existence of two antagonistic powers seeking to limit and control their confrontation.[4] Some Western commentators have played down the significance of START II, given that a very substantial strategic arsenal will remain on both sides even after implementation (roughly at a level before the strategic arms control process began at the end of the sixties).[5] But it could be argued that even though START II still represents some of the old logic of arms control, it is a significant move in the right direction. One of the key provisions of START II is the elimination of multiple warheads on land-based missiles. This constitutes a qualitative restructuring of the arsenals that substantially enhances stability at a much reduced level and to a large extent takes the competitive element out of the maintenance of a nuclear deterrent force.

But there is a good case to be made that this does not go nearly far enough. *The end of the Cold War should in principle also mean the end of the strategic nuclear confrontation.* This would require standing weapons down from prompt response postures and more radical reductions in the arsenals. The agreement of January 1994 between the United States and Russia not to target strategic weapons at each other is a symbolic gesture along those lines, but it is not technically significant and it is unverifiable. A verifiable way to adopt a non-threatening posture for both sides would be to stand all land-based nuclear forces off alert, remove the warheads from the missiles and store them separately. So far neither the US nor the Russian government have been willing to engage in serious measures to 'de-alert' their strategic arsenals.

The technical aspects of START

In order to get a sense of the current direction of strategic arms control, it is useful to outline some of the technical aspects of the accords so far achieved in the START framework. In 1991, when the START I agreement was concluded., the United States and the former Soviet Union had deployed a total of 10,875 and 10,271 strategic nuclear warheads respectively. After the first START Treaty has been implemented in 2001 these will have been reduced to at most 6,000 on both sides.[6] The provisions of START I can be summarised as follows:

- The total number of strategic nuclear delivery vehicles (ICBMs, SLBMs and heavy bombers) and associated launchers is limited to 1,600.
- The total number of warheads deployed is limited to 6,000, with a sublimit of 4,900 on ballistic missiles (ICBMs and SLBMs) and 1,540 on heavy missiles (only the Russian SS-18 currently counts as a heavy missile). No more than 1,100 warheads may be deployed on mobile missiles.
- Under the START I 'counting rules' agreed, warheads on ballistic missiles count as one, whereas the entire load of gravity bombs or short-range attack missiles (SRAM) (carried on a heavy bomber) counts as only one weapon. For Air-Launched Cruise Missiles (ALCM), it has been agreed that both sides can deploy 20 per bomber which will only count as 'ten warheads'.[7]
- Various future developments have been precluded: new types of heavy ICBMs, ICBMs with more than ten warheads, heavy SLBMs and their launchers, rapid reload ICBM launchers and ALCMs with multiple warheads are banned under START.[8]

START II envisages a further reduction in two phases. During the first seven years after ratification of the treaty both sides will cut their strategic arsenals to between 3,800 and 4,250 warheads each. By 1 January 2003 both sides must reduce their strategic nuclear warheads on both sides to a total of 3,500.(This provision was altered by a protocol proposed at the Helsinki Summit in March 1997 to extend the implementation deadlines until 31 December 1997 in view of the failure of the Russian parliament to ratify the treaty by then). Arguably the most important feature of the treaty is the elimination of land-based missiles with multiple warheads. From the American point of view, the elimination of the SS-18 is particularly welcome. Half of the SS-18 force is due for removal under START I, the remainder under START II.

This means that in future Russia will have just single-warhead ICBMs. 105 of the older SS-19 can be retained in service. They currently have six warheads and will have to be 'downloaded' to carry just one. The rest of the Russian ICBM force will consist of single-warhead SS-25 or its successor, the Topol-M, designated SS-27. The United States ICBM force will consist entirely of 'downloaded' single warhead Minuteman III missiles. The MX 'Peacekeeper' missile, subject to much political controversy in the early 1980s, will be scrapped.

The total number of warheads carried by submarine based nuclear missiles (SLBMs) is limited to 1,750 by the treaty. They could still be MIRVed. The United States has deactivated the last remaining submarines carrying *Poseidon* C-3 missiles and is expected to retain some of its *Trident* I (C-4) and *Trident* II (D-5) missiles. These will be downloaded to some extent. Russia is expected to scrap some of the older missiles and retain the SS-N-18, SS-N-20 and SS-N-23 in service on the *Typhoon* and *Delta* submarines.

Strategic bombers constitute the third 'leg' of the so-called nuclear 'triad'. The United States will cut its bomber force substantially. The B1 bomber has been converted to conventional use, although in return for allowing Russia to retain some SS-19 missiles the US is allowed to use B1 bombers as a nuclear weapons platform as some of the older B 52s are taken out of service. The Russian TU 160 *Blackjack* will be deployed in only token numbers. The same applies to the American B2 'Stealth' bomber.[9]

Table 5.1 Russian and US strategic forces before and after START I and II

US Strategic Nuclear Warheads
(Projected figures after implementation of agreements)

	Pre-START (1991)	START I	START II
ICBMs (Intercontinental Ballistic Missiles)			
Minuteman II	450	0	0
Minuteman III	1,500	900	500
MX (Peacekeeper)	500	500	0
Total	2,450	1,400	500
SLBMs (Submarine launched Ballistic Missiles)			
Poseidon (C-3)	1,920	0	0
Trident I (C-4)	3,072	1,536	768
Trident II (D-5)	768	1,920	960
Total	5,760	3,456	1,728
Bombers			
Total	2,665	1,065	772
Overall totals	10,875	5,921	3,500

Soviet/Russian Strategic Nuclear Warheads

	Pre-START (1991)	START I	START II
ICBMs			
SS-11	326	0	0
SS-13	40	0	0
SS-17	188	0	0
SS-18	3,080	1,540	0
SS-19	1,800	105	105
SS-24	890	890	0
SS-25/27	288	588	399
Total	6,612	3,258	504

SLBMs			
SS-N-6	192	0	0
SS-N-8	280	0	0
SS-N-17	12	0	0
SS-N-18	672	576	0
SS-N-20	1,200	720	720
SS-N-23	448	448	448
Bulava	0	0	336
Total	2,804	1,744	1,744
Bombers	855	820	752
Overall totals	10,271	5,687	2,760

Note: These figures represent one amongst several possible configurations of future strategic nuclear forces under the START treaties

Russian foreign policy debates and the prospects of START ratification

Whereas START I was readily ratified by the Russian parliament, since it was the instrument of the denuclearization of the non-Russian Newly Independent States, START II has proved more controversial.

It is important to be aware of the fact that the rush to negotiate and sign the START II Treaty was also driven to a significant extent by the collapse of the Soviet Union. As early as October 1991, before the formal dissolution of the USSR, the Russian leadership issued an internal document on its nuclear policy. It insisted on the rapid and complete denuclearization of the non-Russian former Soviet republics and also advocated cutting all ties with military R&D establishments outside Russia, especially the *Yuzhnoe* missile production facility and other plants in Ukraine, in order to avoid technical dependency on other countries, losing technical information to the West and in the end having to financially support Ukraine and other former Soviet republics.[10] The retirement of the SS-18 and the SS-24 by the end of their normal service life, the two modern ICBMs with multiple warheads, was a natural consequence of this stance. As the only modern ICBM manufactured in Russia was the single-warhead SS-25 *Topol*, the Yeltsin government was receptive to American pressure to abolish MIRVed ICBMs in START II.

A detailed critical analysis of the START II accord was published by the well-know civilian analyst of military affairs (and member of the Duma) Alexei Arbatov.[11] He argues that Russia concluded the agreement too hastily, the

United States was determined to keep too great a part of its strategic arsenal intact, and the outcome is inequitable. He points out that MIRVed landbased ICBMs form the backbone of the Russian strategic missile force (with more than 60 per cent of strategic warheads deployed in this manner) whereas the United States has a mere 18 per cent of its strategic warheads deployed on MIRVed ICBMs. On the other hand, the United States can retain its sea-based MIRVed counterforce system, the Trident II (D5). Not only does Russia not possess a sea-based system equivalent to the Trident D5 (especially in terms of hard target kill capability), but its sea-based weapons are much more vulnerable to ASW (anti-submarine warfare).[12]

Central to Arbatov's argument is the view that START II eliminates the foundation of Russia's strategic deterrent which was based on a time-urgent counterforce capability configured to a launch-on-warning posture. This was based on the assumption that in the age of highly accurate counterforce systems even hardened systems could not survive a determined, large-scale first strike. Early warning and command and control systems were designed to enable such a posture to be operationalised. Mobile ICBMs such as the SS-25 are not well suited to launch-on-warning, although their mobility makes them less vulnerable.[13] START II will thus effectively require the abandonment of the basic principles of Russian strategic force doctrine. At the same, it will require a costly expansion of its single-warhead missile force.

This general point was made by various critics of the START II accord. Thus Vice-Admiral Rudolf Golosov argued that as a result of START II '... the structure of the US strategic triad remains virtually unchanged. But Russia has to drastically change the structure of its own strategic forces ...'[14]

Colonel Petr Belov made the same point. After the Bush-Yeltsin agreement he criticised the decision to scrap the SS-18 and rely almost exclusively on the SS-25 in future.[15] In an article after the signing of START II he expressed the view that the mobility of the SS-25 does not ensure its invulnerability because redeployment is slow, bearing in mind the nature of Russia's terrain and poor road system, and that road/rail-mobile systems are vulnerable to accidents and sabotage.[16]

Russian strategic planners in the SRF and the General Staff are still preoccupied by the US-Russian strategic balance. The problem that preoccupied them as START II was signed was that during the first seven-year phase of START II drastic reductions in MIRVed ICBMs are required (to a level of 1200 warheads, with only 650 on heavy missiles, i.e. the SS-18). This means that the number of MIRVed launchers will have to very drastically cut, to a level of at most 120. On the other hand, the projected production rate of SS-25 (and its successor, the SS-27 *Topol M*) will not be adequate to restore what is considered an acceptable balance with the United States for some time. Russian military planners foresee a 'window of vulnerability' for its land-based force lasting from the end of the first phase of START II implementation until the year 2010. It is assumed that if a certain imbalance exists in the number of ICBMs deployed on both sides, the United States can take out even mobile SS-25s using a barrage of nuclear warheads targeted at the patrol area of the road-mobile ICBMs.[17]

Russian strategic analysts are also concerned that START II does not impose any restrictions on nuclear-tipped sea-based cruise missiles. Although the United States has withdrawn unilaterally all sea-launched cruise missiles (SLCMs), the conventionally-armed *Tomahawk* cruise missiles are an important element of the US Navy's arsenal. Russian analysts fear that the United States could either use conventionally armed cruise missiles to target land-based missile silos (with a good hope of destroying them in the event of war) or replacing the conventional with nuclear warheads in a crisis. Finally, Russian analysts claim that after the implementation of START II the United States will retain the ability to reconstitute its ballistic missile force much more quickly than Russia. This is based on the notion that the United States can keep the 'buses' for the MIRVed warheads on the Minuteman III which will be replaced by single warheads. This would provide a rapid 'upload potential' if the United States chose to abandon START II at any time in the future. Since Russia's ICBM force would largely consist of single-warhead missiles which were designed to have only one warhead, a Russian response to such a move would be costly, requiring either new MIRVed warhead designs for the SS-25/27 force or even the deployment of new missiles.

Despite these concerns, it is nevertheless remarkable that while political opposition to START II has been very sustained, the military has been more moderate in its attitude and has generally supported START II, albeit without great enthusiasm. This is a consequence of the fact that drastic reductions in the number of strategic warheads will be necessary and START II conforms reasonably well with the direction of the modernisation of the Russia's strategic forces. The Soviet era workhorses of the ICBM force, the SS-19 and SS-18, will have to be scrapped because of they are reaching the end of their operational life and the infrastructure that created them is no longer available. A reduction in the concentration of warheads on missiles and mobility combines to provide reduced vulnerability. Igor Sergeev, who became commander-in-chief of the Strategic Rocket Forces in 1992 and Minister of Defence in 1997, has consistently supported the START process in the context of a transition to a pure second-strike posture to replace 'launch under attack' (*vstrechno-otvetnii udar).*[18] The de-MIRVing of American and Russian ICBMs would make a substantial contribution to reducing the vulnerability of land-based missiles. Given fixed warheads ceilings, distributing the number of permitted warheads over the maximum number of delivery vehicles also reduces vulnerability.

At the Helsinki summit in March 1997 Presidents Clinton and Yeltsin discussed the possibility of a START III agreement with reductions to levels of 2,000-2,500 warheads.[19] On the assumption the after 2010 Russia will ultimately move to a level of at most 2,000 strategic warheads at best, the Russian military has been rather keen to ensure movement towards START III. Indeed, START III would fit the anticipated configuration of a moderenised Russian strategic arsenal better than START II and would prevent the opening up of a significant quantitative gap vis-á-vis the United States.

Economic Issues Relating to START II

There is a clear perception in the Russian government and sections of the political and intellectual élite that the Russia will not be able to maintain a strategic nuclear force beyond post-START II levels. The modernisation of strategic nuclear forces would be too costly and would require the rebuilding of large-scale production and engineering facilities currently located in other former Soviet republics, especially Ukraine.[20] Indeed, Russia has difficulty in maintaining its existing force. There is a shortage of personnel due to declining numbers of conscripts and poor working conditions for SRF officers, with the result that missile combat crews are staffed at only 50-60 percent of the required level. Morale in the SRF is quite low due to stressful working conditions, exacerbated by low pay as well as food and housing shortages. Maintenance of the missile force has become less regular, with the result that the combat readiness has been impaired and a substantial number of missiles have been taken off alert.[21] For this reason, START I implementation has proceeded rapidly and began in fact before ratification of the treaty.

To justify the size of reductions in Russian strategic forces, the political authorities, including the Chief of the General Staff, have emphasized the extent to which the United States will reduce its arsenal under START II. The government's argument is that without START II Russia will have to reduce its arsenal without securing comparable reductions by the US.

Analysts from academic institutes and the nuclear industry have pointed out that disarmament is also expensive and technically difficult. Russia has to physically destroy the silo and rail-mobile launchers for nearly 200 MIRVed ICBMs. It has to convert up to 90 SS-18 silos so that they can only house smaller single-warhead missiles. It has to physically destroy more than 300 SS-18 missile airframes. The dismantlement of a very large number of nuclear warheads, the storage of large amounts of fissionable materials and radioactive waste products pose technical problems that require investment in new facilities. There is no clear concept yet as to what will happen to all the weapons grade plutonium recovered from warheads in the long term. Similarly, the dismantlement of missiles and the reprocessing of highly toxic rocket fuels poses a problem. There are too date no reliable estimates of the costs of dismantlement. Internal analyses by the strategic rocket forces command suggest that in the initial stages the implementation of the treaty would result in net costs, and that savings could only be expected after the year 2000.[22] (This estimate has to be revised given that START II was not ratified by January 2000). The costs of START II implementation would increase markedly if it resulted in a determined effort to build up the naval leg of the strategic nuclear forces, along with the surface naval forces required for its protection. The United States has provided assistance under the Co-operative Threat Reduction programme for strategic missile and warhead dismantlement.[23] However, opponents of the treaty argue that such assistance does approach the real costs of disarmament.

What is politically especially sensitive is that the burden of disarmament is unequal. In order to implement START II, the United States has to scrap the MX *Peacekeeper*, scrap the older Minuteman II and download the Minuteman III missiles so that instead of three they will carry only one warhead. They will also download some of their submarine based missiles. However, there will be no need to deploy new systems and therefore the US has to bear no procurement costs to implement START II. In this sense, for the United States START II implementation is relatively straightforward. This is because the existing structure of the US arsenal fits very well with the agreement. Russia, on the other hand, will have to completely restructure its arsenal. A large portion of its most modern missiles will have to be scrapped. In order to take advantage of the START II limits, it would have to manufacture and deploy a large number of single-warhead missiles (the SS-25/27). It could also maintain the modern elements of its sea-based force and expand it by implementing existing plans for a new missile-carrying submarine with a more modern SLBM. The expansion of the strategic bomber force is also an option under the terms of the treaty. In practice the latter two options seem impractical. The strategic bomber force was decimated by the break-up of the Soviet Union and its remains are suffering from severe neglect due to shortage of spare parts and fuel. Heavy bomber production has ceased completely. The current operational status of the long range aviation force is very much in doubt. Similar problems afflict the strategic naval forces. Hardly any SSBN patrols are currently taking place. Strategic missile submarine production has ceased, although a new submarine, the *Borey* is under development. Furthermore, many older nuclear submarines need to be decommissioned. It is therefore doubtful that Russia has affordable options to maximise its force under the START II limits. This issue has not escaped the opponents of START II in the Russian parliament.[24]

The outlook for Russia's capability to manufacture and finance sophisticated strategic nuclear weapons systems in the future is not looking promising. It is unlikely that the resources to expand naval forces will be found; the trend is towards the closing down of production facilities. Likewise companies which were involved in missile production are finding it difficult to maintain this part of their activities as the government is increasingly unable to pay for existing orders. On balance, the economic arguments would favour large-scale reductions, and it is preferable that this process proceeds in an orderly fashion.

The politics of START II ratification

When efforts began to obtain parliamentary approval of the ratification of START II, the government was aware that its analysis of the strategic rationale would not find much support.[25] It therefore sought to defend START II in terms of the established criteria of strategic arms control. The influence of the military industries and traditionalists in the Russian parliament resulted START II ratification becoming a test case for the foreign policy orientation of the Yeltsin government which many of its critics saw as being too pro-Western and not taking sufficiently account of Russian national interests.[26] Among conservative and traditionalist opposition deputies there was and persists the perception that START II means that Russia has to give up the most potent weapons in its arsenal whereas the United States retains some of its most modern and capable systems and that Russia is being pushed into giving up its position as a global strategic nuclear power. There is also an argument which is expressed in parliamentary and military circles that Russia should restructure its strategic nuclear arsenal according to national security priorities without the constraints of arms control, even if it means reductions to levels below those of START II in some categories of forces and rely on the political environment to compel the United States and others to follow suit with unilateral reductions of their own arsenals. Some ultra-conservatives from the nationalist and communist camps have described the large reductions in the Russian nuclear potential as form of high treason. General Boris Tarasov, for example, from the *Otchizna* (Fatherland) faction in the Russian parliament (pre-October 1993) described START II as a humiliation of Russia and surrender to a hostile superpower.[27] Until February 1993, the Ministry of Foreign Affairs lobbied hard for START II ratification; after that the issue was temporarily dropped as the power struggle between the President and the Parliament intensified. President Yeltsin finally submitted the START II Treaty for ratification to the Duma on 20 June 1995. He designated Foreign Minister Andrei Kozyrev and Defence Minister Pavel Grachev as his START II representatives for the Parliament. The International Affairs Committee of the Duma was assigned overall responsibility for START II and was to co-operate with the Defence Committee on this matter. Hearings were held on 11 July 1995. Representatives from Ministries of Foreign Affairs and Defence, the armed services (The Strategic Rocket Forces, the Navy and the Air Force) and the State Committee for Defence Industry were invited to give testimony. Although the contents of the statements made to the Duma is not known, those present have confirmed that the tenor of discussion was almost uniformly positive. However, the Chairman of the Defence Committee Sergei N. Yushenkov stated after the hearings that ratification would depend on three conditions: the unconditional implementation of the 1972 ABM Treaty, a time table for the implementation of START II which corresponds to Russia's economic possibilities, and the provision of adequate funds for the maintenance of Russia's strategic nuclear arsenal.

The debate about theatre missile defences and moves in the US Congress to resolve this issue unilaterally clearly influenced the Russian debate about START. The debate about NATO expansion and the implication that nuclear weapons could in future be deployed in Poland or the Czech Republic likewise affected that debate on START II. It proved impossible to move further before the Duma elections on 17 December 1995. Prospects for START II ratification did not improve with the Parliament (State Duma) elected in December 1995.[28] Officials interviewed in May 1994 still were very optimistic and convinced that START II would be ratified once all the formalities with regard to START I had been completed and implementation had begun.[29] Following parliamentary elections Russian foreign policy shifted noticeably, with a greater emphasis on Russia's national interests and the reassertion of Russia's leading role in the former Soviet Union. There was also substantial opposition to START II among influential leaders of the military-industrial complex.[30] START II became very much a hostage of relations between the West and Russia as well as the internal relations between the Duma and the President.

In the aftermath of the financial crisis in August 1998 START II ratification received new momentum. The Russian State Duma Defence Committee urged ratification because Russia cannot afford to maintain its nuclear forces at a higher level. The committee said Moscow would need Rbl 700 billion ($38.7 billion) to maintain Russia's nuclear arsenal at START I level of 5,000 nuclear warheads until 2007-2010.With the defence budget set at Rbl 82 billion for

1998, the committee took the view that keeping the force at this level is beyond its capability. First Vice-Prime Minister Yuri Maslyukov, previously associated with hardliners on the military-industrial complex that opposed the treaty, became an ardent lobbyist in favour of START II. START II is likely to be followed by a START III Treaty with reductions to a limit of 2,000-2,500 warheads on each side. The Allied attack on Iraq (Operation Desert Fox) in December 1998 however received such a negative reaction in Russia that Duma proceedings on START II were halted again. As a result of the Kosovo crisis and Russia's renewed military campaign against Chechnya US-Russian relations experienced serious difficulties that impeded any progress in START II.

All indications are that Kosovo had a very profound implication on thinking about national security in Russia in general and the role of nuclear weapons in particular. The effectiveness of high technology weapons, the scale of destruction caused and the readiness of NATO to intervene in a local conflict in Europe all raised the spectre of possible interventions in the various conflicts on the territory of the former Soviet Union. A special meeting of the Security Council on 29 April 1999 adopted a range of measures relating to nuclear weapons policy. The precise content remains classified, but it appears that the decision whether or not stay in the informal regime adopted in 1991 has been postponed until the year 2000. Likewise decisions on strategic force modernization were postponed until 2000, but whereas since July 1998 the Security Council had only considered force modernisation options that were in accordance with START II and III, the possibility of START non-compliant force posture which includes MIRVed ICBMs is no longer being ruled out.[31] It should be said that the decision of the United States to deploy a National Missile Defence system to guard against accidental launches and missile attacks from 'rogue states' such as North Korea has a major impact on Russian thinking on strategic arms control.

In the aftermath of Kosovo and faced with persistence of the stalemate in Russia over START II the governments of the United States and Russia held more intense talks about START III as a means of by-passing the problem of START II. Formal negotiations about START III began in August 1999.

When Vladimir Putin took over as Acting President after Boris Yeltsin's surprise resignation on 31 December 1999, he soon began to signal that he wanted to resume co-operation with the West. After Putin was confirmed as President in the general election the START II Treaty was finally ratified by the Duma in April 2000. While this has saved the whole START process for the time being, the effect of other issues, such as US ballistic missile defence programmes on strategic arms control remains to be seen.

Ballistic missile defence and arms control

Ballistic missile defence has been an important factor in strategic arms control. Russia has the only operational anti-ballistic missile (ABM) system in the world which is deployed around Moscow. It consisted initially of 100 launchers employing two types of missile, the *Galosh* and the SH-08 (*Gazelle*). The *Galosh* was designed to detonate a nuclear warhead above the atmosphere and destroy incoming warheads. The *Gazelle* was a high-acceleration missile for interception inside the atmosphere. The modernized Soviet ABM system around Moscow (based on the technology of the *Topol*) essentially raises the level of Soviet BMD technology to the standard of the now dismantled US *Safeguard* system and provides a limited capability against hostile missile launches. For example, the system can be expected to perform well against the very limited Chinese strategic missiles. American, and even French and British strategic forces are well capable of saturating and penetrating the Moscow defences.[32]

During the Gorbachev period the official position on strategic defence was based a complete rejection of SDI (the Strategic Defence Initiative) and any deviation from the ABM Treaty.[33] In 1990, as the strategic relationship with the West was changing, these capabilities were increasingly defended on the basis of ballistic missile proliferation in the Third World. Indeed, there were hints that the Soviet Union might be interested in expanding ballistic missile defences to defend against accidental launches or 'third country blackmail', so long as the systems are not space-based and remain a limited, 'thin' system.[34] After the disintegration of the Soviet Union, the Russian leadership became interested in co-operation with the United States to develop an integrated GPALS system (Global Protection against Limited Strikes) could serve to defend against the emerging ballistic missile threats from the Third World.[35] This new interest in strategic defence reflected a desire to obtain access to US technology as well as realize the potential of Russian technology. For example, Russian military experts believed that the S-300 (SA-10) air-defence missile was more capable of defending against tactical missiles than the US *Patriot* that was used in Gulf War.[36] The SA-12 *Giant* has also been tested successfully in an ATBM (anti-tactical ballistic missile) mode.[37] The establishment of a joint US-Russian early warning centre agreed by Presidents Bush and Yeltsin was a first step in the direction of such co-operation. The enormous technical difficulties and substantial costs involved however cast considerable doubt about such projects. To establish even a 'thin' defensive system on a nationwide basis or deploy space-based interceptors (known as 'brilliant pebbles') would put a prohibitive strain on Russia's limited resources. There was by no means unanimous support in Russia's political and military establishment for such close technical co-operation with the United States.[38] This reflected in part continued distrust of the United States.[39] There was also an unwillingness to accept a reduction in the funding of other military programmes in favour of ballistic missile defence (BMD).[40] In addition there was scepticism with regard to using the SA-10 and the SA-12 as the basis for a missile defence system given its limited technical capabilities. It is unlikely to be effective against modern ballistic missiles, and the performance of the *Patriot* even against the *Scud* which is based on a design from the 1950s at the time of the Gulf War has turned out to be less impressive than at first believed.[41] This problem was exacerbated by the gaps in the integrity of the strategic early warning system based on large phased array radars on the periphery of the former Soviet Union caused by the disintegration of the union.[42]

The official position of Russia was not without its ambiguities. Former Russian defence minister Pavel Grachev linked the implementation of strategic arms reductions with continued adherence to the ABM treaty.[43] The Bush-Yeltsin statements of June 1992 made no reference to the ABM Treaty and thus the question of the possible extent of co-operation on strategic defence remained unclear. This was particularly the case since the Clinton administration cut the budget for BMD and disbanded the SDI Office (SDIO), shifting the emphasis ground based interceptors for ATBM (anti-tactical ballistic missiles).[44]

With all these reservations, however, it must be emphasized that Presidents Bush and Yeltsin did lay the foundation for co-operation in strategic defence. According to the joint statement:

> The two presidents agreed that their two nations should work together with allies and other interested states in developing a concept for such a system as part of an overall strategy regarding the proliferation of ballistic missiles and weapons of mass destruction.[45]

In the United States, the lack of technical progress with SDI and the changed security environment resulted in a scaling down of ballistic missile defence and a shift of focus. It was recast as a programme to rapidly develop and deploy mobile interceptors that can defend against tactical ballistic missiles in regional wars. Currently the United States can field *Patriot* air defence missiles modified to intercept ballistic missiles of limited range and speed. The Gulf War demonstrated both a clear need for theatre missile defence in such conflicts and the limitations of the capabilities currently in existence.

The core of the TMD (theatre missile defence) programme is the theatre high-altitude defence system (THAAD). In addition to that there are a range of projects for space-, air-, land- and sea-based systems. The programme has three principal objectives:

- To provide the United States and its allies with a capability to limit the damage caused by the use of ballistic missiles (with conventional, chemical, biological or nuclear warheads) in regional conflicts. It is believed that certain states in the Third World are deploying ballistic missiles of increasing range and accuracy and that over the next ten years these may become a significant regional threat.
- To lower the political costs of regional conflicts and thus strengthen the resolve of the US or its allies when considering the use of military force. The possession of a large number of accurate medium range missiles could be a deterrent against US involvement unless it had the means to counter or at least degrade such a capability.
- To maintain a substantial superiority in the military technology available to the United States compared with that of regional powers.

The architecture of the TMD currently in development is envisaged as follows.

The first layer of defence will be provided by long-range exoatmospheric interceptors (a missile which intercepts an incoming warhead outside the earth's atmosphere). This is the THAAD and/or a sea-based naval TMD. It is hoped that the first THAAD prototype will be available in 1996 and the system will be operational three to four years later.

The second layer of defence is to be provided by a short-range endoatmospheric interceptor (a missile which intercepts an incoming warhead inside the earth's atmosphere) such as the *Patriot*. The *Patriot* system is to be substantially upgraded with the *Erint* missile. Another option will be the sea-based *Standard* missile supported by the *Aegis* radar.

Russian commentary on the US TMD programme has been rather muted. This reflects the tension between the traditional anxieties US high technology weapons programmes which usually express themselves in pressing for adherence to the ABM Treaty one the one hand and the desire for a strategic partnership with the United States which will bring tangible benefits for Russia on the other. Official talks took place between Russia and the United States about what is permissible under the ABM Treaty.

Theatre Ballistic Missile Defence and the ABM Treaty

The ABM (Anti-Ballistic Missile) Treaty of 1972 limits missiles that 'counter strategic missiles'. It does not limit anti-aircraft missiles, anti-satellite systems or anti-tactical ballistic missiles as such. Anti-tactical or theatre missile defences constitute a 'grey area', however, since they may provide a limited capability also against strategic missiles.

Any deployment of theatre missile defences thus requires an agreement with Russia on what is permissible under the ABM Treaty. Some US officials advocated a unilateral declaration that TMD do not violate the ABM Treaty. Clearly there are elements of the US military who seek to pursue theatre defences without restraint. In November 1993 the Clinton administration proposed a 'clarification' that would have allowed the planned programmes to proceed, but this was not accepted by the Russians. In view of the possible consequences on relations with Russia and the fate of the START II Treaty in particular the Clinton administration sought a negotiated solution.

There is evidence that there was some re-thinking in the General Staff in Moscow about the ABM Treaty and the possible virtues of joint research with the United States into ballistic missile defence. This was partly prompted by the presence of strategic nuclear weapons on the territories of Kazakhstan, Ukraine and Belarus. For a time even some academics who were previously staunch supporters of the ABM Treaty seemed to favour modifications of the treaty and joint collaborations with the United States in the field of ballistic missile defence. Sergei Blagavolin from IMEMO argued that the changed nature in the strategic relationship with the United States meant that since there was no longer a system of mutual deterrence a system of protection against limited strikes could not threaten international stability.

However, soon a more sober mood set it. Sergei Rogov from the Institute for the United States and Canada argued that those who supported the development of ballistic missile defences in collaboration with the United States were clinging to illusions. The United States would not be prepared to engage in a major technology transfer. There was no hope of an international control over space-based strategic defence systems. More importantly, no affordable system would provide any significant protection against a missile attack. Furthermore, Rogov argued that there was no significant missile threat to Russia from third parties that would require such a major investment of resources. The main threats that Russia faced were local and ethnic conflicts in which ballistic missile defence had no role to play. Similar arguments were made by Georgi Arbatov.

It became clear that the while the enthusiasm among civilian analysts for collaboration in TMD was short-lived, the military establishment likewise was for the most part not very enthusiastic about going down the route of abandoning the ABM Treaty or allowing more liberal interpretations of it. For one thing it also recognised that Russia would be unable to afford the development of high technology ballistic missile defence systems, and co-operation with the United States would remain limited. Indeed, simply to restore the early warning radar network of the former Soviet Union would be difficult. In the near term it was unthinkable to recreate this system on Russian soil and the only hope lay in negotiating access to the radars situated in Ukraine, Azerbaijan and Latvia. The consequence would be that a relaxation of the restraints on ballistic missile defence technology would allow the United States to acquire a significant lead over Russia in yet another area of critical military technologies. Particular anxiety was attached to the space-based components. The dividing line between anti-tactical missile systems and systems capable of intercepting strategic delivery systems is blurred for the systems of higher performance which are being developed. This is necessarily so because tactical ballistic missiles more advanced than the *Scud* or its modified Iraqi version, the *Al Hussein*, with ranges of between 1000 to 3000 km, would have re-entry vehicle sizes and velocities of the same order of magnitude as so-called strategic weapons. The next generation of US early warning radars, linked in with the Defence Support Programme satellite network enhanced to enable mid-course tracking of ballistic missiles and a new generation of high acceleration interceptors would form the basis of the system that could be transformed into a nationwide strategic defence system at relatively short notice. This clearly is the old 'SAM upgrade' problem - i.e. the American fear that the Soviet Union might upgrade its air defence system into a nationwide ABM system - in reverse. It can be described as the Russian fear of a 'theatre defence upgrade'. It is clear that the Russian military does not want the United States to develop a theatre ballistic missile defence that could have significant ABM capabilities against strategic delivery vehicles. In other words, it does not want new space-based elements of target acquisition and battle management systems, and it does not want the US to develop and deploy interceptors significantly more capable than the *Patriot* or the S-300V. The context are the strategic force reductions mandated by the START treaties. Strategic defences could further degrade the already reduced capabilities of Russia's strategic nuclear arsenal to a point where Russia's assured second strike capability might be seriously at risk. Thus Russian defence minister Pavel Grachev linked the implementation of strategic arms reductions with continued adherence to the ABM treaty and thereby poured cold water on the idea of a joint programme.

Nevertheless, in 1994 both Russia and the United States reaffirmed their common interest in developing and deploying effective theatre ballistic missile defences on a co-operative basis. They agreed to conduct joint exercises of theatre missile defence and early warning systems. This indicates that at a political level there continued to be a strong commitment to strategic co-operation. However, with regard to strategic defence it is quite clear that the military objections to any dilution of the ABM Treaty have not been overridden, and the various efforts at establishing co-operation with the United States in the field of ballistic missile defence have remained without substance.

The Russian insistence that theatre ballistic missile defences must not be permitted to undermine the ABM treaty meant that a clarification of what is permitted under the treaty was required. The Clinton administration proposed that a missile defence system should only be considered subject to the restrictions of the ABM Treaty if it has been demonstrated to be able to intercept targets flying a faster than 5 km/sec. The Russians agreed to this, with the important condition that the interceptors themselves should not be faster than 3 km/sec. Any faster interceptors should be classified as ABM systems. This was unacceptable to the US navy and air force who are developing systems with faster interceptors. On 23 October 1995, the United States and Russia agreed that TMD systems would be tested only against targets with a velocity of less than 5 km/sec and a range of less than 3,500 km, and that interceptors with velocities of 3 km/sec or less would be regarded as in compliance with the ABM Treaty. An agreement regarding interceptors with higher velocities was deferred.

Another problem relates to proposals to introduce space-based systems for tracking ballistic missiles. To intercept a missile successfully, the target must be detected, located and acquired. Radars are vulnerable to attack and are not useful for discriminating between real warheads and decoys. Exoatmospheric interceptors can be fully effective only if the targets are tracked for some time in space before they re-enter the atmosphere. Both problems can be solved by the deployment of space-based sensors. The US Ballistic Missile Defence Organisation and the US Space Command favour the deployment of a system called *Brilliant Eyes*. This would consist of between 12 and 40 low-orbit satellites with infra-red and visible spectrum sensors. They could be used to provide data for the ground-based radars and the calculations of intercept trajectories especially for longer range missiles. Such a system would clearly be capable of being used to track strategic missiles. It would therefore represent a direct threat to the ABM treaty regime. On the other hand, the effectiveness of any theatre ballistic missile defence system will remain very restricted without space based sensors. The pressure to deploy space-based sensors will become irresistible once THAAD reaches the deployment stage.

Russia and the United States did eventually resolve their differences and reached a 'TMD demarcation agreement'. This was a package of measures consisting of the following:

- A Memorandum of Understanding that extends the ABM Treaty to three other former Soviet republics with ABM facilities on their territory, Belarus, Ukraine and Kazakhstan.
- the 1995 agreement on low-velocity TMD interceptors.
- a high velocity TMD interceptor agreement. This involves mostly elements that were already present in the 1995 discussions, namely the agreement not to test TMD systems against targets that exceed a velocity of 5 km/sec and a range of 3,500 km. Moreover neither the United States nor Russia will deploy either low-velocity or high velocity TMD systems against each other, or deploy TMD systems that would pose a realistic threat to the strategic forces of the other side. It was also agreed that the parties would not develop, test or deploy space-based TMD interceptors or TMD systems based on other physical principles (eg. lasers).[46]

Although this set of agreements was a substantial breakthrough, it did not remove the issue of ballistic missile defence from the list of possible stumbling blocks in arms control, because by 1999 a national consensus had formed in America, including all parties and the administration, that the United States should deploy a thin 'National Missile Defence' (NMD) system to guard against accidental launches and attacks by 'rogue states' with limited ballistic missile capabilities, such as North Korea or Iran. Conservative politicians in the US advocate openly that if Russia does not agree to modifications of the ABM Treaty, the United States should abandon the Treaty.

The Russian political and military elite is uncertain how to respond to NMD, but the concern that such as system would significantly affect the strategic balance. There seems to be little support for a symmetrical response, i.e. the deployment of an NMD by Russia itself. The most obvious answer would be to maintain the deployment of some ICBMs with multiple warheads. The Commander of the Strategic Rocket Forces, Vladimir Yakovlev, has stated that the Topol-M could be equipped with three MIRVed warheads as a response to NMD.[47] This means that National Missile Defence could precipitate the collapse of the START regime, even though START II has finally been ratified. Ballistic missile defence therefore still remains a serious problem in US-Russian strategic relations.

Conclusion

During the early years after the dissolution of the Soviet Union, it looked as if arms control would play a critical role in global co-operative denuclearization. The START process finally delivered the promise given by the nuclear powers in the nuclear non-proliferation treaty (NPT) of substantial (if not total) nuclear disarmament. The denuclearization of the non-Russian former Soviet republics helped to keep the non-proliferation regime intact. The Comprehensive Test Ban Treaty and the Fissile Material Production Ban would constrain the further development of nuclear weapons both in nuclear and non-nuclear countries. However, by 1998, these tremendous achievements began to crumble. The ratification of START II seemed unobtainable and even with the extensions of the time limits agreed the regime was running out of time. Fortunately strategic co-operation was resumed after the Russian presidential elections in 2000. However, despite the ratification of START II serious problems are still on the horizon. The United States is committed to make decisions about the procurement of a National Missile Defence System in the near future. The rejection of the CTBT by the US Senate of 13 October 1999 dealt a severe blow to the global arms control and non-proliferation process. The United States and Russia have to continue to make serious efforts to ensure that the entire promising network of arms control agreements that was designed to put US-Russian strategic relations onto a completely new footing does not unravel.

Notes

1. For more details, see Christoph Bluth, *Soviet Strategic Arms Policy Before SALT*, Cambridge: Cambridge University Press 1992.
2. Raymond L. Garthoff, 'BMD and East-West Relations', in Ashton B. Carter and David N. Schwartz, eds., *Ballistic Missile Defence*, Washington DC: The Brookings Institution 1984, pp.275-319.
3. It is generally accepted that at least two warheads need to be targeted at a missile silo to ensure a high probability of its destruction; even then uncertainties persist. For an analysis of first-strike capabilities, see Bruce G. Blair, *Strategic Command and Control*, Washington DC: The Brookings Institution 1985, p.311.
4. Interestingly, the commander of the CIS joint armed forces, Marshal Shaposhnikov, has stated his support for the gradual elimination of all nuclear arsenals and weapons of mass destruction. See FBIS-SOV-92-212, 2 November 1992, citing a report from Moscow Radio Moscow World Service, 1 November 1992.

5. See for example Lawrence Freedman, 'A treaty from the past', *The Independent*, 31 December 1992.
6. This is according to the START counting rules. For more details see Christoph Bluth, 'Military and Security Issues', in Alex Pravda (ed.), *Yearbook of Soviet Foreign Relations - 1991 Edition*, London: I.B. Taurus 1991, pp.227-260; particularly pp.228-230.
7. Robert Einhorn, 'Strategic arms reduction talks', *Survival*, Vol.XXX, No. 5, September/October 1988, pp.387-399; Walter B. Slocombe, Force posture consequences of the START treaty', *Survival*, Vol.XXX, No.5, September/October 1988, pp.402-407. These 'counting rules' do not apply to the START II Treaty where each actual warhead is counted as one.
8. Richard Burt, 'The Strategic Arms Reduction Talks' - A look at the end game and beyond', *NATO REVIEW*, May, Vol.38, August 1990, pp.24-27. As mentioned above, no agreement was reached on SLCMs. The issue remained unresolved except for unilateral declarations limiting each side to 880 SLCMs without verification.
9. Much of this analysis is based on *The Military Balance*, op.cit., pp.222-229, which was published before the signing of START II but after the Bush-Yeltsin agreement. Considerably less reliable are figures cited in newspaper reports of the START II accord; see *Financial Times*, 30 December 1992; *The Independent*, 30 December 1992 and 4 January 1993; *The Times*, 4 January 1993.
10. Nikolai Sokov, *Russian Strategic Force Modernization*, Oxford: Rowman & Littlefield Publishers 2000, p.93; the contents of this document have become known due to a published letter from Sergei Rogov and Andrei Kokoshin to Russian Foreign Minister Kozyrev, which repeated much of the content of the document signed by Yuri Petrov, Yuri Skokov and Yuri Ryzhov.
11. Alexei Arbatov, 'START II, Red Ink and Boris Yeltsin', *Bulletin of the Atomic Scientists*, April 1993, pp.16-21.
12. For more detail on the relative vulnerability to ASW, see Christoph Bluth, *Soviet Strategic Arms Policy Before SALT*, Cambridge: CUP 1992, Chapter 6.
13. During the Gulf War of 1991 the destruction of mobile missile launchers even in conditions of complete air superiority turned out to be a much more difficult task than anticipated. See Martin Navias, *Saddam's Scud War and Ballistic Missile Proliferation*, London: Brassey's 1991, pp.28-35; Lawrence Freedman and Efraim Karsh, *The Gulf Conflict 1990-1991*,

London: Faber & Faber 1993, pp.307-309. Russian criticisms about the supposed 'invulnerability' of mobile missiles is discussed below.
14. *Pravda*, 23 February 1993, p.3.
15. Petr Belov in *Rossiskaia Gazeta*, 3 November 1992, p.4; the article is scathingly critical of the technical capabilities of the SS-25 in particular. It should be noted that one reason for Russia to get rid of the SS-18 in the long-term is that it is manufactured in Ukraine.
16. For more detail, see Belov, ibid.; he notes 10 instances in which SS-25 missiles deployed on road-mobile launchers have actually toppled over.
17. Based on interviews with Russian military experts.
18. Nikolai Sokov, *Modernization of Strategic Nuclear Weapons in Russia: The Emerging New Posture*, Monterey Institute for International Studies 1998, cns.miis.edu.
19. Discussions about START III intensified in 1999. With regard to START and the ABM Treaty, see 'Russia: Rodionov Voices 'Concern' Over US Calls To Leave ABM Treaty', Moscow Interfax 1754 GMT 14 May 1997.
20. Of the modern ICBMs, only the SS-25 is manufactured entirely in Russia at the plant in Votkinsk. The SS-18 and SS-24 relied on facilities in Ukraine (the Yuzhmash Plant and the Pavlograd Mechanical Plant). See Leonard S. Spector, Mark G. McDonough with Evan S. Medeiros, *Tracking Nuclear Proliferation*, Washington DC: Carnegie Endowment 1995, p.77.
21. Igor Sergeev, 'Raktenye voyska strategicheskogo naznacheniia: problemy stroitel'stva i reformirovaniia', *Voennaia mysl*, No.6, 1993, pp.12-18; Igor Sergeev and Aleksandr Dlinin, 'Poletenye zadaniia rakete nuvelye, no smysl dezhurstva ne izmenislia', *Krasnaia zvezda*, 17 December 1994, pp.1-2; see also John W.R. Lepingwell, 'Is START Stalling?', in George Quester (ed.), *The Nuclear Challenge in Russia and the New States of Eurasia*, New York: M.E.Sharpe, 1995, pp.100-124.
22. Based on interviews in Moscow. Sorokin cites Anatoli N. Svetikov from the SRF who confirmed this judgement; Konstantin E. Sorkin, 'The Nuclear Strategy Debate, *Orbis*, Winter 1994, pp.19-40, p.33.
23. See chapter 6 for details.
24. Vladimir Iakimets, 'SNV-2 dlia Rossii - asimmetrichyi START, perekhodnyi period, kolichestvennye I kachestvennye faktory', in Moscow Carnegie Centre, *Dogovor SNV-2: perspektivy ratifikatsii*, Moscow: Izdatel'stvo Erebus 1995, pp.77-91; V.I. Krivokhizha, E.N. Kuznetsov, I.A. Nikolaichuk, *Dogvor SNV-2 i iadernaia stabil'nost'*, Moscow: RISSI 1994.

25. Based on interviews in Moscow.
26. Suzanne Crow, 'START II: Prospects for Implementation', *RFE/RL Research Report*, Vol.2, No.3, 15 January 1993, pp.14-18.
27. Sorokin, op.cit., p.33.
28. At the time of writing the attitude of the Duma elected in 1999 is unclear.
29. Interviews in Moscow, May 1994.
30. John W.R. Lepingwell, 'START II and the Politics of Arms Control in Russia', *International Security*, Vol.20, No.2, Fall 1995, pp.63-91.
31. Nikolai Sokov, *Russian Strategic Modernization*, Oxford, Rowman & Littlefield 2000, pp.164-165.
32. For an assessment of Soviet ABM systems, see Jeanette Voas, *Soviet Attitudes towards Ballistic Missile Defence and the ABM Treaty*, Adelphi Paper 255, London: Brassey's for IISS 1990.
33. The evolution of Soviet policy towards SDI is analyzed in Karen Puschel, 'Can Moscow live with SDI', *Survival*, Vol. XXXI No.1., January/February 1989, pp.34-51.
34. Major General V. Belous in *Sovetskaia Rossiia*, 23 March 1990, p.5.
35. John Lepingwell, 'US-Russian Cooperation in Missile Defense, *RFE/RL Research Report*, Vol.1, No.33, 21 August 1992, pp.49-56.
36. B. Bunkin, *Krasnaia Zvezda*, 27 June 1991, p.2; see also the report on the Oborona-92 (Defence 92) exercises which involved the interception of Scud, Smerch and Cruise Missiles and resulted allegedly in a '100-percent defensive umbrella', in FBIS-SOV-92-107, pp.2-3, citing a report from Moscow Teleradiokompaniia Ostankino Television on 21 October 1992.
37. David S. Yost, 'Soviet Ballistic Missile Defense and NATO', *Orbis*, Vol.29, No.2, Summer 1985, pp.281-292.
38. *Izvestiia*, 16 April 1992, pp.5-6.
39. *Krasnaia Zvezda*, 28 April 1992, p.3.
40. In late 1991 responsibility for BMD was transferred from the PVO (Air Defence) Troops to the newly formed *Strategic Deterrent Forces*. This may mean that there is no concerted institutional interest representing the interests of strategic defence, since the strategic deterrent forces are preoccupied with maintaining the integrity of strategic offensive forces.
41. For a critical assessment of the *Patriot*'s performance in the Gulf War, see Theodore A. Postol, 'Lessons of the Gulf War Experience with Patriot', *International Security*, Vol.16, No.13, Winter 1991/92, pp.119-171.
42. For more detail, see Lepingwell, op.cit., p.50. It should be noted that the radar system has been affected by other problems; the Krasnoyarsk radar had to be dismantled because it violated the ABM Treaty. The construction

of the Mukhachevo radar in Ukraine was abandoned due to environmental concerns and it is conceivable that attempts to build new radars on Russian territory may encounter similar difficulties. The 'over-the-horizon backscatter radars' (OTH-B) have experienced severe technical problems.

43. *Krasnaia Zvezda*, 23 June 1992, pp.1-2.
44. See the report in *New Scientist*, 3 April 1993, p.7 The budget for BMD in 1994 has been scaled down from $6.3 bn dollars to $3.8 billion.
45. *US-Russian Statement on a Global Protection System*, 17 June 1992, (US Information Service).
46. Monterey Institute of International Studies, *Nuclear Successor States of the Soviet Union,* No.5, March 1998, p.27.
47. *Nazavisimaia gazeta*, 12 February 1998, p.1.

6 Co-operative Threat Reduction: Safe and Secure Dismantlement of Nuclear Weapons

The end of the Cold War has transformed the international security environment fundamentally and in a paradoxical fashion. While the global confrontation of the Cold War was based on the enormous threat of the large-scale use of strategic nuclear weapons, it was characterised by a relatively stable regime of nuclear deterrence and the political stability of the principal groups of states that were involved in this conflict. The fear of the consequences of nuclear war had a fundamental ordering effect on the international system and resulted in the suppression of conflict on the European continent. At the same time the international system as a whole and Western Europe in particular remained under the permanent threat of imminent large-scale military conflict.

The disappearance of the threat of a major war in Europe which threatened to escalate to a global nuclear conflict has without question enhanced the security of all European states immeasurably. However the social and economic dislocation and the disintegration of the political structures in the Communist countries, especially the former Soviet Union, which accompanied the end of the Cold War have created new and unprecedented dangers. As the conflicts in the former Yugoslavia and on the territory of the former Soviet Union have shown, the paradoxical consequence of the end of the Cold War is that while the threat of war has receded from Western Europe, real conflicts involving the use of military force have erupted. In other words, the international system has moved from a situation of a large-scale threat and high political stability to one of a low threat and low political stability.

At the root of the problems is that the states which emerged from the dissolution of the Soviet Union are not stable. The collapse of the Communist political order has resulted in a degree of anarchy as a stable democratic political system has not yet emerged in any of the former Soviet republics. Although the old decision-making structures of the Communist system have disintegrated, the transition to a liberal democratic state is far from complete. Indeed, with the loss of power of the CPSU and the disintegration of the union Russia and became a territory that lacked many fundamental institutions of state and the process of state-building is still on-going. Russia is passing through a profound economic and social crisis. The need to convert a huge industrial complex which is primarily geared to military production and to the requirements of an efficient high technology economy that is competitive at world level and based on market principles requires and extensive period of economic transformation at a gigantic scale. So far this has been exceedingly poorly managed. The consequence has been a perpetual crisis in governmental finances and the inability of the government to mobilise national resources, as well as a drastic decline in living standards in the general population and the rise of organised criminal activity.

The logic of 'thinking the unthinkable' which was developed by the radical proponents of nuclear deterrence in the early years of the nuclear era assumed that the two major nuclear powers had their arsenals and their military establishments under tight control. Theoretical models of nuclear deterrence generally assumed that in a bipolar conflict the two nuclear powers could be considered as 'rational actors'. The bipolar Cold War system appeared stable because nuclear deterrence regulated international conflict, while the stability of democratic and communist societies enabled the development of social and technical mechanisms for controlling a large number of nuclear weapons.

Indeed, during the Soviet period the government controlled, as much as possible, every aspect of life. Political, economic, scientific and cultural activities were strictly organized along the lines and within limits set by the Communist Party leadership which developed an elaborate network of social controls. The vast military-industrial complex was shrouded in secrecy and all military establishments were well protected. This was especially for true for nuclear weapons and all installations involved in their design, production, storage, maintenance and deployment. Thus during the Cold War one of the principal requirements for nuclear deterrence, namely that the strategic nuclear arsenals are strictly controlled, was firmly believed to apply both for the United States and the Soviet Union.

During the final stages of the Gorbachev period in the Soviet Union political reform and economic *perestroika* provided a catalyst for political developments to weaken and eventually displace the Communist Party of the Soviet Union as the locus of central power. At the same time the local political elites in the fifteen Soviet republics gained ground. The escalation of the conflict between Armenia and Azerbaijan over Nagorno-Karabakh highlighted both the weakening of the centre of power in Moscow and the potential collapse of the authoritarian control during the final years of the Soviet period. The social and economic dislocations that accompanied this process have created an environment in which nothing of value can be considered secure from loss. This is alarming especially with regard to the military-industrial complex. The huge arsenal of advanced nuclear and conventional weapons, as well as the very large number of small arms produced and deployed or stockpiled by the former Soviet Union represents a potential security risk of enormous magnitude in an environment where governmental control over all institutions in society has become weak and uncertain.

In 1990 Soviet decision-makers had become aware of the vulnerability of tactical nuclear weapons deployed on Soviet territory itself. Soviet academics were already discussing with Western experts the problems regarding the control over nuclear weapons in the event that the Soviet Union should break up. However, no actions were taken to address this problem. In the United States it was the coup of August 1991 which galvanised the concerns of the academic community, especially at the J.F. Kennedy School at Harvard University, and the Bush administration regarding to potential consequences of the break-up of a nuclear superpower.

Fundamental to any action by the US government was an assessment of the threat and the available instruments to deal with it. A report by scholars from the J.F. Kennedy School of Government entitled *Soviet Nuclear Fission* published in the autumn of 1991 brought this issue to public and government attention. It identified the following risks:

1. The break-up of the Soviet Union into its 15 constituent republics would result in the creation of new nuclear states, including four (Russia, Belarus, Ukraine and Kazakhstan) with strategic nuclear weapons. This would raise profound questions about the nuclear non-proliferation treaty regime (NPT), which did not envision the creation of new legitimate nuclear powers. More seriously, the nature of the governments in the newly independent states was uncertain. Moreover it was estimated that there existed considerable potential for political and even military conflicts on the territory of the former Soviet Union. Nuclear weapons were seen as an unpredictable and potentially very dangerous element of such conflicts.

2. In times of political and social upheaval, nuclear weapons might fall into the wrong hands. Tactical nuclear weapons were seen as particularly problematic, given that many of them were deployed in crisis regions and were not adequately protected against unauthorised use.

3. Storage sites for weapons grade nuclear materials had inadequate systems for materials control and accounting and were not sufficiently protected. Consequently there was a threat for the diversion of nuclear materials. The risk of proliferation also extended to other high technology weapons components, including delivery systems, and to nuclear expertise. As funding for the nuclear weapons complex collapsed, it was perceived that of the 100,000 people employed by it might look for better paid employment elsewhere, such as in states seeking to acquire nuclear weapons.

Traditional defence and arms control approaches clearly were completely unable to meet this range of perceived threats. Based on the assumption that the government of the Soviet Union (later the governments of the newly independent states, and especially Russia which still controlled most of the territory and most of the weapons), recognized the problem but was unable to resolve it with its own resources, a new programme was initiated designed to deal with it on a co-operative basis. This was a radical and ambitious approach because in essence it meant that instead of pursuing defence policy by the procurement of weapons and their integration into armed forces on the basis of a national strategy, it was based on assistance for the physical protection and dismantlement of the weapons of another country. It would involve in providing direct financial and technical assistance in dealing with the most sensitive military installations in the former Soviet Union.

The origins of the Co-operative Threat Reduction Programme

The Co-operative Threat Reduction was inspired by the report of the Harvard group, led by Ashton Carter which highlighted the dangers of the impending Soviet collapse for nuclear safety and security and was the initiative of Senator Sam Nunn (Democrat, Georgia) who had a long-standing interest in the security and safety of nuclear weapons.[1] The catalyst was the Moscow coup in 1991 during which the President of the Soviet Union temporarily lost control over the nuclear arsenal. Sam Nunn and Les Aspin, Chairman of the House Armed Services Committee attempted to obtain authority for the transfer of $1 billion in humanitarian aid for the Soviet Union from the budget of the US Department of Defence which was designed to include measures to address concerns about weapons of mass destruction in the Soviet Union. This measure was defeated. Consequently Nunn together with Senator Richard Lugar arranged for Ashton Carter to brief a number of key senators on their study on nuclear weapons in the Soviet Union as the prelude to a new initiative called the Soviet Nuclear Threat Reduction Act of 1991 which was adopted as an amendment to an unrelated bill (the Arms Export Control Act) and signed into law on 12 December 1991.[2] Section 212 of the Act, which defined what came to be know as the 'Nunn-Lugar Co-operative Threat Reduction Programme', authorised the transfer of $400 million from the budget of the Department of Defence for co-operation with the Soviet Union to provide for the safety and security of nuclear weapons. This was to be accomplished through the following measures:

- the destruction of nuclear, chemical and other weapons of mass destruction
- provision for the safe and secure transportation and storage of weapons to be destroyed
- the establishment of verifiable safeguards against the proliferation of weapons of mass destruction.

The Department of Defence was designated as the implementing agency. Several conditions attached to the spending authorisation caused serious problems with the recipient country (or countries). The first was the 'buy American clause' which stated that 'where feasible' US technology and expertise should be used. Others consisted of the requirement of the recipient countries to fulfil certain obligations, such as observing arms control agreements, internationally recognized norms of human rights and verification that funds were used as agreed by the United States and the recipient country.[3]

The 1993 Defence Authorization Act extended the scope of the Nunn-Lugar programme. It was recognized that it would be in the national security interest of the United States to:

- facilitate the safe transportation, storage and dismantlement of nuclear weapons and other weapons of mass destruction
- prevent the proliferation of nuclear weapons, nuclear material and expertise
- aid the process of demilitarisation in the former Soviet Union, including defence conversion
- continue and widen the programme of military-to-military contacts.[4]

The Act authorised the transfer of an additional $400 million dollars for the Nunn-Lugar programme.

Since then the programme has been an integral part of the annual Defence Authorization Act. 'Nunn-Lugar' became synonymous with the Co-operative Threat Reduction (CTR) Act on 1993 which was established by the 1994 Defence Authorization Act and which defined the authority to implement the programmes outlined above. Significantly, the CTR involved the appropriation of new funds rather than the authority to transfer funds from existing appropriations as before. In 1995 and 1996 an additional $400 million and $298 million were appropriated for CTR activities.

This reflects the increased priority that relations with Russia and nuclear non-proliferation received in the Clinton administration. The Secretary of Defence, Les Aspin, was a co-sponsor of the 1991 attempt to provide demilitarization assistance to the Soviet Union and his Deputy William Perry (who later himself became the Secretary of Defence) was a defence conversion expert from the Centre of International Security and Arms Control at Stanford University and an enthusiastic supporter of the Nunn-Lugar programme. Authors of the initial Harvard report on *Soviet Nuclear Fission*, such as Ashton Carter and Graham Allison, joined the Department of Defence. Carter was appointed assistant secretary of defence and put in charge of what the Administration called the Co-operative Threat Reduction programme.

The high priority accorded to the programme by the Administration did not protect the programme from the various bureaucratic and political minefields that such a bold initiative is likely to encounter very effectively. Apart from the fact that many aspects of the programme sooner or later ran into powerful congressional opposition, both the Bush and the Clinton administration had difficulty in putting together an interagency process that would implement the programme in a manner designed to effectively achieve its objectives. The partial disarray on the US side was complemented by the difficulties of negotiating with the foreign partners, especially the Russians. For an initiative designed to address an international problem of the utmost urgency, the progress in implementing CTR moved forward at a glacial pace, a fact that was much criticised both by proponents and detractors of CTR. By the end of FY 1993 the Department of Defence had only spent (i.e. obligated) $470 million of the $800 million in transfer authority for the Nunn-Lugar programme. Ashton Carter testified before Congress that 1993 had been 'the year of negotiation' and that after 25 bilateral implementing agreements had been signed with the partners in the NIS 1994 would be the year of implementation. Congress, exasperated by the delay, voted not to renew $330 million in transfer authority from FY 1992 and 1993 which had expired. The loss of such a large sum of money to the programme did not say much for the way in which it was being implemented.

Many of the factors of delay internal to the United States were a consequence of the precise nature of the legislation and not entirely the fault of the administration. The programme was designed on the basis that most of the funds were to be spent in the United States. In the course of negotiations with the NIS Nunn-Lugar funds were increasingly used as an incentive for the NIS to participate in accordance with the objectives of the programme. The 'buy American' clause set limits to the ability of the Administration to use funds in this way. Moreover, it generated a negative perception in the NIS and especially Russia and undoubtedly had a negative impact on the willingness of the Russian government to participate. All this was exacerbated by the fact that normal Department of Defence procurement procedures were used. Rose Goettemoeller, who as Director for Russia, Ukraine and Eurasia on the National Security Council was deeply involved in the Nunn-Lugar programme, has defended practice on the following grounds:

> The Nunn-Lugar legislation essentially required a "buy American" strategy that was readily served by off-the-shelf purchases; these were also more easily accomplished through the Department of Defense (DOD) procurement rules which that agency saw as necessary to implementation of the program.[5]

A close analysis of the various aspects of CTR will show that this statement is not quite accurate; CTR assistance did go beyond just purchasing off-the-shelf items and following DOD procurement rules undoubtedly contributed to the delay in beginning serious implementation[6] of the programme. Indeed, this single feature of the programme meant that it was virtually impossible to spend significant amounts of money in the first few years even if all the other problems had been speedily resolved by all sides.

Congress varied in its enthusiasm for CTR, but continued to provide support. In 1995-96, the House of Representatives cut the programme by half, only to be reversed by the Senate where the 'Nunn-Lugar II' amendment was approved. Clearly there is a conservative element in the US legislative which is critical of all forms of arms control and financial support for Russia. Moreover there is a sentiment that assistance for nuclear dismantlement frees funds for strategic arms modernization in Russia, suggesting that the United States is supporting the maintenance and development of Russian strategic nuclear forces. This is why the administration continues to emphasise that CTR is not 'aid' in any form. Congress also attached important conditions to CTR which cannot be waived by the President. They require certification by the President or his representative, the Secretary of State, every year that recipients of CTR funding are in compliance with all arms control agreements, are not using components of dismantled nuclear weapons in the production of new weapons, are not engaged in military modernisation exceeding legitimate defence requirements, and observe internationally recognized human rights, including the protection of minorities. As a consequence, various issues not related to nuclear safety, such as arguments about the CFE Treaty or Russian intervention in Chechnya threaten the continuation of CTR funding.

Critics of the slow pace of CTR implementation, such as Thomas Cochran from the National Resources Council, were without doubt justified. In 1991 the Harvard report had painted a picture of 'unprecedented dangers' that had arisen as a result of social and political disintegration of the Soviet Union. The follow-on report urged decisive action to prevent nuclear proliferation, deal with the danger of the unauthorised use of nuclear weapons and the 'leakage' of nuclear materials. After five years of Nunn-Lugar, the larger political issues of the nuclear status of the non-Russian Newly Independent States had been resolved, but the dangers cited in those reports had not been alleviated at all. The funds allocated were relatively small compared to the scale of the problem. As the social disintegration of Russia had progressed, the security and safety of nuclear weapons and materials in Russia had substantially declined further. Jason Ellis, generally very supportive of CTR, asks why 'a new procedure designed to meet a short-term security need' was not created.

Implementation of the Co-operative Threat Reduction programme

The Harvard report and its successor laid out the priorities for nuclear weapons safety and dismantlement in terms which at least in broad outlines came to be mirrored in the programme that eventually evolved from the Nunn Lugar initiatives and will be discussed below under the main categories of activity.

The 'safe and secure dismantlement of nuclear weapons' (NSSD) was one of the principal concerns of the authors of the two Harvard reports and subsequently became a major focus of CTR. The second report introduced the concept of 'co-operative denuclearization'. It was never made clear exactly what this meant. While the authors did not recommend that the United States and Russia should go down to a level of 'zero', it implied a gradual co-operative reduction to very low numbers and the elimination of nuclear weapons as a factor in international politics. Other authors were less reticent, including the so-called Canberra commission, and recommended global nuclear disarmament. Co-operative denuclearization was seen as a means to accomplish two objectives: One was to complete the process of strategic disengagement between the Cold War superpowers by addressing the issue of the nuclear arsenals. Although nuclear weapons had been integral to conduct of the Cold War, no new regime had been put in place that codified nuclear weapons policy in the security relationship after the Cold War, leaving the strategic nuclear relationship virtually intact. The other objective was to deal with the issues of the safety and security of nuclear weapons in the geographic region that was once the Soviet Union. The withdrawal of these weapons from the non-Russian Newly Independent States and their consolidation in central locations was seen as an important element. The reduction in their number and especially the dismantlement of tactical nuclear weapons was an important element of this process.

Co-operative Threat Reduction, as conceived by the Clinton Administration, embodied all these elements within a framework based on the assumption that both the United States and Russia would continue to maintain a substantial (albeit reduced) arsenal of strategic nuclear weapons. The threat was said to emanate not from the maintenance of nuclear arsenals per se, but the dangers arising from the chaotic circumstances in Russia and the other Newly Independent States. *Safe and secure dismantlement* was designed to address two areas of concern: The *security* of nuclear weapons, i.e. the problem of unauthorised access to nuclear weapons during storage and transport, and the *safety* of nuclear weapons storage and dismantlement (i.e. the risks of nuclear contamination). The emphasis on *dismantlement* made this programme attractive to Congress since it had the effect of reducing the number of nuclear weapons potentially threatening the United States. This supported the notion of CTR as a part of US defence policy and established a direct linkage with strategic arms control policy which was designed to achieve major reductions in strategic nuclear warheads.

While dismantlement undoubtedly deals with the security issue, because a dismantled weapon cannot, by definition, be subject to unauthorised use, there was some question, however, whether dismantlement was the right way to deal with the safety problems. The dismantlement of at least 2,000 nuclear weapons per year generated large amounts of plutonium and highly enriched uranium (HEU) which need to be stored. Some experts expressed the view that it would be safer to leave these materials, which also posed substantial security and safety risks, in weapons. In the Clinton Administration this issue was not controversial; the judgement was made that dismantlement of nuclear weapons had to be an integral part of this process.

The first priority of the Clinton administration in this field was deal with the problem of the nuclear weapons outside Russia, i.e. in Belarus, Ukraine and Kazakhstan. CTR played a critical role in persuading Ukraine to give up nuclear weapons. This had three elements: The first was the assurance that within the context of the programme weapons transported from Ukraine to Russia would actually be dismantled, and Ukrainian observers had the right to oversee some aspects of this process. The second was that it was possible to carry out part of the dismantlement process, especially the destruction of missiles, on Ukrainian soil. Perhaps the most important of all was the fact that CTR assistance provided a financial incentive. The promise of CTR assistance in concrete dollars was an integral part of the package (which included the provision of nuclear fuel for use in power stations from Russia) that enabled President Kravchuk to obtain the agreement of the Ukrainian parliament for the deal whereby all nuclear warheads would be removed from Ukrainian territory. Similarly Belarus and Kazakhstan expected and received CTR assistance in return for giving up their strategic nuclear weapons. While it may be argued that this went beyond the purposes of CTR as originally agreed, there was little objection in Congress. The denuclearization of the non-Russian Newly Independent States, until it was achieved, was the top priority of the CTR programme, and the yardstick of its success. It could be argued that the denuclearization of the non-Russian NIS remains the most important tangible success of the Nunn-Lugar programme.

The main direction of the efforts of CTR in its initial phases seems to have been simply to permit implementation of START I. Thus the denuclearization of Belarus, Ukraine and Kazakhstan was what was required of these countries under the Lisbon Protocol of May 1992 which set out how the Soviet successor states who inherited the Soviet strategic nuclear arsenal would implement the treaty that had been signed while the Soviet Union was still in existence.[7] In Russia, he issue was more complicated given that Russia was going to continue to maintain a sizeable strategic nuclear arsenal. At the same time the scale of dismantlement activities was enormous by comparison. This programme came to be referred to as 'Strategic Offensive Arms Elimination'.

Strategic offensive arms elimination and nuclear weapons protection

The possibility that nuclear weapons from the arsenal of the former Soviet Union might fall into the wrong hands or that command and control over nuclear weapons in Russia might be lost has exercised Western experts and some policymakers since 1990. It is important here to distinguish between tactical nuclear weapons and strategic nuclear weapons, since the problems of command and control as well as security and safety are different for the two categories.

It is generally believed by experts that command and control over strategic nuclear forces is relatively secure and that only the military high command could launch strategic nuclear weapons. This is based on what is known about the complex system of permissive action links (PALS - electronic security devices that require the input of a multidigit code to arm the weapons) and authorisation procedures called the KAZBEK system. It is symbolised by the so-called nuclear suitcases (called CHEGET) that contain electronic terminals to permit the transmission of authorisation codes. Three nuclear suitcases are normally in operation, held by the President, the Defence Minister and the Chief of the General Staff. In the event of an early warning signal there would be an emergency teleconference of the top leadership to decide on the response. The purpose of the system is to ensure that permission for a nuclear strike has to be given by the top leadership while at the same time enabling a rapid response to a nuclear attack. It is generally assumed that the high military command in the General Staff would be able to initiate the launch of ICBMs if it chose to seize control of the arsenal, because otherwise there would be no retaliatory capability if the national command authority (the President and the Defence Minister) were incapacitated or killed in a first strike. Moreover, the General Staff holds all the codes and provided the inputs into the Kazbek system and for this reason alone would be able to subvert the chain of command. This was vividly illustrated during the 1991 coup when President Gorbachev's nuclear suitcase was removed and disconnected from the system. Even though the military leadership thus clearly could seize command and control over nuclear weapons and launch or threaten to launch at the United States, such a scenario currently lacks plausibility. The uncertainty about Russia's future political stability, however, gives rise to concern, because in the event of civil conflict or a military coup control over the nuclear arsenal or part of it might be lost. There have been recent reports that the technical system, including the telecommunications network, used for nuclear control is breaking down and that officers operating the system could easily subvert the control mechanisms.

Tactical nuclear weapons present a somewhat different picture. The unauthorised delivery of tactical nuclear weapons to a territory outside the former Soviet Union is difficult because of the short range of launchers (tactical missiles, artillery) and/or their vulnerability (aircraft). On the other hand, many tactical nuclear weapons do not possess permissive action links and therefore could be armed and detonated by unauthorised persons.

This illustrates that the security of nuclear weapons remains a major problem area. Launch sites for Intercontinental Ballistic Missiles (ICBMs) are heavily protected by passive defences such as barbed wire, electrified fences, motion centres mine fields and other unknown facilities which are said to require specialised equipment to move across. The guards on duty have the order to physically eliminate anyone who does not respond to the first order to freeze and await the arrival of guards. The forces defending the missile launch centres are said to be sufficient to deal with a large and well-organised attack. This does not mean that ICBM launch sites can be considered to be completely safe. The officers of the Strategic Rocket Forces have also experienced severe social problems, such as lack of housing and scarcity of food. Local authorities have at times refused to permit food supplies to pass to the missile bases, causing the officers to go on strike. The length of the duty shifts for SRF officers has been extended. The absolute loyalty of the service personnel can therefore not be taken for granted.

If ICBM launch sites are still relatively secure, this cannot be said of the storage sites for strategic and tactical nuclear areas. As a result of the withdrawal of warheads from other parts of the former Soviet Union the existing storage sites are filled with warheads to about 60 per cent beyond the capacity than they were designed for. There is no money for building new facilities and even facilities under construction are not being completed. There are several problems:

- The security of the sites is inadequate. Some are guarded by civilians and protected by passive defences. The example of large-scale thefts from conventional weapons depots is an indication of the dangers.
- There is no adequate accounting for all the warheads, many of which were withdrawn under emergency conditions and dumped at the sites. There are persistent reports of missing warheads, such as 23 warheads which disappeared from a depot of Komsomolsk-na-Amure in March 1992 and 12 warheads based in East Germany which could not be accounted for prior to all withdrawal of warheads from Eastern Europe.
- Warheads from Soviet nuclear weapons production require regular maintenance. Some warheads in Ukraine for example became critically unsafe. They had become highly radioactive and had dangerous concentrations of hydrogen. It is unclear if the regular servicing of all these warheads can be guaranteed under present circumstances. Accidents, resulting in large-scale radioactive contamination by scattering the nuclear materials through the countryside, cannot be ruled out.
- The transportation of nuclear weapons constitutes a potential risk. Ordinary goods are intercepted and seized by criminals on a regular basis. A determined attempt to seize nuclear weapons cannot be ruled out and therefore all measures need to be taken to ensure transport of nuclear warheads is secure.

As a consequence, the destruction of strategic nuclear weapons and the protection of nuclear warheads were identified as core tasks for co-operative threat reduction. The programmes for strategic offensive arms elimination (SOAE) and nuclear weapons, protection, control and accounting (WPC&A) address two related, but distinct problems. The principal purpose of SOAE is to provide assistance with the implementation of START I (and START II, if it is ever ratified and/or implemented) which requires the elimination of missile launchers and delivery vehicles. It also includes assistance to deal with the conversion or safe deposition of liquid rocket fuel, which constitutes a major environmental hazard. While it might be argued that SOAE is in some sense peripheral to the main purpose of CTR, as it does not directly address the problems of the 'leakage' of nuclear weapons or materials, it is nevertheless essential for the stability of the political framework that enables CTR to proceed. From the point of view of Congress, it means the CTR makes a concrete contribution to the process of the elimination of weapons that are targeted at the United States and thereby justifies the entire programme as a positive contribution to the national security of the United States. From Moscow's perspective, the cost of arms control in general and that of the dismantlement of strategic delivery vehicles in particular is prohibitive and financial support from the United States for dismantlement is essential to maintain support for arms control and its implementation. WPC&A provides assistance for the safe and secure transport and storage of nuclear warheads removed from the deliver vehicles. SOAE and WPC&A together account for close to three quarters of all CTR expenditure.

Progress in strategic arms elimination

The elimination of strategic nuclear weapons in the newly independent states is an enormous task. In comparison with other CTR activities, however, it is relatively straightforward since both the objectives and the implementation are for the most part both technically well understood and politically non-controversial. In Russia, about 200 silos, 1,400 missiles and 50 strategic bombers are to be eliminated by 2007 (if START II is to be implemented).[8] The provision of equipment and services to dismantle ICBMs started in 1994. The equipment provided included cranes, tool carriers, bailers, cutting and other industrial tools and scrap handling equipment. In Russia, dismantlement was carried out, using the equipment supplied, by Russians without direct involvement of foreign staff and companies. In Kazakhstan, Ukraine and Belarus, the United States played a more direct role in the entire process of defueling missiles, removing them from launchers and destroying the silos. In Kazakhstan, all the work has been completed. 104 SS-18s were returned to Russia, 147 ICBM launchers were eliminated and 1,400 strategic nuclear warheads were transported to Russia.. All ICBM silos were destroyed and 178 nuclear weapons test tunnels were sealed. In Ukraine, denuclearization was completed with the return of all nuclear warheads to Russia. The elimination of 130 SS-19 missile silos was completed in December 1998, and all the missiles were destroyed by February 1999. Ukraine is not intending to destroy all the SS-24, but wants to retain them or use as space vehicle launchers. However, all of the SS-24 have been removed from their silos, and the destruction of the silos is to be completed in 2001. In addition, 3 heavy bombers have been destroyed, while the remaining strategic bombers and all ALCMs were transferred to Russia after an agreement by Russia to pay for their return. In Belarus, all CTR activities came to a complete halt in March 1997 after a severe downturn in US-Belarusian relations following the election of President Lukashenka. Fortunately, by this time all nuclear weapons, including all SS-25 ICBMs (which were not supposed to be destroyed in any event) had been withdrawn to Russia. The United States had provided equipment to assist in the destruction of SS-25 launch positions, and CTR funding was to assist with the eliminated of 1,000 metric tons of liquid rocket fuel and 9,000 metric tons of oxidiser. However all US equipment has been withdrawn and all dismantlement activity has apparently ceased.

The total scorecard for SOAE by the end of 1999 therefore is that 4,854 strategic warheads have been taken out of service, 373 ICBMs have been destroyed, 354 ICBM silos have been eliminated and 52 bombers destroyed. In addition, 46 SLBMs have been eliminated, 12 strategic missile submarines (SSBNs) have been destroyed and 191 nuclear test tunnels/holes have been sealed. The programme is well on target to achieve all of its principal objectives by 2003, and there is every reason to believe that if START II will be ratified, the objectives set for 2007 will also be achieved.

Two important gaps exist in the development and construction of the nuclear weapons elimination infrastructure which SOAE is committed to put in place. One is the elimination of a very large quantity of rocket fuel. With the commissioning of two oxidizer conversion facilities in Krasnoyarsk krai the first step has been taken, but this problem, which in view of the toxic properties of the fuel is extremely important from an environmental point of view, needs to be resolved.

The other gap is the elimination of up to 916 motors from solid-fuel ICBMs and SLBMs. Initially a plant was to be constructed by Lockheed Martin in Perm, but this project was stopped by local resistance due to environmental concerns. Russia now plans to locate this plant in Votkinsk, but some local resistance is beginning to emerge at that location as well. It is unlikely that the plant will be in operation before 2001.

The launcher dismantlement process itself has resulted in technology proliferation risks, as John Lepingwell and Nikolai Sokov have pointed out, because components of missiles could be of interest for countries developing ballistic missiles.[9] This is illustrated by the discovery of gryoscopes from Soviet-made SLBMs in Iraq.[10] Although these SLBMs were not dismantled as part of the SOAE programme, this example emphasises the potential risk of component leakage and technology proliferation as an unintended consequence of missile dismantlement. While it is claimed that sensitive components are destroyed by Russian and Ukrainian specialists in the presence of US representatives, it remains unclear whether there are adequate procedures in place to account for all sensitive components and provide for their destruction.

Without a doubt, strategic offensive arms limitation is the most successful element of the Co-operative Threat Reduction programme. It not only is set to achieve all of its objectives but it also accounts for the politically most visible achievement of the entire programme, namely the denuclearization of Belarus, Ukraine and Kazakhstan.

Nuclear weapons safety and security

Among one of the issues identified in the early stages of the Nunn-Lugar programme was the problem of safe and secure transportation of warheads from remote locations of the former Soviet Union.[11] In the view of the Russian military, the most vulnerable element of the nuclear weapons life cycle was transportation.[12] As conflicts began to break out in parts of the former Soviet Union and with the rise of organised crime and the precipitate decline in the authorities to maintain control this vulnerability appeared to assume more and more alarming dimensions. There were persistent reports of warheads having disappeared (albeit unconfirmed by the Russian government). Apart from the actual theft of warheads, one nightmare scenario was an attack by armed gangs on a train carrying nuclear warheads, result in the penetration of weapons casings by projectiles and the large-scale contamination of the countryside by highly toxic and radioactive plutonium. One of the first projects was the design of a railcar for secure warhead transportation. This project suffered from all the problematic features that affected Nunn-Lugar projects more generally. First the Department of Defence sought to procure the railcars in the United States, in line with the general trend to spend as much CTR money in the US was possible. This resulted technical problems which eventually led to the procurement of rail-car conversion kits. Other elements of this programme were the supply of armored blankets, communication equipment and emergency response equipment. The delays meant that it was not available for the withdrawal of tactical nuclear weapons from the non-Russian NIS which was completed by May 1992. It did become available for the removal of strategic nuclear warheads from Ukraine and Kazakhstan, and for the transportation of warheads within Russia between storage depots and dismantlement facilities. Russian commentators on CTR universally expressed support for this aspect of the programme.[13] In 1995 the programme was expanded on the basis of several agreements between the Russian Ministry of Defence and the US Department of Defence with additional funds for measure to improve the security of warheads for the entire military 'chain of custody' over nuclear warheads. $20 million was provided to improve the security and accounting of nuclear weapons, of which $17 million was to be used for security of transportation and $3 million to enhance the security of facilities. In June 1995 another $12 million was promised; $10 million for security of transportation and $2 million for the storage of nuclear warheads and fissile substances. One element of this package was the plan to purchase so-called 'supercontainers' to store weapons before dismantlement and procure computerised systems to improve the methods of accounting for nuclear weapons.[14] Great Britain and France participated in this programme by providing warhead containers and (in the case of the United Kingdom) special trucks for transporting nuclear weapons.

By 1999 the system to provide for comprehensive accounting of warheads with computers set up to track warheads in transit and storage was at an advanced stage of development. So far, 100 computers have been provided and by the end of 2000 another 150 are to be delivered and integrated with network servers. Some of the funds were also to be used to train Russian personnel in nuclear warhead security. In 1999 the construction of a Security Assessment and Training Centre (SATC) was completed in Sergiyev Posad (north of Moscow). The purpose of the SATC is to enable a team of Department of Defence and Ministry of Defence personnel to test and select systems needed to upgrade physical security at Russian nuclear weapons storage sites, establish a personnel reliability programme (including polygraphs, drug and alcohol test kits) and to provide a central location for guard force training systems and system maintenance. After the official test and evaluation of components and the construction of the guard force training facility have been completed in 2000, the SATC will become fully operational.[15]

Any attempt to evaluate the WPC&A programme comes up against the problem that the lack of evidence of stolen warheads is not necessarily conclusive, given that one the one hand there are persistent rumours that warheads have gone astray and on the other there is no confirmation and possibly no means to confirm it. In the absence of clear evidence to the contrary, it appears that efforts to provide secure transportation for a very large number of warheads has been successful. There is however a continuing concern about nuclear warhead storage sites. The security of nuclear warhead storage sites varied greatly throughout Russia. Some sites were equipped with what was called Technical Means of Guarding (Tekhnicheskiye Sredstva Okhrany - TSO)[16] involving armed guards and a whole range of active and passive security measures. Estimates about the proportion of sites equipped with TSO prior to the allocation of CTR funds to warhead storage security vary greatly, with Russian civilian analysts suggesting that only 3-5 per cent of all sites had the high level of security.[17] Such an estimate can only be a guess given that the total number of sites is not known with complete accuracy. As John Lepingwell and Nikolai Sokov have pointed out, under WPC&A, physical protection upgrade sets have been provided for 50 sites, but Western experts estimate that there perhaps 80 nuclear weapons storage sites in use.[18] The paradox is that while the number of storage sites may be greater than officially stated, most of those sites are near military bases and hold tactical weapons, and there is not sufficient storage space for all the warheads withdrawn from non-Russian NIS. Russian specialists estimated that the centralised storage sites for tactical nuclear weapons were filled to 167 per cent of their nominal capacity, resulting in a neglect of normal security and safety procedures.[19] It has also been stated that some sites are quite purely guarded with only civilians in charge.[20]

Details about nuclear weapons storage sites in Russia remain classified and the extent to which physical protection upgrades have been put in place remains a matter of trust. There is no agreed measure yet to verify the implementation of security upgrades. The increased emphasis on tactical nuclear weapons in Russian military doctrine means that Russia will most likely seek to maintain, if not increase, the number of weapons near operational bases. Suggestions to move weapons to well-guarded central facilities far removed from delivery vehicles are likely to be ignored. The security and safety of tactical nuclear weapons therefore remains a central concern for the foreseeable future.

Nuclear warhead dismantlement

The withdrawal of tactical nuclear weapons from the Central and Eastern Europe and the non-Russian former Soviet republics and the strategic arms reduction process has created the requirement for the dismantlement of thousands of nuclear warheads. Unlike ballistic missiles and other strategic weapons platforms, nuclear warheads are not subject to any arms control regime. There has not been any formal exchange of information on warhead stockpiles and consequently US intelligence has only been able to make estimates of the Russian stockpile with a very considerable margin of uncertainty. Verification of nuclear warhead stockpiles and dismantlement would require very intrusive measures far beyond what is commonly referred to as national technical means. Russia is especially sensitive about guarding the technical design secrets of its warheads and would object to any access by foreign inspectors that would allow such information to be revealed.

Nevertheless it is apparent to both the US and the Russian governments that in order for the whole array of arms control and co-operative threat reduction agreements to achieve their objectives, the issue of warhead dismantlement has to be deal with in some way. The United States has a keen interest in verifying that Russia's stockpile of tactical weapons is irreversibly dismantled. The demonstrable reduction in the size of Russia's warhead stockpile will be essential to maintain continued political support for co-operative threat reduction in the long term. Russia is interested in ensuring that the United States will dismantle warheads removed from Minuteman missiles and strategic bombers as they constitute a 'break-out' potential from the START regime (i.e. they will allow the United States to rapidly reconstitute their ICBM force with MIRVed warheads in the event that a decision is made to abandon arms control commitments).

The most formidable challenge that attempts to develop warhead dismantlement transparency regimes face stems from the insistence of the US and Russian governments that sensitive warhead design information remains secret. There are three operational levels at which inspections can be carried out: the unclassified level, the classified level and the 'nationals only' classified level. The latter is based on the view that some information cannot be shared between the United States and Russia even through classified channels because of the fear of revealing advanced warhead design features, including possibly vulnerabilities. Obviously verified dismantlement of nuclear warheads has to be mutual requiring Russian access to US nuclear dismantlement facilities and vice-versa. So far it has not been possible to agree what level of observation can take place at an unclassified level, what information can be shared at a classified level and what technical procedures will permit transparency without sharing information that the countries do not want to reveal.

Another set of problems arises as a consequence of the structure of the warhead production complexes in the United States and Russia. Russia as four warhead assembly/disassembly facilities (called serial production facilities) at Arzamas-16, Penza-19, Sverdlovsk-45 and Zlatoust-36. The Avangard Electromechanical Plant at Arzamas-16 (Sarov) was the first Soviet plant to mass produce nuclear warheads, and currently older nuclear warheads and warheads removed from missiles dismantled under START I are dismantled there. Dismantlement of tactical nuclear weapons removed from Ukraine was begun there. Penza-19 (Zarechniy) manufactures electronic components for nuclear warheads in addition to the assembly/disassembly of the warheads themselves. The Elektrokhimprobor Combine at Sverdlovsk-45 (Lesnoy) is engaged in the final assembly of warheads and is also one of the largest dismantlement sites. The Instrument Making Plant at Zlatoust-36 (Trekhgornyy) produces nuclear warheads and ballistic missile re-entry vehicles. The Nuclear Complex Reconfiguration Programme, adopted by the Russian government in 1998 envisages that all work on the dismantlement of nuclear warheads at Arazamas-16 and Penza-19 will end by 2003. The storage of HEU and plutonium is managed at Chelyabinsk-65 and Tomsk-7.[21]

By contrast, in the United States the dismantlement of warheads and storage of plutonium pits takes place in one location, the Pantex facility outside Amarillo, Texas. The Y-12 plant at Oak Ridge Tennessee disassembles HEU secondaries.

This raises two problems in relation to a warhead dismantlement transparency regime. The first is that of reciprocity; monitoring in Russia would require access to a larger number of facilities then in the United States. Russia might demand access to other facilities by way of 'equal treatment'. The second is that whereas in the United States the dismantlement of weapons and the management of nuclear weapons components and fissile material is entirely under civilian control (i.e. Department of Energy), in Russia the 12th Directorate of the Ministry of Defence is involved in all warhead management operations. This may raise complications in the implementation of any agreement as the collaboration of Minatom (the Ministry of Atomic Energy) and the Ministry of Defence in CTR has often been problematic. With a sufficient degree of political leadership, however, it should prove possible to deal with these problems in a manner acceptable to both sides.

The first attempt to put in place a regime of transparency in warhead dismantlement was initiated at the summit in January 1994 when presidents Clinton and Yeltsin agreed to co-operate to ensure that transparency and irreversibility of the process of reduction of nuclear weapons. This set in motion the 'Safeguards, Transparency and Irreversibility' (STI) initiative with the main objective of ensuring that fissile materials from dismantled warheads would not be recycled into new weapons. A joint working group was established in May 1994 to consider the details. The main elements of the initiative were the following:

The Agreement for Co-operation

This was to be the legal instrument that would permit the governments of the United States and Russia to exchange sensitive and highly classified information in accordance with the requirements of the US Atomic Energy Act. While the United States and Russia generally agreed on the protection of sensitive information to be exchanged, the negotiations proved very difficult and did not reach a conclusion.

Stockpile data exchange procedures

The thinking behind the proposals for stockpile data procedures was that information should be exchanged on the stockpiles of fissile materials and nuclear warheads. No strict verification regime was envisaged, but a system of spot checks was to be instituted to provide some level of confidence regarding the information provided. In time such exchanges would allow the accumulation of fairly reliable data on which a transparency regime could be based.

Mutual Reciprocal Inspections (MRI)

The idea of MRI was that non-intrusive techniques to determine that after the dismantlement process a declared item contained contains HEU or weapons-grade plutonium whose dimensions (shape and mass) are consistent with a warhead component. Some promising techniques were developed and demonstrated by US and Russian experts, but not agreement on specific MRI procedures was reached.

Limited Chain of Custody (LCC)

Specific excess warheads or fissile materials from dismantled warheads were to be monitored by placing seals and tags on containers and using remote monitoring techniques. No specific measures were developed.

In the autumn of 1995 it became evident that STI required a level of access to sensitive information that the Russians were not ready for. The Russian government ceased all discussions about STI after an internal policy review.[22]

The collapse of the formal STI negotiations was not the end of efforts to create a transparency regime. These efforts continued as part of the so-called Laboratory-to-Laboratory Programme (described in the next chapter) that involved direct contracts between US and Russian nuclear weapons laboratories and were designed to promote material protection, control and accounting of fissile materials. US nuclear weapons experts, under the aegis of the Department of Energy, had already conducted studies of the problem. One of these studies was distributed to interested experts (although it was not officially made public) and thereby established basic principles for the analysis of warhead transparency. This was a report dated May 1997 and entitled *Transparency and Verification Options: An Initial Analysis of Approaches for Monitoring Warhead Dismantlement.*[23] The first discussions about transparency between the labs were held at an arms control workshop in Chelyabinsk-70 in late 1995. Consequently a contract was signed in 1996 for a joint study by the Sandia National Laboratories and Chelyabinsk-70 on warhead dismantlement transparency funded at about $400, 000. The purpose of the project was to maintain a technical dialogue on warhead dismantlement with Russian experts, develop a common understanding of the technical basis for transparency and build a community of expert advocates for dismantlement transparency among Russian weapons designers.

The first study was considered successful and additional contracts were concluded during the period 1996-98. The November 1997 meeting in Chelyabinsk-70 had representatives from Minatom, the Institute of Automatics, the Institute of Impulse Technologies, and the four nuclear warhead dismantlement plants. A wide range of representatives from the US Department of Energy and the various weapons labs attended.

The work on warhead dismantlement transparency was restricted to hypothetical scenarios, technical transparency measures and modelling. This was due to the sensitivity of the subject matter. The general plan involved four phases: (1) preliminary studies, (2) advanced studies, (3) technology demonstration in the laboratory and (4) technology demonstration at a nuclear dismantlement plant. By 1998 the DOE budget for this programme reached a level of $10 million and the work had reached phase three.

Before the programme could get to the stage of deploying a prototype transparency system it was disrupted by a more general clampdown of Russian security services on the sharing of information on nuclear weapons-related matters. In November 1998 the contracts were first disrupted and then slowed down. No further progress can be reported by mid-2000.

Dismantlement and the future of the stockpiles

The whole dismantlement process has to be seen in the context that both sides are committed both to a substantial reduction in the number of weapons deployed and to the indefinite maintenance of nuclear weapons capabilities at a substantial level. The black hole of the dismantlement process is the Russian stockpile of tactical nuclear weapons. The United States has 1,000 tactical nuclear warheads either deployed or in reserve, and another 1,500 are to be dismantled. The Russian stockpile is estimated at 5,700, with another 4,000 to be dismantled. If tactical and strategic warheads are to be brought down to similar levels on both sides, Russia would have dismantle an estimated 11,300 warheads under START II conditions and 13,300 to achieve START III levels, whereas the United States would have to dismantle a mere 1,179 under START II and 4,026 under START III (assuming US hedge stockpiles of 2,644 or 2,270 respectively). Two important issues arise from this. The first is that the maintenance of nuclear weapons capabilities requires the continued production of nuclear warheads. This affects Russia much more than the United States, for two reasons. One is that the implementation of START requires the deployment of a significant number of new single-warhead missiles, and these will be new ICBMs (*Topol M*). This will require the manufacture of new warheads as well. The other is that the maintenance and life-cycle of Russian nuclear warheads is considerably shorter; the service life of a Russian nuclear warhead is 10-12 years (at most half that of US manufactured warheads). This means that the tactical stockpile, for example, will diminish or will have to be replenished. Russian production of warheads has diminished to about 10 per cent of its 1990 level, but the capacity remains to manufacture about 3,500 warheads per year. The United States, by contrast, has lost the capacity to mass produce nuclear weapons since the closure of the Rocky Flats plant in Colorado in 1989 for environmental reasons, and only a small scale capacity to manufacture a handful of warheads exists at Los Alamos National Laboratory. On 23 June 1994 US Vice-President Al Gore and Russian Prime Minister Viktor Chernomyrdin both countries agreed to cease the manufacture of plutonium for use in warheads. Russia agreed to close down all of its 13 graphite moderated reactors the produced plutonium by the year 2000. All reactors except for three dual-purpose reactors have been shut down; two are at Tomsk-7 and one at Krasnoyarsk-26. They supply heat and electricity for the local population and Russia has suggested that the United States should assist with the provision of alternative before they are closed down.[24] In the meantime Russia has agreed that plutonium from the three reactors will not be used in the manufacture of warheads. Both Russia and the United States have supported an international fissile materials production ban. All this means that if Russia continues to produce warheads, the fissile material must come from existing stocks, either storage sites or older warheads. All of these sources will be a violation of the objectives of any STI regime that may be agreed. So far it is completely unclear how arms control is going to be reconciled with future stockpile management in Russia. This is fundamental conceptual problem at the heart of the co-operative threat reduction process.

The second problem is the cost of dismantlement. In the United States the dismantlement of one warheads costs approximately $100,000, and the Russians have indicated that their costs are similar.[25] Oleg Bukharin and Kenneth Luongo have pointed out, however, that this is unlikely given that MINATOM's annual budget for defence programme is $400,000, while the dismantlement programme alone would have swallowed up $200,000 assuming the reported dismantlement rate of 2,000 per year. Clearly salary and other costs are at a much lower level in Russia. Whatever the true cost, however, the economic difficulties in Russia may make it difficult to maintain dismantlement rates and implement transparency regimes. Bukharin and Luongo suggest that the simplest mechanism of US financial support for Russian warhead dismantlement would be to pay a fee for every irreversibly dismantled warhead.[26] This programme would emulate to some extent the HEU deal. However, it will have no chance of being seriously considered by Congress until there is an agreement for safeguards, transparency and irreversibility, which also requires issues about the future Russian nuclear stockpile to be resolved.

Submarine dismantlement

Since the early 1960s, the Soviet Union constructed 244 nuclear submarines (including ballistic missile and attack submarines). During the Soviet period hardly any of these vessels were decommissioned. In the unusual event that a vessel developed reactor problems it was usually scuttled at sea. Three submarines with nuclear weapons and reactors were lost and sank to the bottom of the ocean.

In the late 1980s a significant proportion of the Soviet fleet was due for decommissioning. The Soviet Union was not prepared for the full dismantlement, fuel disposition and long-term reactor compartment storage.

Russia inherited this problem in 1991 which was exacerbated by the severe decline in the economy. The inability of the Russian Navy to support the size of the existing fleet due to the lack of resources resulted in an accelerated decommissioning. Nuclear submarines were usually powered by two HEU-fuelled reactors. The fuel constitutes a potential environmental and proliferation risk of enormous proportions. Security at the naval sites with stockpiles of HEU declined as the civilian and military staff had to cope with low wages and understaffing, just as the rest of the economy. There was an accumulation of decommissioned submarines at naval sites, while the dismantlement rate was minuscule (between three and six per year). By the end of 1999 180 submarines had been decommissioned, but less than one third had been de-fuelled.[27]

Submarine dismantlement and securing naval fuel was an obvious area for CTR. In line with its mandate the early DOD programme in the field of submarines concentrated on assistance for missile and warhead dismantlement and the provision of technology for SSBN dismantlement. This activity took place at three shipyards where Russia declared that SSBNs would be dismantled: Nerpa (Murmansk), Zvezda (Bolshoi Kamen) and Zvezdochka (Severodvinsk). Between 1995-98 five SSBNs were dismantled with CTR support. The low number of dismantlement projects convinced US officials that this element of CTR was not achieving its objectives. Instead of the previous principles which, given congressional restrictions, used US equipment and did nothing to ameliorate the situation of Russian workers, work on dismantlement was contracted out to Russian shipyards on the basis of delivery, just as would be the case for US contractors. The pilot project was a contract with the Zvezdochka facility in Severodinsk in March 1997, to dismantle a de-fuelled submarine for $4.25 million. Since then the dismantlement of SSBNs has been agreed at four shipyards, and by 2003 the total number of SSBNs dismantled is to reach 31. The cost per submarine is about $10 million, less than half the cost of SSBN decommissioning in the United States. Without a doubt the fact that the DOD has managed, despite difficult regulations imposed by Congress and suspicions on the Russian site, to facilitate the dismantlement of such a large number of SSBNs is very impressive. There are still 80 nuclear submarines in the Northern Fleet and 60 in the Pacific Fleet not covered by this programme. They still represent a significant threat of proliferation and environmental contamination.

Conclusion

The Co-operative Threat Reduction programme has become an established feature of US-Russian strategic relations. The denuclearization of the non Russian former Soviet republics was a stunning achievement for the programme. Its contribution to the viability of the START regime by supporting the safe and secure dismantlement of nuclear weapons and their delivery vehicles is evident, even if it is not nearly as comprehensive as might have been hoped for. The most important problem faced is undoubtedly the safety and security of weapons-usable fissile materials. This is the subject of the next chapter.

Notes

1. For more detail, see Sam Nunn, 'Foreword: Changing Threats in the Post-Cold War World', in John M. Shields and William C. Potter (eds.), *Dismantling the Cold War*, Cambridge, MA: The MIT Press 1997, pp.ix-xx; see also Richard Combs, 'U.S. Domestic Politics and the Nunn-Lugar Program', in Shields and Potter (eds.), op.cit., pp.41-60.
2. 'The Soviet Nuclear Threat Reduction Act of 1991' (Title II, Public Law 102-228).
3. Jason Ellis, 'Nunn-Lugar's Mid-Life Crisis', *Survival*, Vol. 39, No.1, Spring 1997, pp.84-110; see also Combs, op.cit.
4. Ellis, op.cit., p.87.
5. Rose Gottemoeller, 'Presidential Priorities in Nuclear Policy', in Shields and Potter (eds.), op.cit., pp.61-81, p.64.
6. Ellis, op.cit., p.88.
7. Based on conversations with British government officials. However, these reports remain speculative an no warhead has ever appeared. Evgennii Maslin, head of the 12th Main Directorate of the Ministry of Defence in Russia has stated that so far not a single nuclear device has been stolen or has disappeared in Russia. See *Yaderny Kontrol*, No.5, 1995, p.12.
8. John Lepingwell and Nikolai Sokov, *Assessment of Delivery Vehicle Elimination and Weapons Protection, Control and Accounting*, unpublished paper, Monterey Institute for International Studies 1999.
9. Lepingwell and Sokov, op.cit.
10. Vladimir Orlov and William C. Potter, 'The Mystery of the Sunken Gyros', *Bulletin of the Atomic Scientists*, Vol.54, No.6, November/December 1998.

11. Graham Allison, Ashton B. Carter, Steven E. Miller and Philip Zelikow, *Co-operative Denuclearization*, Cambridge MA: CSIA 1993, pp.91-92.
12. According the General Evgeny Maslin, chief of the 12th Main Directorate of the Ministry of Defence which is in charge of nuclear warheads. See Vladimir Orlov, 'Interview with Gen. Maslin', *Yaderny Kontrol*, March 6, 1995, p.2.
13. See for example Alexander A. Pikayev, 'The CTR Program and Russia: Is a New Start Possible? A Russian View', in John M. Shields and William C. Potter (editors), *Dismantling the Cold War*, Cambridge, MA: MIT Press 1997, pp.103-140.
14. 'Perry adds $20 million to Support Dismantlement of Russian Weapons', *Post-Soviet Nuclear and Defense Monitor*, Vol.2, No.16, 25 April 1995, p.3; 'Defense Minisitry receives $24 Million for Weapons Dismantlement', *Post-Soviet Nuclear and Defense Monitor*, Vol.2, No.20, 12 Jul 1995, p.2; see also Pikayev, op.cit.; Graham T. Allison, Owen R. Coté, Richard A. Falkenrath and Steven E. Miller, *Avoiding Nuclear Anarchy*, Cambridge, MA: MIT Press 1996, p.89.
15. Thomas Kuenning, *Co-operative Threat reduction Program: Overview and Lessons Learned*, Presentation at the Monterey Institute for International Studies, December 1999.
16. *Krasnaia Zvezda*, 18 March 1992, p.3.
17. POSTFACTUM News Agency Weekly Military Digest, 30 March 1992.
18. Lepingwell and Sokov, op.cit., p.9; Joshua Handler, *Russian Nuclear Warhead Dismantlement Rates and Storage Site Capacity: Implications for the Implementation of START II and De-alerting Initiatives*, CREES Report No. AC-99-01, Princeton: Woodrow Wilson School, Princeton University 1999.
19. Anton Surikov and Igor Sutyagin, *Nuclear Weapons in the Former Soviet Union: Safety and Security Aspects*, unpublished paper, London: RIIA 1994.
20. Surikov and Sutyagin, op.cit.
21. Oleg Bukharin, Thomas Cochran and Robert S. Norris, *Making the Russian Bomb: From Stalin and Yeltsin*, Boulder, CO: Westview Press 1995, pp.50-52. Oleg Bukharin and Kenneth Luongo, *US-Russian Warhead Dismantlement Transparency: The Status, Problems, and Proposals*, PU/CEES Report No.314, available at www.princeton.edu/~ransac
22. Bukharin and Luongo, op.cit., p.3.
23. Bukharin and Luongo, op.cit.

24. See Bukharin, Cochran and Norris, op.cit., p.52; for more detail see *Nuclear Successor States of the Soviet Union*, No.5, March 1998, MIIS & Carnegie, Endowment for International Peace, pp.29-30.
25. Hearings before the Committee on Armed Services, United States Senate, 150th Session on S.936, Part 7, Strategic Forces, February 27, March 5, 12, 19, April 16, 1997, Washington DC: USG Printing Office, pp.98-99
26. Bukharin and Luongo, p.11.
27. James Clay Moltz, *Assessing U.S. Assistance Programs for Submarine Dismantlement and the Naval Fuel Cycle*, unpublished paper, MIIS: Monterey 1999.

7 Co-operative Threat Reduction: Dealing with Nuclear Proliferation

Securing fissile materials in the former Soviet Union

While the security and safety of nuclear warheads is important, the security risks posed by fissile materials is much greater because the threat of diversion of materials is much greater. The Soviet Union produced in total an estimated 1,200 tons of highly enriched uranium (HEU) and 170 tons of plutonium for direct use in nuclear weapons. According to estimates by the U.S. Department of Energy, in addition to the fissile materials in nuclear warheads, 650 tons of weapons-usable fissile material (HEU and plutonium) is stored on the territory of the former Soviet Union.[1] This material can be found in a range of military and civilian facilities, with varying degrees of security. About 5 kg of plutonium or 15 kg of HEU is required to make a nuclear weapon.[2] The threat of the unauthorised diversion of nuclear materials results from a combination of factors. The first is that there is a perception, not totally unwarranted, that this material is extraordinarily valuable. It is expensive and difficult to produce. For terrorists existing stockpiles are probably the only plausible source of fissile materials; for states that have a clandestine programme to develop nuclear weapons the purchase of weapons-grade nuclear materials provides a short-cut to the acquisition of a weapons capability. According to some reports, Iran has sent 'buying teams' in to the former Soviet Union to acquire anything useful for its nuclear weapons programme.[3] The second is the socio-economic dislocation in the country which affects all areas, including the nuclear weapons complex. As personnel working at nuclear weapons and materials storage sites are not paid for months at a time, the need to find other sources of money is overwhelming. This has resulted, for example, in soldiers selling weapons and ammunition, and the temptation to steal and sell fissile materials is undeniable. The third factor is that security of sites where fissile materials are located, such as it is, was designed to prevent outsiders from gaining access; during the Soviet period the notion that staff of the facilities would try to divert nuclear materials was simply not conceived of. In addition, it has become clear that many sites at which significant amounts of HEU or plutonium are stored have no better security than ordinary industrial facilities. Moreover, if small amounts were gradually removed, the loss might never be detected. This was proven in Podolsk where a worker stole one and a half kilograms of HEU over an extended period, and the theft was never detected during inventories as the amounts lost were within acceptable limits.[4] At the Institute of Physics and Power Engineering at Obninsk, plutonium and HEU used to fuel the fast critical assemblies was stored in the form of tiny disks that workers could easily slip into their pockets, making this site a prime candidate for thefts by insiders. During the so-called Project Sapphire, when the United States removed 600 kg of HEU that had been discovered in Kazakhstan, 104 per cent of the amount declared in the inventory was discovered. Soviet specialists routinely kept a margin of fissile material over and above the declared inventories in order to be able to account for any losses that occurred during processing. This is in line with the general principle that inventories were not geared towards security, but rather to the maximisation and meeting of production targets. In terms of the total fissile material produced by the Soviet Union, a margin of 4 per cent represents enough material to manufacture 4000 weapons, according to Allison et al. [5]

These dangers are not theoretical; since the dissolution of the Soviet Union a lively illicit trade in radioactive materials has developed and significant diversions of weapons-grade fissile material have indeed occurred. Some of the instances where the material was recovered by the authorities are discussed below in more detail in the context of the general problem of the diversion of nuclear materials and the smuggling of radioactive substances. There is no question that the safe and secure storage of properly accounted for fissile material (called materials protection, control and accounting - MPC&A) must be accorded the highest priority in the Co-operative Threat Reduction programme.

The MPC&A element of the Nunn-Lugar programme was very slow to get off the ground, despite the fact that the urgent need for it was perceived quite early. Until 1996, MPC&A operated on two different levels. The first was the government-to-government level, which on the Russian side involved Minatom (the Ministry for Atomic Energy). The second was called the lab-to-lab programme. It originated with an initiative from the Los Alamos Nuclear

Laboratory but has since been managed by the Department of Energy with active participation by other US nuclear laboratories (including Sandia and Livermore).

The first agreement, signed on 2 September 1993 after very protracted and frustrating negotiations, provided $10 million for the development of a modern MPC&A system at the Electrostal fuel fabrication facility near Moscow. However, Minatom insisted that US assistance should only be used to provide for MPC&A for civilian LEU (low enriched uranium) fuel fabrication. The United States was not interested, given that LEU is not considered a proliferation risk, and request access to the HEU line at Elektrostal. This was declined by the Russians on the grounds that it was used to manufacture naval fuel and the US could not be given access (just as Russians were denied access to US naval fuel facilities). They offered to permit the US to develop model MPC&A systems at the Novosibirsk LEU line in addition to Elektrostal, but the US declined. In the meantime an agreement was developing whereby the United States would purchase last quantities of HEU (i.e. 500 tons) from dismantled Russian nuclear weapons. This would require the large-scale blending down of HEU to LEU in Russia prior to transportation to the United States. Under the Nunn-Lugar programme, another $20 million were allocated in early 1994 to provide MPC&A at the Sverdlovsk blending facility where the downblending was to be undertaken. These plans were vetoed by Minatom and later it was claimed that Russia put in place its own MPC&A systems at the Sverdlovsk facility.[6] Minatom also refused to supply a list of the sites most at risk, so MPC&A at the government-to-government level seemed to be going nowhere fast. In January 1995 Thomas Cochran from the Natural Resources Defence Council in Washington, DC denounced the MPC&A programme under the aegis of Nunn-Lugar as a complete failure, noting that only $1 million of the $30 million allocated had been spent and no improvement in the security of weapons-grade materials had occurred.[7] Cochran blamed initial resistance in the Department of Defence to Nunn-Lugar, the 'buy American' policy, the lack of interest in fissile material security in the DOD's Office of International Security Policy and poor management by the National Security Council in co-ordinating Nunn-Lugar efforts. There is no doubt that given the urgency of the task, the Nunn-Lugar programme as a whole and MPC&A in particular took a long time to begin meaningful work, losing $330 million in the first two years due to the failure of the DOD to obligate the funds before the end of the financial year. Critics have also argued that the fact that much of the funding was spent in the United States created a sceptical attitude in Russia, and quite clearly the incentive for co-operation was not as great as it could have been. However, the Russian reluctance to co-operate had deeper reasons; the idea of allowing

Americans access to its most secret military installations, whose existence was only recently a highly classified state secret was still problematic.

Towards the end of 1994 the Russian side became more flexible and agreed to allow US assistance in the creation of MPC&A systems at three sites with large amounts of weapons-grade material: Electrostal (the HEU fuel fabrication line), the Mayak Chemical Metallurgical Combine at Chelyabinsk-65, the Institute of Physics and Power Engineering (IPPE) at Obninsk, the Luch Scientific Production Association at Podolsk, the Scientific Research Institute for Atomic Reactors (Dmitrovgrad) and the fuel rod and pellet fabrication plant at Novosibirsk. But despite that agreement US experts were repeatedly denied permission to carry out surveys at the agreed facilities, which is necessary before MPC&A upgrades can be developed. This problem was only resolved at the meeting of the Gore-Chernomyrdin Commission in June 1995, which had become the main channel for dealing with US-Russian issues. An agreement was signed by US Energy Secretary Hazel O'Leary and the Russian Minister for Atomic energy Viktor Mikhailov to permit work to be undertaken on all the sites agreed under the government-to-government programme. It is widely believed by US officials that an advance payment of $100 million dollars as part of the HEU purchase agreement played a critical role in bringing about the agreement. The initial surveys were completed with two months at all of the five designated sites and eventually MPC&A upgrades were installed. At the Institute in Obninsk, a Russian Safeguareds Training and Methodology Centre was established to train Russian MPC&A specialists. US officials consider this extremely important, because the philosophy of the Nunn-Lugar programme has to be that ultimately Russia has to provide itself for the safety and security of fissile materials. The United States can provide financial assistance, some assistance with equipment and most important, training and a change in the 'safety culture' of Russian personnel.

The lab-to-lab programme began in February 1992 with a meeting between the directors of the Los Alamos and Lawrence Livermore National Laboratories and the directors of two nuclear weapons production facilities in Russia, Arzamas-16 and Chelyabinsk-70. Initially the relationship between the labs concentrated on technical co-operation in research, bringing fresh funds to Russian scientists while allowing US scientists access to Russian expertise at low cost. In April 1994, as concern was growing at DOE about nuclear smuggling, the Undersecretary of Energy Charles Curtis directed the nuclear weapons labs to include nuclear material protection, control and accounting in their joint activities with Russian labs. DOE provided $2 million for these activities which were not subject to the stringent rules of the Nunn-Lugar programme, i.e. the funds could be spent on Russian equipment and services.

Partly as a result of the enthusiasm of the scientists in Russia and the United States and partly because of the different funding rules the lab-to-lab programme made more rapid progress than the government-to-government programme.

At Arzamas-16 the lab-to-lab programme developed a demonstration MPC&A system using small samples of nuclear materials at non-sensitive areas, using mostly Russian-made equipment. The principles of this system were to be applied to other areas and other facilities. The enthusiasm of the scientists came to be shared by managers of nuclear enterprises, and in May 1995 the equipment was moved to Minatom headquarters on instructions from Minister Mikhailov to be shown to government officials. As a result a number of major institutes under the jurisdiction of Minatom expressed interest in participating in the programme.

The other showpiece of the lab-to-lab programme was the Kurchatov Institute in Moscow, where the Sandia National Laboratory led an effort to improve the security of Building 116 that contains more than 150 pounds of HEU in two reactor assemblies. This required the installation of fairly elementary measures, such as secure fences and locks. Sensors to detect intrusion, remote cameras, a portal control and monitoring system, interior alarms etc. were also installed, and a physical inventory of the fissile material was conducted. The system at Kurchatov was also used as a model demonstrated to many other officials.[8]

While the government-to-government programme failed to produce tangible results for two years, the lab-to-lab programme produced these demonstrable achievements within six months. MPC&A programmes subsequently were initiated at a range of facilities in Russia's nuclear weapons complex, including Obninsk, Mayak, Krasnoyarsk-26, Sverdlovsk-44, Chelyabinsk-70, Avangard, Penza-19, Sverdlovsk-45, Zlatoust-36 and Tomsk-7. In 1995, $15 million were provided for lab-to-lab activities by the Department of Defence ($7 million) and the Department of energy ($8 million). The increase in activity was reflected in the funds obligated in 1996 which amounted to $25 million from DOE for government-to-government projects in Russia and $45 million for lab-to-lab programmes in Russia and other NIS.[9] By August 1996, the Department of Energy was involved in projects at 44 different facilities in the Newly Independent States.

On the American side a fundamental shift in the approach to the management of MPC&A occurred in 1996. Co-operative Threat Reduction had been managed by the Department of Defence, where the emphasis, despite Ash Carter's and Bill Perry's support for the whole range of CTR activities, had been on defence-related matters such as ballistic missile and warhead dismantlement and security. In order to defuse the internal conflicts in the

Department of Defence about the priorities of the programme the then Deputy Secretary of Defence John Deutch devised an arrangement whereby DOD would divest itself of the more controversial non-defence related elements of the programme. This process has become known as the 'balkanization' of CTR.[10] As part of this process, MPC&A became the responsibility of the Department of Energy, whereas non-proliferation programmes came under the aegis of the State Department. DOE received a one time payment from DOD for MPC&A projects in FY 1995 (in addition to $30 million of FY 1992-94 funds which had already been transferred) and was supposed to find its own funds from then on. In FY 1996 DOE requested $70 million for MPC&A in the NIS and $95 million in FY 1997, increasing to $137 million for FY 1998. In order to ensure interagency co-ordination on MPC&A, the National Security Council established an MPC&A interagency working group. So far, 'balkanization' does not seem to have had a negative affect on MPC&A funding or operations.

The long-term disposition of fissile materials

When the concept of 'safe and secure dismantlement' was born with the Nunn-Lugar programme, a major issue that exercised the experts from the beginning was the problem of the disposition of the nuclear materials that would emanate from the dismantled warheads. Indeed, one of the contradictions of the programme was that the drive to increase international security by dismantling nuclear warheads in Russia had the potential for creating greater insecurity by increasing the stockpiles of fissile materials. The options available for HEU and plutonium were quite different. Uranium is commonly used in the civilian nuclear industry in the United States and throughout the world in a form not suitable for weapons use. Thus the United States proposed the very bold idea to buy 500 metric tons of HEU from dismantled Russian nuclear warheads for $12 billion over 20 years. The HEU (containing 92 per cent or more Uranium-235) would be blended down in Russia to LEU (uranium enriched to about 4.4 per cent) before being shipped to the United States. The purchase would be made by the United States Enrichment Corporation (USEC - previously owned by the government and under the aegis of the Department of Energy, but now a private corporation).[11] The agreement was signed on 18 February 1993. However, a number of difficulties arose about the terms as they related to US trade laws, the price (which appeared high for a privatised corporation), profit sharing by Ukraine, Belarus and Kazakhstan and the question of an advance payment to Minatom of $100 million. This issues were eventually resolved (Russia agreed to compensate the other NIS in the form of LEU fuel rather than cash) and USEC took delivery of LEU equivalent to 6 tons of HEU in 1995, followed by 12 tons in 1996. In November 1996 USEC and Minatom signed a contract amendment governing prices and quantities to be purchased that significantly increased the amounts to be acquired annually. The HEU equivalent to be purchased was 18 metric tons in 1997, 24 in 1998, and 30 tons in 1999, 2000 and again 30 in 2001. Thus by 2001 USEC will have purchased about a third of the total of 500 tons.[12]

One important issue that touched both on the trade law and the threat reduction aspects of the deal was the problem of verification that the material purchased by USEC did in fact derive from dismantled nuclear weapons. There was suspicion that Minatom might seek to palm off LEU from other sources given the weakness of the global market for uranium.[13] At the 30 June 1995 meeting of the Gore-Chernomyrdin Commission Minatom agreed to the following verification measures: Samples would be taken at the point when HEU would be introduced and the point at which blending with LEU (enriched to 1.5 per cent) would take place. These samples could then be used to verify the final product. Final details of the verification measures, which involved monitoring at the Ural Electrochemical Combine (Sverdlovsk-44), the Krasyonarsk Electrochemical Plant and Tomsk-7 were negotiated throughout 1996. An important element of these negotiations was that the Russians insisted on reciprocal monitoring rights at the Portsmouth Gaseous Diffusion Plant owned by USEC where the Russian material was to be processed, as well as the facilities where it was to be made into reactor fuel. The final annexes to the agreement were signed by early May 1996. Thus the HEU deal can be described as of the major success stories of co-operative threat reduction which constitutes an important and real contribution to international security.

Plutonium disposition is a different kind of problem. In principle, weapons-grade plutonium could also be used as fuel if it is mixed with uranium to produce mixed oxide (MOX) fuel rods for use in light water reactors (LWR). However, the industrial capacity to convert plutonium to MOX on the scale required does not exist. MOX is also not an economic fuel to use in LWR. Long-term secure storage facilities will therefore have to be constructed until there an agreed method for disposing of the plutonium has been developed.[14] In order to deal with this problem, the US and Russia are also co-operating in the establishment of a storage facility at Mayak (Chelyabinsk-65) with a modern MPC&A system for the long-term storage of nuclear material from dismantled warheads. After much delay and controversy, this facility is now under construction. It is designed to have a capacity of 25,000 containers to store 50 metric tons of plutonium. This is equivalent to fissile material from 6,250 dismantled warheads. The Bechtel company has been awarded the contract for the construction, but Russian labour and materials are being used. The first wing is to be completed in FY 2001 and the container storage wing by 2002. The facility will have state-of-the art MPC&A supported by a special paramilitary unit to combat nuclear smuggling.[15] The construction of this facility has generally been recognized as an important contribution to fissile material security; criticism has focussed largely on the inordinate delays in getting this project underway, and there are also concerns that if strategic arms control proceeds the storage capacity may prove inadequate. While making a significant contribution to fissile material security, both the HEU deal and the Mayak storage facility may not do quite enough to resolve the problem, and may turn out to be too little too late.

Assessing the achievements of co-operative efforts to secure fissile materials

The Russian Federation

The problem of securing fissile material is of a different character in Russia compared with the other NIS since Russia still has an active nuclear weapons programme, is engaged in the process of dismantling a large number of warheads and still operates nuclear-powered submarines, whereas the other NIS have no nuclear warheads and the sensitive sites on their territories are either civilian sites or sites no longer part of a military weapons programme. Russia also has by far the largest number of sensitive sites on its territory. The continuing military relevance of the Russian nuclear complex and has been one factor which has continued to inhibit co-operation in providing for the protection of fissile materials. One manifestation of this is the refusal by Russia to supply inventories of fissile materials, which is a prerequisite for establishing MPC&A covering the totality of fissile materials stored at any facility.

According to estimates by the Department of Energy, approximately 50 tons of fissile material have been placed under enhanced security facilities and one ton of material has been transferred from smaller, more vulnerable sites to more secure facilities.[16] Given that about 650 tons of material are stored in the NIS in total (most of which is on Russian territory), it is quite clear that so far most of Russia's fissile material remains stored under conditions without MPC&A system upgraded under the Department of Energy programme. Although the HEU purchase programme is reducing the amounts stored in Russia, more fissile material is emanating from the 2000 warheads that are dismantled every year. It is hard to argue that despite all the worthwhile initiatives and MPC&A demonstrations that nuclear material stockpile in Russia have become more secure. Given the general deterioration of the socio-economic conditions, it is likely that they have become less secure. To provide a general picture of the state of affairs, we will briefly look at the various facilities where nuclear weapons-grade materials are stored.[17]

The most substantial improvements to security of any facilities in Russia's nuclear weapons complex have taken place at two nuclear weapons laboratories, the All-Russian Scientific Research Institute of Experimental Physics (VNIIEF) at Arzamas-16 (now called Sarov) and the All-Russian Scientific Research Institute of Technical Physics (VNIITF) at Chelyabinsk-70 (now called Snezhinsk).

It is estimated that at VNIIEF there is more than a ton of nuclear-weapons usable material. The Department of Energy has been engaged in joint work with VNIIEF to implement MPC&A upgrades at its research site which contains at least six reactors (of which two have been shut down) and critical assemblies as well as considerable amounts of HEU and plutonium (although not all the materials stored in Sarov is included). Installation of the MPC&A system, including vehicle and personnel access control, material control and accounting for fissile materials in the reactors, critical assemblies and storage areas and monitoring of nuclear materials moved between buildings on the site, was completed in march 1997 Additional work fo the experimental; testing facility and the industrial Facility at Sarov is in progress.[18]

The VNBIITF was involved in the design of nuclear warheads, and the manufacture of experimental and prototype warheads. Six US nuclear weapons laboratories were involved in upgrading physical security and the development of more rigorous material accounting procedures at the Pulse Reactor Facility in Snezhinsk. By December 1997 portal monitors to detect attempted thefts of nuclear materials had been installed to cover all pedestrian pathways and vehicle access routes.[19] Special security forces were established by the Russian government to ensure the physical protection of nuclear facilities at Sarov, Snezhinsk and Trekhgornii (Zlatoust-36).

VNIIEF and VNIITF have clearly become the showcases for MPC&A in Russia. The Russian specialists at the two labs have acquired considerable expertise and are able to devise procedures and manufacture equipment that can be used to upgrade other facilities in Russia. For example, VNIITF has been contracted to provide security upgrades at the Ural Electrochemical Combine (Sverdlovsk-44). Two major training programmes were created with assistance from the DOE. One of these is the Russian Methodological Training Centre (RMTC) for Nuclear Material Control and Accountability at the Institute of Physics and Power Engineering in Obninsk. By late 1998 more than 1,000 specialists from the NIS had received training in Obninsk.[20] Another programme was created at the Moscow engineering and Physics Institute in 1997 which offers a master's degree in Nuclear Materials Safe Management, Protection, Control and Accounting which covers both the technical aspects of MPC&A and the political issues of non-proliferation. VNIITF is planning to create a second MPC&A training centre as demand seems to clearly outstrip supply, and hopes to obtain partial funding from the European Union.[21]

Safeguards and security upgrades have also been put in place at three major and eleven smaller civilian research facilities. The larger sites are the Scientific Production Association Luch (NPO Luch) in Podolsk, the Scientific Research Institute of Atomic Reactors (NIIAR) in Dmitrovgrad and the Kurchatov Institute in Moscow. Another notable initiative is the Material Conversion and Consolidation programme, whereby HEU from the NPO Luch in Podolsk and the Scientific Research Institute for Instruments in Lytkarino will be blended down from 90 per cent enrichment to 17-19.5 per cent. By September 1999 the first 100kg of HEU had been downblended, and there is an agreement that at least one ton of HEU should be downblended in FY2000. There is also an effort to convert HEU-fuelled research reactors to operate on lower enriched fuel called the Reduced Enrichment Research and Test Reactor (RERTR) programme, but no conversion of any reactor cores has yet taken place due to technical and political problems.[22]

Despite these successes one has to be absolutely clear about the fact that the bulk of Russian military nuclear weapons-grade materials have not yet been subject to upgraded MPC&A. The next stage of the programme was to extend it to serial warhead production facilities. These are the Avangard Electromechanical Plant at Arzamas-16, the Start Production Association (Penza-19), Elektrokhimpribor (Sverdlovsk-45) and the Instrument Making Plant (Zlatoust-36). In 1998 the Department of Energy and Minatom agreed in principle to include these facilities in the MPC&A programme. However, no work has yet taken place at these sites.

Political developments have hindered progress, and access to secret facilities has become a major stumbling block. Since 1993 the attitude of the Russian authorities with regard to access to defence industrial installations and information about defence matters has hardened. This resulted to the decision in 1999 that the United States would not initiate any new projects until the access issue was resolved.

Other NIS

It should be mentioned that there have been significant MPC&A activities in other Newly Independent States. These activities are in principle different because none of these countries have active nuclear weapons programmes, although the fundamental requirements for MPC&A are the same. Storage of weapons-grade fissile materials is much more limited outside Russia. Countries that have received DOE assistance for MPC&A include Belarus, Ukraine, Georgia, Latvia, Uzbekistan, Kazakhstan and Uzbekistan. In Belarus significant weapons-usable fissile materials are stored at the Institute of Energy Problems (IEP) at the Sosny Science and Technology Centre; there are 1.9 tons of HEU with 40kg of over 90 per cent enriched uranium and about 330 kg over 20 per cent enriched (i.e. deemed as weapons usable). Upgrades of MPC&A were completed in 1996, prior to the cut-off of CTR funding to Belarus.[23]

In Ukraine weapons-usable fissile material is located at three facilities: The Institute of Nuclear Research in Kiev, the National Science Centre, Kharkiv Institute of Physics and Technology and the Sevastopol Institute of Nuclear Energy and Industry. The Department of Energy was involved in MPC&A upgrading at the three sites between 1994-99, and declared the completion of its work in January 1999. The projects at Kharkiv and Sevastopol, although the basic requirements were achieved, raised concerns. The working relationship between the Ukrainian scientists and the American specialists was poor, there were administrative problems (such as equipment being detained in customs for 19 months) and technical problems. There is some pessimism that the equipment installed will be maintained adequately. For this reason Emily Ewell Daughtry and Fred Wehling have noted the importance of including the Ukrainian sites in the Site Sustainability and Operations programmes planned by the DOE.[24]

In Georgia, fissile material was located at two institutions in Georgia prior to 1998: the Georgian Institute of Physics in Tbilisi and the Vekua Institute of Physics and Technology in Sukhumi (Abkhazia). For a number of years in the early 1990s 10 kg of 90 per cent HEU were located at the Institute of Physics without any serious protection, a matter of serious concern especially as the civil war broke out. In August 1995 half of the fresh fuel at the Institute was transferred to the Uzbek Institute for Nuclear Physics. In 1996 DOE instituted MPC&A measures to protect the remaining fuel, but eventually all remaining fuel was removed with the help of specialists from the Oak Ridge national Laboratory for storage in Scotland in April 1998 (Operation Auburn Endeavour). At Vekua, there was a small amount of 90 per cent enriched HEU (about 2 kg).The facility was abandoned by Georgian scientists in 1993 when Abkhazian rebels took control of Sukhumi. Russian officials discovered in 1997 that there was no trace of the nuclear material which has disappeared.

In Uzbekistan fissile materials are located in two places - the Institute of Nuclear Physics (INPh) at Ulugbek near Tashkent, and the Photo

Radioelectrical Technical Plant in Tashkent. MPC&A upgrades were undertaken at the INPh which operates a VVR nuclear research reactor that was fuel by 90 per cent enriched HEU. It is being converted to run on 36 per cent enriched fuel. Uzbek officials are satisfied with the physical protection upgrades, most of which were completed in October 1996. It should be added that although unauthorised diversion of material could occur in Uzbekistan, the social order in that country has not deteriorated as sharply as in other former Soviet republics.

Kazakhstan had an important place in the nexus of the Soviet nuclear complex, primarily because of its nuclear test site and missile launch sites. Weapons-usable material can now be found at three locations in Kazakhstan: The National Nuclear Centre's (NNC) Institute of Atomic Energy in Kurchatov City at the Semipalatinsk Test Site, NNC's Institute of Atomic Energy in Alatau just outside Almaty (the former capital of Kazakhstan and the Mangystau Atomic Energy Combine in the Caspian Sea port city of Aktau. Prior to 1994 there was a significant amount of weapons-grade HEU stored at the Ulba Metallurgical Plant near Ust-Kamenogorsk in the North East of the country. This material was removed by the United States to the Oak Ridge Y-12 Plant in Tennessee at the behest of the Kazakhstani government in October 1994 (the famous Operation Sapphire).[25] The most important nuclear site in Kazakhstan is the BN-350 fast breeder reactor in Aktau. It was shut down in April 1999. Initially it was planned to remove the spent fuel containing more than 3.5 tons of plutonium to Russia, but in 1997 it was decided to move the fuel to the Semipalatinsk Site for long-term storage. The Department of Energy put in place a programme for secure transport but no fuel has been moved and Kazakhstani authorities believe the fuel should stay at Aktau. Although MPC&A upgrades at the facility were completed in 1998, the fuel remains vulnerable at a facility that now has few staff and there is doubt as to whether the physical protection equipment is being used properly. Thus the nuclear fuel remains at risk. The Institute of Atomic Energy operates four nuclear reactors. A VVR-K reactor at Alatau that operates on 36 per cent enriched HEU was restarted in 1998 after having been closed down for nine years. Physical protection upgrades have been installed but it is unclear that all these systems are operational and the materials must still be considered at risk.

The success of MPC&A programmes in the various Newly Independent States has been uneven. While they do not represent nearly the same problem as the facilities of the Russian Federation, there remains the risk of the diversion of some significant quantities of weapons-usable material. The main challenge for the future is to sustain the programmes that have been initiated. In this context, it should be noted that in the spring of 1999, responsibility for the non-

Russian NIS was moved from the MPC&A programme to the Office of International Safeguards in the DOE. It is unclear how this will impact on their inclusion in new DOE activities such as the Site Operations and Sustainability programme. It is critical that MPC&A activities outside Russia continue and are sustained.

Nuclear Smuggling

The illicit diversion of nuclear materials and the danger of fissile materials being acquired by terrorists or 'rogue states' is considered by many one of the most serious threats emanating from the territory of the former Soviet Union. Since the Soviet collapse there have been hundreds of reported incidents of illegal trafficking in radioactive substances. For example, the German Federal Intelligence Service (Bundesnachrichtendienst) reported 512 incidents between 1992 and 1996.[26] Most of these relate to low level radioactive materials that do not come from the nuclear weapons complex, but from medical facilities and other more accessible sources. Many of the incidents involving scams, where the material offered cannot be delivered or is worthless, the most famous being the peddling of 'Red Mercury', a mythical substance allegedly essential to the development of nuclear weapons stealth technology and missile guidance systems.[27]

However, considerable evidence has now accumulated to show that there is 'leakage' of fissile materials from the former Soviet nuclear weapons complex. The following are the most prominent incidents:

- In 1992 1.5 kg of HEU was stolen from the Luch Scientific Production Association at Podolsk, Russia, by an employee. An engineer by the name of Leonid Smirnov filled thirty 50g vials with HEU without being detected. Smirnov was accidentally apprehended during an investigation of battery thefts and the HEU was recovered. Smirnov had not been able to find a buyer.
- On 29 July 1993, 1.8 kg of HEU enriched to 36 per cent in the form of two fuel rods was stolen by two naval servicemen at a naval base storage facility of the Northern Fleet at Andreeva Guba, Murmansk region. Russian security forces recovered the fuel rods and arrested the culprits.[28]
- In Tengen, near Konstanz at the Swiss border 8 g of plutonium were found which consisted of 99 per cent plutonium-239. This is more highly enriched plutonium than is normally found in nuclear weapons. It is believed by experts that it was produced for research purposes (to standardise fission

cross sections) at Arzamas-16. The plutonium was stored in the garage of a man by the name of Adolf Jaeckle who was being investigated for counterfeiting, and the discovery of the nuclear material was accidental.[29]

- On 13 June 1994, undercover agents obtained 800 mg of HEU enriched to 87.7 per cent (probably originating from Obninsk in Russia) from a Slovakian trader, Gustav Illich, in Landshut, Germany. The material had previously been stored in a metal cylinder at a bank in Prague. Illich and his supplier, a Czech trader by the name of Vaclav Havlik, were subsequently arrested on 14 July 1994 at a sting operation during which Havlik handed over a pellet of low enriched uranium.[30]
- The most prominent case was the discovery in August 1994 of 580 g of MOX in Munich on an airliner from Moscow. This contained 363g of plutonium that was close to weapons-grade material. It appears that two Russian nationals, O.V.Asafiev and E.V.Baranov, sold the mmateiral to a Columbian, Justiniano Torres Benito and two Spaniards, Julio Oroz and Javier Bengoechea Arratibel. Some political controversy was caused by the revelation that this had been an unauthorised 'sting operation' by the German Intelligence Services. German intelligence officers actively procured the radioactive material. There is no evidence of any other prospective customer. Although the Russian government initially denied that the material originated from a Russian facility, analyses by the Los Alamos National Laboratory and Euratom confirmed that the material was likely to have come from the Institute of Physics and Power Engineering in Obninsk. There was a report in February 1996 that the then Russian Foreign Minister, Evgeny Primakov, sent a report to Bonn from the Russian Federal Counterintelligence Service confirming that the material was from Obninsk.[31]
- At the Sevmorput Shipyard in the Rosta District of Murmansk, 4.5 kg of HEU (enriched to 20 per cent) was diverted from three fuel rods at a storage facility for submarine reactor fuel. The culprits were apprehended and the material recovered as they were searching for a buyer.[32]
- In December 1998, the Russian Federal Security Service reported that a group of employees at one of the nuclear facilities in Chelyabinsk Oblast had attempted to divert 18.5 kg of radioactive materials that could have been used in the production of nuclear weapons. The attempt was averted and the perpetrators apprehended.[33]

The market in nuclear materials appears to be primarily supply driven and there is not much evidence of serious buyers. But this should not give rise to complacency. First of all the ease with which radioactive materials can be acquired is worrisome, and there are cases where hundreds of kilograms of LEU were diverted and never recovered.[34] It must be noted that the cases where materials were seized took place in Europe or Russia. The potential illicit export route to the south has never resulted in any arrests, but this where it is suspected a real market might exist. The lack of arrests may simply be a consequence of the fact that Western law enforcement agencies are unable to operate in these areas. Another aspect of this problem relates to the illegal export and trafficking in so-called dual-use materials, i.e. materials which are needed for the manufacture of nuclear weapons but which have non-nuclear civilian uses. There is evidence that Iran has actively sought access to such materials; the best known example is the attempt to acquire beryllium from the Ulba Metallurgy Plant near Ust-Kamenogorsk in Kazakhstan.

Efforts by the US administration to deal with this problem have taken the form of export control assistance programmes. Responsibility for the funding of export control co-operation with the Newly Independent States has been with the State Department since FY 1996. As a result of the processes whereby export control are administered in the United States, several other agencies are involved in aspects of export control assistance, including the Department of Commerce and the Department of Energy.

State Department funding for export control assistance is co-ordinated through the Nonproliferation, Anti-Terrorism, Demining and Related Programmes (NADR) and the Nonproliferation and Disarmament Fund (NDF). The NADR funds long-term projects in export control regime building. The Nonproliferation and Disarmament Fund was established by section 504 of the 1992 Freedom Support Act and it is part of the Bureau of Nonproliferation at the Department of State. The NDF supports effort to halt the proliferation of weapons of mass destruction (WMD), their delivery vehicles and limit the spread of advanced conventional weapons. One of the more specific goals of the NDF is to help establish or strengthen export control systems.[35] Other US government agencies can apply for funding to the NDF for activities related to the goals of the NDF.

The Department of Commerce is involved in supporting internal export control compliance programmes at US companies. Its activities in Russia have focused on assisting Russia in the development of such programmes, especially (after new export control regulations came into effect in Russia in 1998) internal compliance programmes at companies that trade in sensitive technology. These activities are conducted by the Nonproliferation and Export Control Programme (NEC) of the Bureau of Export Administration in the Department of Commerce. The NEC works with all NIS and Central European countries.

The Department of Energy is involved in export control assistance in the nuclear sector and been involved in relevant programmes since 1995 at all the various levels of co-operation with Russia and the other NIS. It seeks to assist in the development of licensing procedures, establishing and strengthening export control legislation and regulations and increase awareness among industry leaders and government officials.[36]

The Department of Energy initiated a programme in 1998 called the 'Second Line of Defence' (SLD) which is an additional element of DOE's MPC&A programme, working with the Russian State Customs Committee and procuring Russian detection equipment for border crossings and checkpoints. The priority has been given to the southern border of Russia, where nuclear material might be smuggled to Middle Eastern countries or South Asia. Equipment has been installed at the Sheremetevo I airport in Moscow from which many flights to other airports within the Soviet Union originate, and six border crossings, mostly along the border with Kazakhstan, the Caspian Sea area and in the Far East are to receive equipment in due course. The Department of Defence is involved with the FBI and the US Costums Service in a counterproliferation programme focussing on the development of customs regulations and law enforcement.

The US export control assistance programmes have contributed much to provide a legal and institutional basis for export controls in Russia, Ukraine and Kazakhstan, and to some extent in Georgia and Belarus, in relation to nuclear, missile technology and dual-use equipment.

Co-operation in export control could be undermined by policy differences. The export of weapons and weapons technology, although sharply reduced by comparison with the Soviet period, is important both in terms of the hard currency earned and the support it provides for Russia's ailing arms industries. Many of Russia's clients, such as Iran, Syria, and Libya are considered 'rogue states' by the United States and are subject to sanctions. Although Russia would not sanction the export of nuclear weapons technology or weapons-grade fissile materials, there have been very controversial issues, such as the sale of missile technology to India (which was aborted), the sale of aircraft and submarines to Iran and assistance with the construction of four light water nuclear reactors. Various countervailing pressures exist, one the one hand to conform with international regimes and accommodate the concerns of the US administration (shared to some extent by the General Staff in Moscow) and on the other to act in Russia's national interest and earn much-needed funds for the arms industry and the Ministry of Defence. The result is that while the Russian government has continued to co-operate with existing international conventional arms transfer control regimes (including the Missile Technology Control Regime, the

Wassenaar Arrangement on export controls of conventional weapons and dual-use technologies as well as the arms embargo against the former Yugoslavia and Iran), it is a policy that is constantly under siege and crumbling at the margins. Depending on the balance of power in Moscow and the future course of Russia's relations with the West, some existing restraints could well be abandoned in future.[37]

The effectiveness of export control assistance programmes is limited also by the porousness and sheer length of Russia's southern border which in most respects is still like an internal boundary of the former Soviet Union and is protected only in a token manner. Effective control of the movement of people and goods is therefore not possible in the foreseeable future.

The export of nuclear expertise

The collapse of the Soviet economy has also affected the Academy of Sciences where many scholars, including physicists, are now without jobs and resources to continue their research. It is reckoned that the Soviet nuclear weapons programme employed about 100,000 scientists, of which 2,000 are estimated to have the knowledge to construct nuclear warheads. About 5,000 scientists and engineers can help in the production of fissionable materials.[38] There has been a significant brain drain to the West,[39] and there have also been reports of attempts by Libya and Iran to hire the services of Soviet nuclear specialists.[40] On 20 October 1992 the Russian newspaper *Izvestiia* published what purported to be the contents of a report by the German Federal Intelligence Service (BND). It stated that an unspecified number of Russians were participating in unofficial nuclear projects in Libya. Likewise, several scientists from the CIS have signed contracts with Algeria. Furthermore, since the end of 1991 14 nuclear specialists have been in Iran and 50 engineers and 200 technicians have concluded new agreements to work in Iran after the dissolution of the Soviet Union. The report asserts that the 7,000 scientists who have emigrated to Israel included 40 nuclear specialists.[41] In December 1992 36 nuclear scientists and missile engineers were arrested when they were seeking to go to North Korea. They had been hired at monthly salaries of between US $1,500-$3,000. It is assumed that they were to assist the North Korean nuclear weapons programme.[42] In general, it must be said the combination of very adverse living conditions and the high value of their expertise to certain countries wishing to acquire nuclear weapons may prove irresistible. In 1996 the U.S. Senate's Permanent Subcommittee on Investigations was involved in the investigation of nuclear proliferation risks from the former Soviet Union at the behest of former Senator Sam Nunn. They recovered a solicitation letter sent around the Middle East by a Hong Kong company offering the services of ex-Soviet nuclear specialists.[43] The situation in the so-called secret cities (such as Chelyabinsk-40 near Kyshtym in the Ural Mountains, Arzamas-16 near Sarov and Tomsk-7 in Siberia) where the Russian nuclear weapons production facilities are located, which used to enjoy special material benefits in return for the separation from the rest of the country, is now difficult as government funding has evaporated.[44] The proliferation of nuclear expertise can ultimately not be prevented, but the restoration of at least some of the material privileges these people used to enjoy, or alternatively, the offer of employment in the West (where their expertise could be used for non-military research) would make it less likely. The United States and the European Community also provided funds for the creation of two International Technology Centres (the International Science and Technology Centre [ISTC] in Moscow and the Science and Technology Centre of Ukraine [STCU] in Kiev) to employ scientists from the nuclear weapons establishment (possibly on environmental or nuclear safety projects). By October 1999 the ISTC, which is administered by the State Department, had provided funding for 835 projects to the amount of $231 million, employing some 24,000 scientists and engineers from the former Soviet Union. There is also a great deal of interest in the United States in funding research in CIS scientific and defence-industrial institutions, using both public and private sources of funding, and exploit expertise and research facilities in areas such as plasma physics, high-energy physics and spectroscopy on a low-cost basis (by American standards). The National Science Foundation supports some 40 collaborative research projects involving scientists from the NIS.[45] US defence companies are also investigating the possibility of joint projects with military research establishments in the NIS.[46]

Another initiative to support scientists and engineers in the former Soviet Union is the Civilian Research and Development Foundation (CRDF) which was established by the National Science Foundation with $ 10 million provided by DOD from CTR funds an a contribution from the Soros Foundation in 1995. By the end of 1997 the CRDF had received nearly $26.4 million through contributions from federal agencies, most prominently the State Department, the MacArthur foundation, US industry and cost-share commitments for projects by NIS governments.

The CRDF is a public-private partnership promoting scientific and technical collaboration with the United States and the NIS. Its objective is to assist defence-oriented researchers in the NIS to transfer their skills and experience to civilian science and industry. The CRDF Co-operative Grants Programme funds research by almost 300 joint teams of specialists from the United States and the NIS across a broad range of fundamental and applied scientific disciplines. The CRDF has established regional Experimental Supports Centres (RESC) to boost regional economical development in the NIS with the provision of major research equipment. It also has a Closed Cities Programme to help NIS defence scientists and sensitive nuclear weapons facilities such as Sarov and Snezhinsk to move into civilian R&D. While there are some interesting projects and initatives, it must be emphasized that the scale of CRDF is relatively small; for example, the Closed Cities Programme is funded to the tune of only $400,000.[47]

There are also two programmes in the Department of Energy dealing with the proliferation of nuclear weapons expertise. These are the Initiatives for Proliferation Prevention (IPP) and the Nuclear Cities Initiative (NCI). The IPP which was started in 1994, with the objective to identify and develop non-military applications for defence technologies, and stabilize personnel and resources that represent a proliferation risk by creating jobs for weapons scientists and engineers in the high technology commercial marketplace.[48] Various IPP funding has gone to projects in Russia, Belarus, Kazakhstan and Ukraine. Projects in Russia have received about 85 per cent of the funding. The request for IPP funding for FY2000 was $30 million, but Congress only appropriated $22.5 million (the same amount available in FY1999).

The nuclear cities initiative (NCI) was created in the autumn of 1998 with the purpose of employing displaced workers in the nuclear weapons complex from these cities in new civilian jobs and thereby contribute to the downsizing of the nuclear weapons complex. The initiative aims to create 30,000 to 50,000 jobs by the end of its programme which is intended to last between five and seven years with funding of $550 million in total. By the end of 1999 NCI could report that 100 jobs had been created at an Open Computer Centre in Sarov, and 30 jobs at the Sarov Nonproliferation Centre. A range of projects are in the planning stage, which according to NCI estimates have the potential for generating 262 new jobs in Sarov, 105 in Avangard, 266 in Snezhinsk and 199 in Zheleznogorsk. They include activities like a high level waste system model, kidney dialysis technology, fibre optic production, bottle manufacturing and radioisotope production.[49] For FY 1999 $15 million were appropriated for NIC.

A report from the General Accounting Office released in February 1999 was critical of IPP and NCI as a result of which legislators restricted both the funding and the content of the programmes. Congress stipulated that no more than 35 per cent of IPP funding could be spent at the national labs of the DOE in future. In order to meet serious concerns that CTR funding could in effect fund Russian nuclear weapons programmes, the Defence Authorization Act prohibits the use of funds to supplement or increase the pay of Russian scientists, or fund scientific institutes that are still engaged in work on missiles, chemical or biological weapons, or have made business or scientific contact with a country of proliferation concern (according to determination of the Secretary of Energy). In addition DOE is required to establish new review procedures to ensure that IPP project technologies do not inadvertently contribute to Russian military programmes involving weapons of mass destruction. CTR funds are no longer allowed to be used for defence conversion. Another controversial issue is the payment of taxes in Russia; IPP funds may not be used to pay Russian taxes unless the Energy Secretary reports that this is unavoidable with an explanation of the reason.

Similar restrictions have been put on the NIC programme; funds may only be obligated if the Secretary of Energy certifies that Russia has agreed to close down facilities in the nuclear cities in order to ensure that money only goes to scientists no longer required for the nuclear weapons complex. Congress appropriated only $7.5 million for FY2000 (instead of the $30 million asked for) and restricted activities to the original sites of Sarov, Snezhinsk and Zheleznogorsk (in addition to two serial production plants).

The various programmes to prevent the proliferation of nuclear expertise have been very imaginative, they have made a dramatic impact and have the potential to achieve the whole range of objectives set. The key problem is that the restrictions set by Congress and the level of funding appropriated, in addition to the complexity of setting up these programmes mean that the problem of the 'nuclear brain drain' has been mitigated, but not yet solved and even the small number of successful initiatives have been very slow in getting off the ground. For this reason significant proliferation of nuclear expertise may have occurred. Moreover, a further deterioration in the Russian economy could intensify the problem again. Like many other aspects of CTR, this issue deserves to be taken more seriously.

Conclusion

The overall assessment of the MPC&A programme so far must be that although significant initiatives have taken place, and in many respects the programme is on the right track, the job still remains to be done. *It is particularly disturbing that there is no overall conception of the final goal for the MPC&A programme.* In December 1999 DOE declared that it had identified 400 buildings requiring upgrades at 55 identified sites, but failed to provide a time-frame for such upgrades or even a commitment for the programme to undertake all these upgrades in due course (in 1995 the original time-frame for completing the upgrade at 100 buildings was the year 2002). The mission statement formulated by Assistant Secretary of Energy Rose Goettemoeller in March 1999 refers to the consolidation of material intro fewer buildings, the elimination of excess HEU and the installation of sustainable physical security and accountancy upgrades, but says nothing about the final scope of the programme. The 'Goals for the Next Two Years' announced by DOE are relatively modest and would result, if implemented, in another 113 metric tons of nuclear materials being brought under the scope of the programme.[50] As Thomas B. Cochran pointed out in 1995,[51] weapons-grade fissile materials in the former Soviet Union will not be secure until all facilities where they are stored have the appropriate safety and accounting facilities. Unless political leaders at the highest level agree to a programme designed to accomplish this objective within a well-defined time-frame, the risks posed by the vast quantities of nuclear weapons material in the NIS remains.

Notes

1. Rose Gottemoeller, *The Importance of Sustainability in Securing Nuclear Material in the FSU,* Paper given at the American Nuclear Society Global '99 Conference, Jackson Hole, Wyoming, August 29-September 3, 1999, available at www.dp.doe.gov/nn/mpca/pubs/rosesp2.htm.
2. For more detail, see Owen R. Coté, 'A Primer on Fissile materials and Nuclear Weapon Design', in Graham T. Allison, Owen R. Coté, Richard A. Falkenrath and Steven E.Miller, *Avoiding Nuclear Anarchy*, Cambridge, MA: MIT Press 1996, pp.203-228.
3. In Kazakhstan, containers with beryllium for us in nuclear warheads was found with an Iranian address - the export to Iran was prevented in this case; see William C. Potter, 'Project Sapphire: US-Kazakstani Co-operation for Nonproliferation', in John M. Shields and William C. Potter (eds.), *Dismantling the Cold War*, Cambridge, MA: The MIT Press 1997, op.cit, pp. 345-362. On the Iranian nuclear weapons programme, see Shahram Chubin, 'Does Iran Want Nuclear Weapons', *Survival*, Vol.37, No.1, Spring 1995, pp.86-104.
4. Jessica Eve Stern, 'Co-operative Activities to Improve Fissile Material Protection, Control and Accounting', in Shields and Potter, op.cit, pp. 309-343, p.314.
5. Allison, Coté, Falkenrath and Miller, op.cit., p.38; for a detailed account of Project Sapphire see Potter, op.cit.

6. Thomas B. Cochran, *US Assistance to Improve Physical Security and Accounting of Fissile Materials in Russia*, unpublished paper, Washington, DC: Carnergie Endowment for International Peace 1995; Allison, Coté, Falkenrath and Miller, op.cit., p.81.
7. Cochran, op.cit, p.6.
8. Allison, Coté, Falkenrath and Miller, op.cit., p.84.
9. Jason Ellis, 'Nunn-Lugar's Mid-Life Crisis', *Survival*, Vol.39, No.1, Spring 1997, pp. 84-110.
10. Rose Gottemoeller, 'Presidential Priorities in Nuclear Policy', in Shields and Potter eds.), op.cit., pp.61-81; see also Ellis, op.cit., p.91.
11. There were various problems that affected the negotiations of this deal, including the privatisation of USEC. For more detail, see Richard A. Falkenrath, 'The HEU Deal', in Allison, Coté, Falkenrath and Miller, op.cit., pp.229-292.
12. *Nuclear Successor States of the Soviet Union*, No.5, March 1998, MIIS & Carnegie, Endowment for International Peace, pp.32-33.
13. In October 1997 one canister of LEU from Russia was rejected on the grounds that it was believed it had not been blended down from HEU. See 'Market Impact of Moscow Announcement Uncertain; US Rejects one LEU Cylinder', *Nuclear Fuel*, 15 December 1007, p.2.
14. For more detail on the various alternative methods of the disposal of fissile materials, with various cost estimates, see Ashton B. Carter and Owen Coté, 'Disposition of Fissile Materials', in Allison, Carter, Miller, Zelikow (eds.), *Co-operative Denuclearization*, pp. 117-136.
15. Thomas Kuenning, *Co-operative Threat Reduction Program - Overview and Lessons Learned*, presentation at MIIS, December 1999, p.6; *Nuclear Successor States of the Soviet Union*, No.5, March 1998, MIIS & Carnegie, Endowment for International Peace, p.45.
16. Based on comments by rose Gottemoeller at the CNS-PIR Seminar on Nonproliferation and MPC&A Sustainability in Moscow, 11 November 1999. Based on the account by Emily Ewell Daughtry and Fred Wehling, *Co-operative Efforts to Secure Fissile Material in the NIS: Shortcomings, Successes and Recommendations for the Future*, unpublished paper, Monterey, CA: MIIS 1999.
17. Here I am following the analysis of Ewell Daughtry and Wehling, op.cit. More detail on MPC&A upgrades at all facilities is to be found in the CNS Nuclear Profiles database at www.miis.edu; see also the DOE MPC&A web-site at www.dp.doe.gov/nn/mpca.

18. *Nuclear Successor States of the Soviet Union*, No.5, March 1998, MIIS & Carnegie Endowment for International Peace, p.42.
19. *Nuclear Successor States of the Soviet Union*, No.5, March 1998, MIIS & Carnegie Endowment for International Peace, p.46.
20. www.dp.doe.gov/nn/mpca/frame04.htm.
21. Ewell Daughtry and Wehling, op.cit., p.13.
22. Ewell Daughtry and Wehling, op.cit., p.14.
23. Vyachaslau E. Paznyak, 'Nunn-Lugar Program Assessment: The Case of Belarus', in John M. Shields and William C. Potter (eds.), *Dismantling the Cold War*, Cambridge, MA: MIT Press 1997, pp.167-192.
24. Ewell Daughtry and Wehling, op.cit., p.10.
25. William C. Potter, 'Project Sapphire: US-Kazakstani Co-operation for Nonproliferation', in Shields and Potter (eds.), op.cit., pp.345-362.
26. Rensselaer W. Lee, *Smuggling Armageddon*, New York, N.Y: St.Martin's Press 1998, p.4.
27. In 1996 the DOE stated stated that Red Mercury was a mythical substance that did not exist. See Phil Williams and Paul N.Woessner, 'The Real Threat of Nuclear Smuggling', *Scientific American*, 274, No.1, January 1996, pp.40-41.
28. Joshua Handler, 'Radioactive Waste Situation in the Pacific Fleet' Greenpeace Trip Report, Washington, 27 October 1994.
29. *Nuclear Successor States of the Soviet Union,* No.5, March 1998, MIIS and Carnegie Endowment for International Peace, p.107.
30. *Nuclear Successor States of the Soviet Union,* No.5, March 1998, MIIS and Carnegie Endowment for International Peace, p.108.
31. Mark Hibbs, 'Primakov Confirms to Germany: Munich Plutonium from Obninsk', *Nucleonics Week*, pp.1, 9-10.
32. Lee, op.cit., p.107.
33. Scott Parrish and Tamara Robinson, *An Assessment of U.S. Nonproliferation Assistance to the NIS: Export Controls, Illicit Trafficking, and Braindrain*, unpublished paper, Monterey: MIIS 1999, p.1.
34. *Nuclear Successor States of the Soviet Union,* No.5, March 1998, MIIS and Canergie Endowment for International Peace, p.105.
35. For more detail on the mission and goals of the NDF, see www.ndf.org.
36. Parrish and Robinson, op.cit., p.6.
37. For more detail see Christoph Bluth, *Arms Control and Proliferation: Russia and International Security after the Cold War*, London: Brassey's 1996; Gary Bertsch and Suzette R. Grillot (eds.), *Arms on the Market,*

London: Routledge 1998.

38. For more detail on the workforce of the Soviet defence industry, see Brenda Horrigan, 'How Many People Worked in the Soviet Defense Industry?', *RFE/RL Research Report*, Vol.1, No.33, 21 August 1992, pp.33-39.
39. For an analysis of the extent of the Russian brain drain and attempts to deal with it, see Sarah Helmstadter, 'The Russian Brain Drain in Perspective', *RFE/RL Research Report*, Vol.1, No.42, 23 October 1992, pp.57-60; see also Aleksey E. Levin, 'The First Steps in Russia's New Science Policy', *RFE/RL Research Report*, Vol.1, No.42, 23 October 1992, pp.51-56.
40. Tim Beardsley, 'Brain Drain', *Scientific American*, Vol.266, No.4, April 1992, pp.8-10.
41. *Izvestiia*, 20 October 1992, p.7.
42. *The Sunday Times*, 20 December 1992, p.18.
43. Sam Nunn, *Foreword*, in Bertsch and Grillot (eds.), op.cit., pp. vii-ix.
44. See for example 'The Changing Fate of a Russian 'Secret City'', *RFE/RL Research Report*, Vol.1, No.47, 27 November 1992, pp.50-54.
45. Beardsley, op.cit.
46. 'U.S. Firm Proposes Joint Use of 'Topaz-2'', FBIS-SOV-92-103, 28 May 1992, p.4, citing a report from Moscow Russian Television Network, 13 May 1992.
47. For more details see www.crdf.org.
48. See the official IPP web-site, ipp.lanl.gov.
49. Parrish and Robinson, op.cit., p.9; RANSAC, *Nuclear Cities News*, Vol.1, December 1999, available at www.princeton.edu/~ransac.
50. Kenneth B. Sheeley, *New Strategic Directions in the MPC&A Program*, US DOE, 17 December 1999, at www.dp.doe.gov/nn/mpca/pubs/ksbpaper.htm.
51. Cochran, op.cit., p.9.

8 The Nuclear Challenge

It is said that the road to hell is paved with good intentions. There seems to be no better example that illustrates this proverb than the endeavours by the United States and Russia to define their strategic nuclear relationship after the Cold War. In 1991 a US-Russian strategic partnership was in the making. Strategic arms control was moving ahead with radical cuts in nuclear arsenals, including the elimination of all land-based missiles with multiple warheads. The United States and Russia were working together to secure nuclear non-proliferation on a global basis. The co-operative threat reduction emerged as a unique collaboration to reduce the risk of nuclear proliferation and terrorism in the former Soviet republics. The United States and Russia declared they would not target nuclear weapons at each other.

By the year 2000, however, nothing fundamental has changed with regard to strategic nuclear relations. While the threat of war is low, massive nuclear arsenals are still in place, ready to be launched at very short notice. There are several important factors with regard to the failure of the United States and Russia to deal with the Cold War nuclear heritage.

The failure to adapt to the new international security environment

The end of the Cold War was not simply a realignment of the correlation of forces. It was a change in the nature of the international system. The failure by the political élites of the major states in the global system to come to grips with the meaning of the collapse of Communism and the globalization and demilitarization of security has the result that in Europe and beyond the institutional infra-structure of global security has not been fully reconstructed. It still retains some features and functions that stem from the Cold War period, while new elements that would be required have not yet come into existence.

The failure to understand the nature of the contemporary international system and the implications for national security is pervasive in the West and Russia. The process of NATO enlargement brought all of these contradictions out in the open. NATO enlargement does not threaten Russia, nor does it provide security to the new members against a real and present threat. The gap between the perceptions and the reality allowed this issue to be resolved relatively easily once the inevitability of this process came to be accepted.

It is of course the case that there is an interaction between perceptions and reality that can result in the creation of security risks where none would exist otherwise. This is why it is so important that US-Russian strategic relations are put onto a sound footing.

Russian nuclear policy is a paradigmatic example of how perceptions and hence policy out line with the requirements of national security. Despite the safety and security concerns, and despite far-reaching arms control agreements, Russia has placed renewed emphasis on the nuclear arsenal because of the virtual collapse of its conventional military capabilities and the instability and conflicts on the territory of the former Soviet Union. Of course, a case could be made for 'existential deterrence' according to which in a general sense the fact that Russia has nuclear weapons increases it security. There is a perception that the principal reason why the West and the United States in particular is paying so much attention to Russia is because Russia remains a strategic nuclear power. The idea here is not that Russia should rebuild of a global role. It is rather based on the fear that Russia may become marginalised, and the current political leadership seeks to avoid this at all costs in order to retain and increase the potential for international economic co-operation and aid. These are perceived as essential for Russia to reverse its sharp political and economic decline and achieve a successful transition to modern democratic state with a strong economy based on market principles. Moreover, they are essential for the preservation of the wealth of the country's élites. There is a deep paradox inherent the maintenance of a substantial arsenal of strategic nuclear weapons on the basis of such considerations. It results from the fact that Russia's strategic nuclear weapons are technically the principal military threat to the United States. This produces a plethora of political efforts to reduce or eliminate the nuclear weapons as a factor in relations with the West. On the other hand, a residual threat based on the mere possession of a nuclear arsenal is required to ensure that the West takes Russian concerns seriously.

This is quite different from a doctrine of 'first use' that seeks to operationalise nuclear weapons both in terms of deterrence and military strategy in a regional and global context, such as Russia has adopted. This is troublesome because the kind of conflicts Russia is or might become involved in, such as in Chechnya or Tajikistan, are not susceptible to nuclear deterrence. In other words, a nuclear threat might result in nuclear use. Nuclear weapons have no role in the kinds of conflicts Russia is most likely to be involved in, either in terms of deterrence or military action. In other words, where nuclear weapons are effective, there is no threat, and where there is a threat, they are not effective. This is a fundamental contradiction in the new emphasis on nuclear weapons in military doctrine that remains unresolved. There is a strong perception in Russia that nuclear weapons are vital to its security. In other words, the security nuclear weapons provide for Russia in the present is psychological and not military. This leaves Russia still with the need to find military means to address its actual security risks. Moreover the nuclear weapons complex itself poses a substantial risk to Russia's national security. While a nuclear emphasis in the face of conventional weakness is understandable, it is unclear that the military doctrine as it is evolving represents the most appropriate response to the national security dilemmas that Russia faces. Indeed, the doctrine is dangerous and if operationalised could have catastrophic consequences.

There are similar failings on the US side, and some of the internal debates on NATO enlargement have shown similar tendencies to see Russia still in terms as a potential adversary. Such voices are a minority, however, and certainly the United States government has treated Russia as a partner rather than as a potential adversary. The failure on the Western side is more along the lines of neglect rather than building up the image of a Russian threat. This neglect has expressed itself both in the failure to eliminate remnants of Cold War structures and to create new security structures that include Russia and that are more appropriate to the new international environment. When it comes to nuclear weapons policy, the United States is in a different situation from Russia. While Russian conventional forces are weak, the United States is a military superpower without nuclear weapons given its extraordinary military infrastructure to support high precision strikes with conventional weapons. Despite this, the United States has refused to fundamentally restructure is strategic nuclear arsenal, either unilaterally or on a negotiated basis.

It is important to observe that these failures have their roots in domestic politics.

The failure to appreciate the risks posed by strategic nuclear forces postures

Despite decades of public debate and substantial scientific evidence, military and political leaders in Russia and the United States have failed to admit the risks posed by strategic nuclear force posture. A massive strategic nuclear exchange, resulting in the detonation of nuclear weapons with a combined explosive power of the order of 12,000 megatons of TNT is an extinction-level-event, of the order of the asteroid impact that killed all the dinosaurs. The strategic war plans of the large nuclear powers must never be implemented, and as long as strategic nuclear arsenals are of the order of magnitude that they are (even after START I, II and III) and the war plans envisage rapid launch of the bulk of the arsenal there is a non-zero risk that a nuclear exchange will take place. While those in charge of these arsenals understand that nuclear war must not occur, they are nevertheless ready to implement the war plans under certain circumstances. It may be true that nuclear weapons deterred war with Communist countries, but now that the systemic antagonism between the United States and Russia is over there is a strong case to be made that the risks of a massive nuclear exchange should be eliminated through a process of negotiation between countries who have no reason to go to war or threaten each other. In other words, we must come to grips with the fact that force deployments and war plans are absurd and in themselves pose a danger to international security.

The failure to take timely and effective action with regard to the risks emanating from the former Soviet nuclear weapons complex

The Co-operative Threat Reduction programme is truly remarkable. The very notion of American scientists are working with Russia to safeguard its most secret installations is astonishing and convincing evidence that US-Russian strategic co-operation is possible. However, it is also a disturbing demonstration of the irrationalities of domestic political processes which inhibit an appropriate response to a clear and present danger. Despite the dedication and commitment of those professionals, both scientists and officials, engaged in this programme, and their undoubted skill in identifying the risks and designing ways of dealing with them, the programme has so far fundamentally failed to deal with the risks that it is supposed to avert. Thus only a relatively small proportion of Russian weapons grade fissile materials are covered by the modern materials protection, control and accounting facilities that are being put in place and the risk of the diversion of material is as high as it was when the programme started, if not higher. While a good number of scientists have been provided with non-weapons work, some proliferation of nuclear weapons expertise has undoubtedly occurred. The programme has not been funded at an appropriate level, it was not pursued with nearly enough urgency, and political conditions remain attached that inhibit its work and that have the potential for closing it down.

CTR had the important benefit that it contributed to the safe and secure dismantlement of nuclear weapons and thus to a substantial reduction in the number of Russian nuclear warheads. But Russia still needs nuclear warheads for its nuclear force modernization. It is completely unclear how arms control is going to be reconciled with future stockpile management in Russia. This is fundamental conceptual problem at the heart of the co-operative threat reduction process.

Farewell to US-Russian strategic co-operation?

During the early years after the dissolution of the Soviet Union, it looked as if it might be possible to move towards global co-operative denuclearization. The START process finally delivered at least an instalment of the promise given by the nuclear powers in the nuclear nonproliferation treaty (NPT) of substantial (if not total) nuclear disarmament. The denuclearization of the non-Russian former Soviet republics helped to keep the nonproliferation regime intact. The Comprehensive Test Ban Treaty and the Fissile Material Production Ban would constrain the further development of nuclear weapons both in nuclear and non-nuclear countries.

During the early years after the dissolution of the Soviet Union, it looked as if arms control would play a critical role in global co-operative denuclearization. The START process finally delivered the promise given by the nuclear powers in the nuclear nonproliferation treaty (NPT) of substantial (if not total) nuclear disarmament. The denuclearization of the non-Russian former Soviet republics helped to keep the nonproliferation regime intact. The Comprehensive Test Ban Treaty and the Fissile Material Production Ban would constrain the further development of nuclear weapons both in nuclear and non-nuclear countries. However, by 1998, these tremendous achievements began to crumble. The ratification of START II seemed unobtainable and even with the extensions of the time limits agreed the regime was running out of time. Fortunately strategic co-operation was resumed after the Russian presidential elections in 2000. However, despite the ratification of START II serious problems are still on the horizon. The United States is committed to make decisions about the procurement of a National Missile Defence System in the near future. The rejection of the CTBT by the US Senate of 13 October 1999 dealt a severe blow to the global arms control and nonproliferation process. The NPT regime was damaged by nuclear tests in India and Pakistan. The United States and Russia have to continue to make serious efforts to ensure that the entire promising network of arms control agreements that was designed to put US-Russian strategic relations onto a completely new footing does not unravel. The nuclear challenge will not go away. The shape of the 'second nuclear age' after the Cold War still remains to be defined. The United States and Russia have a special responsibility to ensure that it banishes the nuclear threat as far as it is possible.

Bibliography

Allison, G., Carter, A., Miller, S.E. and Zelikow, P. (eds.) (1993), *Cooperative Denuclearization*, CSIA Studies in International Security, No.2, Cambridge, MA, Harvard University.

Allison, G.T., Coté, O.R., Falkenrath, R.A. and Miller, S.E. (1996), *Avoiding Nuclear Anarchy,* Cambridge, MA, MIT Press.

Allison, R. and Bluth, C.(eds.) (1998), *Security Dilemmas in Russia and Eurasia*, London: RIIA.

Allison, R. (1993), *Military Forces in the Soviet Successor States*, IISS Adelphi Paper No. 280, London: Brassey's.

Arbatov, A. (1992), *Iadernoe Vooruzheniia i respublikanskiy suverenitet*, Moscow: Mezhdunarodnye otnosheniia.

Baker, J.C. and Berman, R.B. (1982), *Soviet Strategic Forces*, Washington DC: Brookings Institution.

Beschloss, M.R. and Talbott, S. (1993), *At the Highest Levels*, London: Little Brown and Co.

Blair, B. (1993), *The Logic of Accidental Nuclear War*, Washington DC: Brookings Institution.

Bluth, C. (1995), *Britain, Germany and Western Nuclear Strategy*, Oxford: Oxford University Press.

Bluth, C. (1995), *The Collapse of Soviet Military Power*, Aldershot: Dartmouth.

Bluth, C. (1992), *Soviet Strategic Arms Policy Before SALT*, Cambridge: Cambridge University Press.

Bomsdorf, F. (1993), *Zwischen Destruktion und Regeneration. Zur Zukunft des postsowjetischen Raumes*, SWP S 389, Ebenhausen: Stiftung Wissenschaft und Politik.

Bowker, M. and Brown, R. (eds) (1993), *From Cold War to collapse: theory and world politics in the 1980s*, Cambridge: Cambridge University Press.

Bukharin, O.A., Cochran, T.B. and Norris, R.S. (1995), *Making the Russian Bomb - From Stalin to Yeltsin*, Boulder, CO: Westview Press.

Campbell, K., Carter, A.B, Miller, S.E. and Zraket, C.A. (1991), *Soviet Nuclear Fission*, CSIA Studies in International Security No.1, Cambridge, MA, Harvard University.

Cooper, J. (1991), *The Soviet Defence Industry*, London: Pinter.

Curtis, M., Diehl, O., Paolini, J., Seydoux, A. and Wolf, R. (1993), *Challenges and Responses to Future European Security: British, French and German Perspectives*, London: European Strategy Group.

Dougherty, J.E. and Pfaltzgraff, R.L. Jr. (1981), *Contending Theories of International Relations*, New York: Harper & Row.

Easton, D. (1965), *A Framework for Political Analysis*, Englewood Cliffs: Prentice-Hall.

Freedman, L. and Karsh, E. (1993), *The Gulf Conflict 1990-1991*, London: Faber and Faber.

Gaddis, J.L. (1992), *The United States and the End of the Cold War*, Oxford: Oxford University Press.

Gilpin, R. (1980), *War and Change in World Politics*, Cambridge: Cambridge University Press.

Herspring, D.R. and Laird, R.F. (1984), *The Soviet Union and Strategic Arms*, Boulder: Westview Press.

Holloway, D. (1994), *Stalin and the Bomb*, New Haven: Yale University Press.

Holloway, D. (1984), *The Soviet Union and the Arms Race*, New Haven: Yale University Press.

Karaganov, S.A. (1992), *Russia: The New Foreign Policy and Security Agenda*, London: Brassey's.

Lee, R.W. (1998), *Smuggling Armageddon*, New York: St.Martin's Press.

Nolan, J.E. (1999), *An Elusive Consensus*, Washington DC: Brookings.

Podvig, P. (ed.), (1998) *Strategicheskoe Iadernoe Vooruzhenie Rossii*, Moscow: IzdAt.

Potter, W.C. and Shields, J.M. (1997), *Dismantling the Cold War*, Cambridge, MA: MIT Press.

Reiss, E. (1992), *The Strategic Defense Initiative*, Cambridge: Cambridge University Press.

Sokov, N. (2000), *Russian Strategic Modernization*, Oxford, Rowman & Littlefield Publishers.

Quester, G. (1995), *The Nuclear Challenge in Russia and the New States in Eurasia*, London: M.E. Sharpe.

Index